LOST
BRISTOL

*

First published in 2006 by
Birlinn Limited
West Newington House
10 Newington Road
Edinburgh
EH9 1QS

www.birlinn.co.uk

Hardback
ISBN10: 1 84158 502 5
ISBN13: 978 1 84158 502 4

Paperback
ISBN10: 1 84158 533 5
ISBN13: 978 1 84158 533 8

British Library Cataloguing-in-Publication Data
A catalogue record for this book is available
from the British Library.

Design Andrew Sutterby

Printed and bound in China by Compass Press Ltd.

LOST
BRISTOL

Victoria Coules

BIRLINN

CONTENTS

ACKNOWLEDGEMENTS

Firstly, I am indebted to my friend Stuart Booth for introducing me to the team at Birlinn Ltd. This is not the first time Stuart has intervened in my writing career and I hope he realises how grateful I am. I thank Susan and Andrew Sutterby, who guided me throughout the writing and production of this book and made working with Birlinn a really enjoyable experience. Of course, there are many who have assisted me with this project, but in particular I would like to thank:

Dr Evan Jones of the Department of Historical Studies, University of Bristol, who was generous with his time and advice on the early maritime history of the city. He gave me access to invaluable papers, both published and awaiting publication, and was kind enough to check the manuscript of some of these chapters. His help is much appreciated.

Oliver Kent who patiently helped me with specific queries and references as well as trusting me with the loan of his own invaluable material that is currently out of print.

John Bryant, who answered my questions promptly and fully.

Andy Davies Coward, who kindly lent me a selection of his own out-of-print material.

History researcher Christine Nicholls, who provided valuable historical information.

In my quest to find out more about Robert Louis Stevenson's link to Bristol, I am grateful for the email correspondence I had with Mark Steeds of the Long John Silver Trust in Bristol (and the Beaufort Arms in Hawksbury Upton!). Eugene Byrne also kindly shared his thoughts on the subject by email and Alan Marchbank from the RLS Club in Scotland was generous enough to telephone me to discuss Robert Louis Stevenson's possible sources for material in *Treasure Island*. Peter Aughton, author of *Bristol: A People's History* also took the time to respond to my queries. I thank

David and Eunice Elsbury, who kindly spent time showing me their superb collection of historical images of Bristol, of which some are reproduced in this book. I am also grateful to Derek and Janet Fisher, of Bygone Bristol, for their kindness and help in supplying some of their images of old Bristol and I thank Keven Flay for his invaluable help in taking some of the photographs. Thank you to Julia Carver and Sue Giles of Bristol's City Museums, Galleries and Archive for their help in providing images.

Thanks also to John Capener and Kensa Budworth for putting up with me when I was researching and writing this book in our shared office, thinking aloud and, at times, covering most available surfaces with notes and papers. Lastly, and most important, I thank my husband, Steve Nicholls, who learned far more about the history of Bristol than he ever needed to know; who walked miles with me to investigate hidden corners of the city; who carefully read the manuscript, making helpful suggestions and who supported me, as always, with humour and love throughout the writing process. It remains to emphasise that any errors and omissions are entirely my own and should be treated as such.

PICTURE CREDITS

David and Eunice Elsbury (pp1, 11, 12, 14, 23, 24, 29, 34, 35, 37, 56, 59, 81, 91, 98, 111, 123, 139, 151, 173, 185, 188, 189, 193, 194, 201, 204), V Coules (pp2, 4, 5, 72, 75, 76, 79, 80, 86, 96, 106, 110, 113, 125, 140, 160, 174, 181, 184), Knight, Charles "The Land We Live In", 1847 (pp3, 48, 61, 99, 136, 137, 202), Hunt, William "Historic Towns, Bristol" 1902 ed Freeman & Hunt (pp8, 15, 16, 28, 36, 89, 100), Bristol's City Museums, Galleries & Archives (pp17, 28, 46, 93, 130, 143, 155, 198), Kevin Flay (pp25, 38, 39, 127, 163, 209), "Mathews new correct plan of the City and suburbs of Bristol 1794" from "Matthews New History of Bristol or Complete Guide and Bristol Directory for the year 1793-1794" (pp41, 133, 144), based on original map courtesy of the University of Texas Libraries, The University of Texas at Austin (pp50), Steve Nicholls (pp68, 196, 203), 'Bygone Bristol', Derek and Janet Fisher (pp84, 107, 149, 154, 158, 159, 168, 171, 172, 186), Foxe's Book of Martyrs (pp105), Long John Silver Trust (pp120).

CHAPTER 1

BRISTOL FOUND

The city of Bristol – indeed, the city and county of Bristol – is a city with a thousand years of history. Yet this history is not blatant; there are no Roman ruins forming a major tourist attraction, no castle dominating the skyline (just a few remains of the castle's foundations), no gleaming spires or medieval banquet halls.

No, Bristol is more reticent about its history. In some places the past is integrated into the city of today, in some places it is lost forever. There are exceptions: the magnificent restoration of the ss *Great Britain*, the Georgian House and Red Lodge under the care of the City Museum, occasional medieval archways or courtyards, glimpses of the past in the corners of churches.

Bristol's river Avon – flowing through the Avon gorge and passing under the Clifton Suspension bridge.

The city is steeped in legend, much of which surrounds its role as a trading port and thriving centre for both merchants and manufacturers, even though commercial shipping no longer berths in the city docks.

Much of Bristol's past is hidden within the modern city, just out of sight but waiting to be discovered. For much of its history, Bristol was England's second city. Its story reflects the story of England and, in places, the story of Europe; its fortunes are those of the shifting circumstances of time. And much of Bristol's success – and, ultimately its demise as a port – is due to its geographical position.

Bristol is situated at the junction of two rivers; the Frome is a small but energetic river that snakes through Gloucestershire and flows into the Avon. As 'Avon' is a Welsh Celtic word for 'river' there are several River Avons in England (or 'River Rivers'). To clarify, the Avon that flows through Bath and Bristol is known locally as the Bristol Avon. Bristol is situated at the furthest point downstream before the river enters the Avon Gorge, which was not bridged until the nineteenth century.

Like most places with an interesting landscape Bristol has its fair share of legends explaining the origin of the Avon Gorge. And like many landscape legends, the story involves giants, in this case Goram and Vincent. There are various tellings of the story but a popular version is that Goram and Vincent were brothers who fell in love with the same woman, Avona.

Avona agreed to marry whichever giant could drain the huge lake that stretched from Bradford-on-Avon to the current site of Bristol. The brothers set about their task with great enthusiasm, Goram digging through the hills at Henbury and Vincent digging through Durdham Downs, creating the gorge

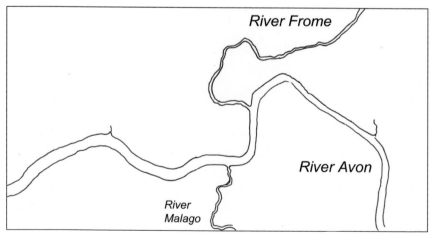

The rivers Avon and Frome with the Malago joining the Avon from the south.

*A view of St Vincent's Rocks from Nightingale Valley on the opposite side
of the Avon Gorge.*

that would drain the lake. Goram was soon bored and tired and, after a few drinks, fell asleep, so Vincent finished the job and won the hand of Avona. When Goram woke up and found he had lost the challenge, he was so distraught he threw himself into the River Severn and drowned. His head and shoulders are still visible as the two small islands of Flat Holm and Steep Holm in the Bristol Channel. Avona gave her name to the gorge that Vincent had built and he gave his name to a part of the gorge, St Vincent's Rocks, located under the cliff where Clifton Suspension Bridge now crosses the river.

Goram left his mark in other ways; a local rock feature in the gorge is known as Goram's Chair and in other versions of the story, Goram cut the chair from the rocks for himself so he could rest from his digging. However, in today's world without giants, the formation of the gorge is explained by the force of water.

The Avon is an enigmatic river. It rises near Badminton, in Gloucestershire, and flows east. Other rivers in this area continue to flow east and eventually join the Thames but the Avon does something different. It flows east for a while, then turns south, makes a huge loop, turns north again to Bath, then north-west to Bristol.

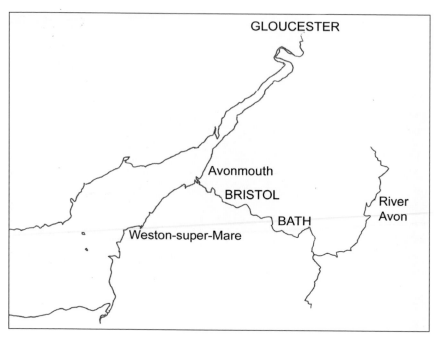

The course of the river Avon

At Bristol, it continues to flow north-west, through the Avon Gorge, which itself is rather curious; the rock of the gorge is carboniferous limestone, which is harder than most limestone. It seems an odd thing for a river to do because cutting through fairly hard rock is not the easiest way for a river to get to the sea, or at least the Bristol Channel. In the landscape of today, it would have made more sense if the river had followed the flat, softer route to the south of Bristol and joined the Channel near Weston-super-Mare.

There are various theories to explain why this scenario did not happen but none are absolutely certain. At the beginning of the twentieth century, one theory suggested that there had once been a huge lake, formed in a distant ice age by glaciers that blocked the natural flow of a river. An outflow from this lake flowed through the carboniferous limestone and carved the gorge. This idea was dismissed until recently, when some deposits were found that had been left by the advancing snout of a glacier. The glacier would have been moving east, possibly blocking or partly blocking the Severn and creating a lake. All this would have happened nearly half a million years ago and, over time, ice ages came and went and the landscape changed, leaving the Avon, its gorge and the legend of the giants.

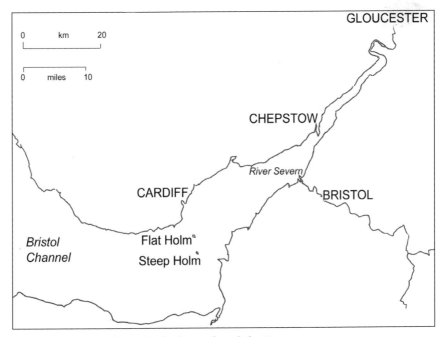

The Bristol Channel and the Severn estuary

The Avon flows into the Bristol Channel at Avonmouth, where it joins the River Severn. The Severn is a powerful river, rising in the depths of Wales at Plynlimon, flowing through England into Gloucestershire, past Gloucester and Sharpness and into the muddy water of the Bristol Channel, also near Avonmouth. But the funnel shape of the coastlines of Wales and North Cornwall and Devon gives it a tidal range second only to the Bay of Fundy in Nova Scotia; the Severn's range can be as high as fifteen metres and at certain combinations of the tide and moon, the force of the tide is so powerful that a two-metre high wave of water is forced up the river at speeds as fast as twenty kilometres per hour, creating the famous Severn Bore, beloved of tourists and surfers.

The tidal waters of the Severn also sweep into and along the narrow gorge of the Avon, so even as far inland as Bristol, the tidal range is fifteen metres – and this has advantages and disadvantages. The tidal flow washes the river clean twice a day but creates a hazard for shipping; vessels risk being dumped in the soft mud of the river bed as the tide recedes.

In ancient times, there was a ford that crossed the river below the cliffs of the gorge, under what is now the Clifton Suspension Bridge, close to the inland end of the gorge. The river's water-levels were unpredictable so an attempt to cross, laden down with baggage while driving livestock, could turn into an expensive mistake.

The original site of the first settlement was the raised area of ground between the River Avon and the River Frome, just upstream of their confluence that is now the shopping centre of Broadmead, High Street and Wine Street. In the early days of the town, this was an area with the natural advantage of high ground. A partial, natural moat created by the loops in the river made it an ideal place to settle and a logical place to build a bridge (which became Bristol Bridge, in place by about AD 1000, as discussed in Chapter 2).

The point where the Frome (pronounced locally as the 'Froom') joins the Avon, a few miles further inland from the end of the gorge, offered a point where the Avon could be easily bridged. It also formed a loop that created a spit of land between the rivers.

The Avon was a natural waterway in the days when it was easier to travel across England by boat than to take a cart or horses across land, particularly when transporting heavy goods. From South Wales and the south-west coast of England to the inland towns of Bath, the Avon was the main route for trade.

The new settlement was a site that could be defended, from threats inland by the natural shape of the river junction and from the sea by the winding Avon Gorge. Where other ports suffered raids from Vikings and pirates, Bristol was as good as impregnable; most positions along the gorge provided a lookout point from which incoming ships could be seen and defensive action taken. Eventually, the Avon Gorge would be Bristol's downfall as a commercial port but for 1,000 years or so, the city enjoyed a security unmatched by any other harbour.

However, giving a date for the origin of Bristol is by no means straightforward and has to be a matter of deduction.

Compared to many other ancient English cities there is much less archeological evidence to give clues about life in the past. The reason is simple – it was easier for early inhabitants to throw rubbish into the river, to be flushed away by the tide, than to let it build up for the eventual discovery of archeologists. The streets of Bristol were by no means pristine, but the twice-daily purging of the Avon gave a natural outlet for much of the day-to-day waste and refuse.

Some idea of the origin of the city can be pieced together from clues. From evidence of settlements at Stokeleigh and Clifton, it seems that there were people living in the area from the Stone Age. By the Bronze Age it appears there was a strong link between Bristol, southern England and Ireland via the Rivers Avon and Severn and the Irish Sea.

Before the Romans arrived, the area was inhabited by the Dobunni tribe of Celts. They were a large tribe, established enough to mint their own coins, and were situated in central and northern Somerset, with the River Avon forming a natural boundary between two factions of the tribe. They took advantage of their position between the prosperous, productive regions to the west and the tribes further east that traded with the continent – a theme that would echo throughout the history of the region. Around central Oxfordshire, mixtures of coins have been found that imply a major trading interface between the Dobunni and the Catuvellauni tribe to the east, and in the more prosperous homes of the Dobunni, continental pottery from Italy and Gaul has been found. The Dobunni were evidently the shrewd busi-nessmen of the Celts and, in the pragmatic tradition of the city of Bristol that followed them, when the Romans arrived, the Dobunni offered their alle-giance to Rome and got on with their trading.

There was no Bristol when the Romans occupied the British Isles. The nearby towns of Aqua Sulis (Bath), Corinium (Cirencester) and, further up the Severn, Glevum (Gloucester) were thriving centres of civilisation but if there was a crossing at the Avon, it seems it was of no real significance to the Romans. The Roman general Ostorius Scapula stationed a garrison at Abona, now the suburb of Sea Mills, where the small River Trym flows into the Avon. Abona was a ferry terminal and trading centre situated on the Roman road that ran across what is now the Downs to Aqua Sulis; there were many fine villas scattered along this road but no trace of a large Roman settlement has been found in Bristol's archeological record.

The first hint of a substantial settlement at Bristol comes from a coin – rather appropriate for a city whose whole reason for being was trade. The coin is in the Royal Collection in Stockholm, probably part of a payment of Dangeld made sometime in the eleventh century AD. Danegeld was a form of pay-off to the Danes first made by Aethelred (the Unready) when it was obvious he could not win the Battle of Maldon against the Vikings in AD 991. It did not take long for the Vikings to realise that extortion was more profitable than war so the practice of being paid to stay away continued, resulting in the people of England being taxed to finance the Vikings' protection racket.

The 'Bristol coin' is a silver penny, as were all the contemporary coins. On one side is the head of Aethelred and on the other the mark and name of the mint operator, Aelfweld, with the name of his location, 'on Bric'. It is possible that the 'on Bric' could also refer to Bridgnorth or Stockbridge but the consensus seems to be that this coin was from Bristol. Silver coins were not used as day-to-day coinage – they had far too high a value – but were destined for the King's treasury, where they could be used as payment of Danegeld. It seems possible that this established route, ending in Stockholm, was the journey the Bristol coin took. If this coin was made in Bristol, the implication is that by 1016, the town was significant enough to have its own mint.

By the time Aethelred's son Edward the Confessor became King (1042), coins from Bristol were clearly rendered as 'Bricsto' or 'Brvesto'.

The next reliable mention of Bristol comes in 1051 with an entry in the Anglo-Saxon Chronicle. It describes the port of 'Brycstowe' as having a well-established trade with Ireland. By the end of the Saxon period, then, the settlement was a thriving town. Some of the Saxon street layout is still evident today – High Street, Wine Street, Broad Street and Corn Street, with St Nicholas Street curving around them, as well as Tower Lane, are all part of the original grid layout.

With William the Conqueror's victory at Hastings, a new order was imposed onto the whole country. When, in 1067, William's forces reached

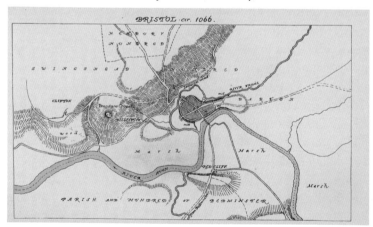

Bristol as it was in 1066. The river Frome creates a loop to enclose the early settlement; between the small town and the Avon is mainly marshy ground.

Bristol, the city showed little resistance; to the citizens, a regime change was only really significant if it affected trade and this philosophical attitude prevailed throughout most of the city's history. That said, although the city did not put up much of a fight, the Normans saw the strategic advantage of the town and set about fortifying it.

The deposed Harold's sons were less accepting of the Norman invasion. The Anglo-Saxon Chronicle tells of how, after the Battle of Hastings, Harold's sons arrived in Bristol:

> And in the middle of this, Harold's sons came by surprise from Ireland into the mouth of the Avon with a raiding ship-army and straightway raided across all that region; then went to Bristol and wanted to break down the town but the townspeople fought hard against them; and then when they could not gain anything from the town they went to the ships with what they had plundered and they went thus to Somerset and went up there.

So by the time the Normans had established themselves in Bristol, the settlement enjoyed a thriving trade and controlled the crossing over the Avon as well as the river's traffic.

The Domesday Book entry for Bristol is disappointing. Bristol is included as part of the entry for the royal manor of Barton Regis; it refers to 'Bertune apud Bristou' or 'Barton near Bristol' which implies that Bristol not only existed but was well known enough to act as a reference point. The entry goes on to state that between Barton and Bristol, 110 marks of silver were paid to the King and 33 marks of silver and one of gold to Geoffrey de Coutances. However, apart from mention of the manor's workforce, there is no other reference to Bristol. Barton Regis gave its name to the area in Bristol now known as Barton Hill, its high-rise flats the first built in Bristol to replace the Victorian slums.

This introduction opens with a reference to the city 'and county' of Bristol – a continual source of confusion to those unfamiliar with the situation. Bristol is not in Somerset, it is not in Gloucestershire, it is a county in its own right. This came about through the application of common sense. As the settlement of Bristol grew it straddled the Avon, which formed the natural boundary between Somerset and Gloucestershire. These counties had their administrative and legal headquarters in Ilchester and Gloucester respectively. Any disputes that needed resolving in Redcliffe, south of the Avon meant a long journey to Ilchester, and likewise anything north of the river required a long day's ride to Gloucester; a dispute between the two sides of the river was an administrative and logistical nightmare.

So, in 1373, Edward III granted Bristol a new charter. At the time, he was busy fighting the Hundred Years War against the French in his attempt to take the French Crown so, like all monarchs embroiled in war, was short of cash. The deal with Bristol suited everyone. For payment from the town of the sum of 600 marks, he conferred the status of 'county' onto Bristol so that it could hold its own courts and administer itself without recourse to Somerset or Gloucestershire.

Quoting from *Little Red Book Vol. I*, Aughton reveals that the charter, dated 8 August 1373, states '... that the said town of Bristol and its suburbs... shall be a county by itself and be called the County of Bristol forever.'

It's likely that the original High Cross was erected to commemorate this charter; it stood at the crossroads where High Street, Corn Street, Wine Street and Broad Street meet. It isn't there any more – it was moved to College Green in 1736 and in 1764 was purchased by Henry Hoare who took it to his estate at Stourhead.

Bristol stayed a county until 1 April 1974. This wasn't an April Fool's joke, but rather, was the formation of the new county of Avon, which incorporated Bristol, Bath, Northavon, Kingswood, Woodspring and Wansdyke. Not a popular move. People in Bristol resented their county status being removed and other towns that were traditionally part of the ancient counties of Somerset and Gloucestershire resented being uprooted to a new-fangled county. Eventually, in 1996, Avon was dissolved and Bristol reverted to its city and county status. Having been a county for 600 years, its incorporation into Avon only lasted two decades and today it once more proudly displays the 'City and County of Bristol' crest on its boundaries.

And the origins of the name? The first reference is that of 'Bricg' or 'Bric', as mentioned above, on the coins. A 'stow' was a settlement, or collection of houses, sometimes described as a 'place of assembly'. The 'Bric' referred to the bridge, so the 'place of assembly by the bridge' became known as 'Brig Stowe' or 'Brigstowe'. Over time, this became 'Bristow' and there it might have stayed had it not been for a characteristic of the local dialect. There is a tendency in Bristol to put an 'L' on the end of words that end in vowels. So, an 'idea' becomes an 'ideal', the 'area' becomes the 'areal', 'Victoria' becomes 'Victorial' and so on. This only seems to occur in the city itself, distinguishing Bristolians from those in the surrounding countryside. And so, Brigstowe and Bristow changed to the name used today, for the city and the county: 'Bristol'.

BRISTOL, HIGH CROSS.

When the original High Cross was moved to Stourhead, a copy was made, shown here installed on College Green. It was later moved to its current position in Berkeley Square.

CHAPTER 2

THE BRIDGE AND THE QUAY

Given that it represents the city's original *raison d'être*, Bristol Bridge is not the most dramatic architectural feature of the city. The swans on the river seem to appreciate the structure more than the citizens; it is a functional bridge, carrying road and foot traffic across the Avon. It has none of the drama and majesty associated with Bristol's more famous Clifton Suspension Bridge, and many people will be pushed to recall what Bristol Bridge actually looks like. It sits on three low stone arches, supported by thick pillars that rest on the medieval foundations of the bridge and has a dignified dark-blue cast-iron balustrade to carry the extra width of the road that was added in Victorian times.

The river divided the settlement of Bristol from the district of Redcliffe, shown here with the distant spire of St Mary Redcliffe and the 'backs', or quays, on the south bank of the Avon.

Bristol Bridge links the junction of Baldwin Street and High Street to Victoria Street, on the other side of the Avon, and it is one of several bridges that cross the river within a few hundred metres of each other. Yet, until the beginning of the nineteenth century, Bristol Bridge, in use by about AD 1000, was the only crossing of the Avon (the nearest bridge was at Keynsham, six miles further upstream) and so was the only link between the two halves of the city. There were several ferries taking passengers, charging a ha'penny a crossing, but livestock and anything on wheels had to cross via the bridge.

With the building of Prince Street Bridge in 1809, St Philip's Bridge in 1841 and Redcliffe Bridge in 1942, all for carrying road traffic, and with Pero's Bridge built in 2000 for pedestrians, Bristol Bridge lost its 1,000-year monopoly and became just another way to cross the river.

The original bridge was built at a natural crossing point just upstream of the confluence of the Avon and the Frome. There is some debate about the exact position of the very first bridge; some speculate that it was a further seventy metres or so upstream from its current position but the consensus is that the original bridge stood on the site occupied by Bristol Bridge today. Made of wood, it was the only route into the town by road from the east and south, as well as the only link across the Avon to connect the two halves of the settlement.

The settlement of Brigstowe grew up around the bridge over the Avon, and a major river crossing point is often reason enough for a town to develop but there was another crucial factor in the settlement's growth. Shipping could navigate up the Avon to load and unload passengers and cargo; Bristol was a natural inland harbour.

There was a slight complication – the tides. At low tide, the natural moorings of the river banks turned into muddy, rocky river bed. As the settlement expanded on both sides of the river, the available moorings on the river bank quickly became cramped and inconvenient so, at the beginning of the thirteenth century, an ambitious plan was hatched to improve the quayside facilities.

The natural flow and curves of the River Avon meant that the Redcliffe (southern) side of the river offered deeper water and softer mooring – oozing mud – when the tide went out. Conversely, the quay on the Bristol (northern) side of the Avon was small and the river bottom stony and hard; ships moored there risked damage to their timbers as they were grounded at low tide. Bristolians decided to do something about it and the result was one of the most ambitious civil-engineering projects of medieval times. The plan was to divert the River Frome so that it joined the Avon further downstream

Bristol's problem as a tidal harbour – as the water level drops at low tide, the Importer *is left stranded on the mud of the river bed, shown with Hotwells and Clifton in the background.*

and created a new, larger, deeper, softer quay for shipping.

This idea was not met with unbounded enthusiasm, however. The rivalry between the opposing sides of the river came to a head; the men of Redcliffe could see that this new quay would take away their advantage and they were not best pleased. Eventually it took the King to get involved, although this wasn't entirely altruistic; Bristol itself was part of the royal manor of Barton Regis and it was in the Crown's interest to develop the port.

Henry II decided to bang heads together and did so with a firm instruction to the residents of Redcliffe. As Bettey shows in *Bristol Observed*, Henry wrote on 27 April 1240:

> . . . to all worthy men dwelling in Redcliffe in the suburb of Bristol, greeting. Whereas our beloved burgesses of Bristol for the common good for the whole town of Bristol . . . have begun a certain trench in the Marsh of St Augustine that ships coming to our port of Bristol may be able to enter and leave more freely and without impediment; which trench indeed they will be unable to complete without great costs.

He went on to stress:

> . . . it may be very useful and fruitful for you for the work of the trench aforesaid to be perfected successfully according as it concerns you together with our aforesaid burgesses, to whom as sharers in the liberties aforesaid, you shall give like efficacious aid as they themselves do, lest the aforesaid work, which we regard as our own, through your defection should receive delay.

In other words, the men of Redcliffe were to help out with the new trench or face the King's wrath.

It took seven years to complete the project, and the cost was enormous, both in man-hours and in hard cash – the final cost was £5,000, a huge amount in those days. The new ditch was 750 metres long, 6 metres deep and 40 metres wide through marshy ground, dug entirely by manual labour. It must have been back-breaking work, the mud and spoils being carried out of the trench in barrow loads taken up timber ramps. They had ropes and pulleys, and primitive cranes to manoeuvre the blocks of stone used to build the quay, but most of the digging work was done by sheer muscle power. It's thought that the spoils from the trench were deposited on the site that

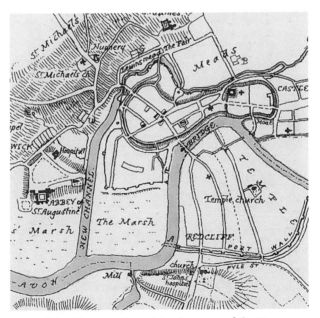

The diversion of the Frome – the original course of the Frome was roughly along today's Baldwin Street.

became the Greyfriars' – Franciscan monks' – site for their friary at Lewins Mead, now the site of Bristol Dental Hospital.

The new quay was a great success. More ships, larger ships, merchant ships – the city was thronging with shipping flying flags from many and varied foreign ports. The new quay was known simply as The Quay and the older moorings downstream of Bristol Bridge was known as the Back; the Back was used more by the coastal vessels that plied their trade in the waters of the Severn and the Bristol Channel, the local trade that gave this stretch of the harbour its current name of Welsh Back.

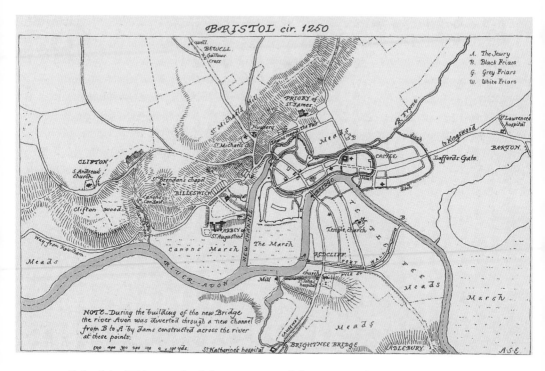

Bristol in 1250 – much of the area around the Avon and the 'New Channel' is marshy ground.

Alongside the building of the new quay, it was already obvious that a new bridge was also desperately needed. Once the new quay was complete, the next task was to build a stone bridge to replace the wooden structure. To do this, the Avon itself would have to be diverted to give access to the river bed in order to build the foundations.

Another ditch was dug, this time across the curve of the river that enclosed Temple Fee, Redcliffe and St Thomas. This was known as the

Portwall ditch and, after the bridge was completed and the river restored to its original flow, the ditch became part of the city's defences.

With most of the river water diverted, the engineers took no chances and built four arches, with columns so thick they created a weir effect in the river. The bridge was similar in design to London Bridge, which had been completed in the early part of the thirteenth century. Although Bristol Bridge was only nineteen feet wide, it was the main thoroughfare into the city and buildings on the bridge were in a prime position to exploit the passing trade; most had a shop on the ground floor. It is hard to see how, given the congestion and general chaos, anyone could browse in the shops but it must have been profitable for the owners. Lined with buildings, the road was cramped and dark. There were thirty houses on the bridge, all built from wood with slate roofs and, straddling the bridge, halfway across, was the Chapel of the Assumption of the Blessed Virgin Mary. And the bridge was built to last. Bettey shows that as late as 1698, the traveller Celia Fiennes wrote, 'The bridge is built over with houses just as London Bridge is but not so big or long, there are 4 arches here.'

The houses were substantial, some of four storeys, some with cellars built into the piers of the bridge. The properties on the bridge commanded the highest rents in the city for the simple reason that the sanitation outlet fed

Detail from Millerd's map of 1673 showing the medieval Bristol Bridge, lined with shops and houses.

directly into the river below so, for the residents, the problem simply went away.

There was, however, a downside to this location. Many of the houses, to increase floor space, were built outwards from the bridge, with bow windows that hung over the river but they did not take account of the crowded moorings and dramatically changing tides. There are stories of masts or bowsprits (the pole that projects forwards from the bow of a ship), forcing themselves up into buildings through the floorboards with the rising tide and, presumably, staying there until the tide went out. Flooding was also a very real threat, so the location had mixed blessings. Livestock were often driven over the bridge and, in the noise and confusion, it was not unusual for animals to panic. There is a story of a large powerful ox that bolted straight through someone's ground-floor parlour and out the other side, through the back window and into the river below.

The shape of the road had a negative camber, whereby the road curved down into the centre so that carts and carriages tended to lean in towards each other as they passed and would make contact and lock together. The result was complete gridlock; as the carriages were untangled, the queue waiting to cross the bridge built up, causing yet more chaos and congestion throughout the city streets. Such major traffic jams may seem depressingly familiar to today's citizens of Bristol.

Writer and satirist Alexander Pope came to Bristol in 1739. Bettey reveals in *Bristol Observed* that concerning this visit Pope wrote to a friend:

> You come first to Old Walls, and over a Bridge, built on both sides like London bridge and as much crowded, with a stronge mixture of Seamen, women, children, loaded Horses, Asses, and Sledges with Goods dragging along, all together without posts to separate them. From thence you come to a Key along the old Wall with houses on both sides and in the middle of the street as far as you can see, hundreds of Ships, their Masts as thick as they can stand by one another, which is oddest and most surprising sight imaginable.

By the eighteenth century, the combination of an increased population spilling outside the city walls, more trade in the city itself and the deteriorating state of the old medieval timber bridge meant that a new bridge was essential. However, the decision to build such a structure set off a train of events that would result in tragedy.

The problem arose initially because of the roads. Cart-loads of goods for market, as well as livestock, riders on horseback and general traffic made the roads mere dust tracks in dry weather and quagmires in the wet. As the city flourished, the population increased and the roads deteriorated until the situation became unworkable.

In 1663, the Turnpike Act was introduced; in order to raise money for repairing and rebuilding roads, tolls were charged and collected at the various gates into the city. Although long-distance travellers were happier with the new improved roadways, local people resented paying for their use. Then came the matter of the bridge.

Although it was easy to agree that something needed to be done, it was less straightforward to make a decision on the course of action to be taken. A committee, or Corporation, of twenty-four was set up to discuss the matter; it was considered that there were two possible ways forward. One was to repair and widen the existing medieval bridge to improve traffic flow; the other option was to build a completely new bridge. The Corporation were leaning towards repairing the existing bridge and proposed they raise the money to do so by a duty on coal, increased rates on houses, a wharfage charge and, of course, a bridge toll.

Yet endless meetings resulted in stalemate and all this time the traffic problem was getting worse. In exasperation, a group of local businessmen decided to take matters into their own hands and proposed a bill to Parliament, allowing them to carry out the construction of the new bridge themselves.

That august body, the Corporation, was galvanised into action once more. The Corporation had run Bristol since the fourteenth century and was an elite group of the city's most wealthy and powerful. Discussions resumed. And they continued. And continued some more. And, seventy-five meetings later, they finally made a decision.

Their decision was to build a new bridge on piers resting on the medieval foundations, based on a design by Bristol architect John Bridges. There was bitter rivalry between the designers of the different plans submitted and although Bridges' design was the one accepted, he suffered continual harassment and criticism. Eventually the experience became so relentlessly unpleasant he left Bristol before the work was finished, leaving another architect well known for his work in Bristol, Thomas Paty, to complete the project.

The new bridge was similar in design to London's Westminster Bridge but its most impressive new feature was a two-metre-high stone balustrade to stop livestock jumping off the bridge and into the river below.

Financed as already described, albeit without the duty on coal, the new bridge opened to pedestrians in 1768 and to horses and vehicles in 1769. The tolls were collected, at a shilling for a laden carriage with horses and a ha'penny for a horse or mule. Crucially, it was announced that the tolls would be collected for as long as it took to cover the cost of the bridge's construction and would then be abandoned in September 1793. At least, that was the original plan.

Tolls are a very convenient way of raising money. The role of administering the bridge and the right to collect the tolls had the potential for considerable profit and, after the promised twenty-four years of tolls, a surprise announcement was made – the toll lease was to be auctioned again at the beginning of September 1793. The previous lease was held by a Mr Abraham Hiscoxe, who had reasonably enough assumed that this was the last year that the tolls would be collected, so was horrified to be told that the tolls were to continue. He knew that this would be deeply unpopular and wanted no part of it – as much for self-preservation as for altruistic reasons.

To make matters worse, the Bridge Trustees refused to publish their accounts; they claimed they had £2,000 in hand but the interest on this wouldn't pay for the lighting and upkeep of the new bridge. Without any further justification they decided to extend the payment of tolls. As Hiscoxe tried to find a way to extricate himself from this, he heard about an idea in circulation that could solve his problem. There was a rumour about a legal loophole, which claimed that if the tolls were suspended, or collection had somehow lapsed for ten days or more, it would take an Act of Parliament to reinstate them. Whether or not this was true wasn't clear, but Hiscoxe felt it was preferable to lose ten days' revenue from the bridge than risk the disapproval – or worse – of the citizens of Bristol. Consequently the tolls would stop as originally planned.

With the tolls due to stop on Saturday 29 September 1793, he reasoned that if he stopped collecting tolls on the morning of Friday the 20th, he would force the 'ten-day rule'. But word had got out, and the night before, a driver taking his cart over the bridge refused to pay and got into an altercation with the toll collector. Eventually the driver was allowed to cross toll-free and, of course, if he could do it, everyone else wanted to do it. So, for nine days, the folk of Bristol enjoyed free passage over the bridge and this new freedom was celebrated by the toll-gates, along with the board displaying the charges, being cheerfully consigned to a bonfire. It seemed that would be that.

The Corporation, however, took a dim view of these proceedings and on the Friday, announced a fifty-guinea reward for information about those who had actually damaged the bridge property. On Saturday 21st, the auction for the toll lease went ahead as planned but the lease did not fetch as much as expected, being bought for the low price of £1,920 by the dubious partnership of Wintour Harris, who was Deputy Chamberlain to the Corporation, and Thomas Symons, an attorney.

A week later, on the morning of Saturday 28 September, new toll-gates were put in place ready for the reinstatement of the tolls the following day. The day of the week was significant because Saturday nights in Bristol were the liveliest of the week – the combination of the weekly pay packet and readily available alcohol in the taverns creating a volatile Saturday-night mob.

Predictably, by the evening, the crowd had gathered, and again the toll-gates were ripped out and thrown on a fire, fuelled by wood brought from Welsh Back. The crowd was excitable, good-natured even, and there was none of the ugliness that can come from these situations. Not at that stage.

The first authority figure on the scene was magistrate George Daubeny. Whether from exasperation, belligerence or sheer panic, his first reaction was to shout at everyone and try to collar an innocent bystander, which resulted in an undignified scuffle.

By the end of the relatively uneventful evening, the crowd was beginning to disperse and the bonfire die down. Meanwhile, however, Mayor Bengough had summoned the militia, a Hereford regiment who happened to be in Bristol guarding French prisoners of war who were languishing in Stapleton Gaol. They marched through the streets, attracting attention and a curious following, so by 11 p.m. there were more people at the bridge than there had been all evening. The Riot Act was read, which did little to diffuse matters. The Riot Act, passed in 1715, stated that if a group of twelve or more refused to disperse after the act had been read to them, ordering them to do so in the name of the Crown, they were guilty of a felony that was punishable by death. However, it seems that many of the fascinated onlookers didn't realise that the act applied to them rather than just the obvious troublemakers; they stayed where they were. Daubeny gave the order for the soldiers to fire over their heads but as the crowd parted, there was a body on the ground. The first life had been lost.

Sunday 29th was supposed to mark a great civic occasion, the start of the new year and the investiture of a new mayor. The formalities started in the morning, in the Council House, where there was some discussion about the events of the night before but no-one seemed unduly perturbed. At midday, men were posted on the bridge ready to start taking tolls and Daubeny was on hand to supervise, but as vehicles approached the bridge, the gathering crowd started chanting 'No toll, no toll' and hustling the drivers not to pay. One cart driver on the Redcliffe side tried to retreat, backing up his horse but, in the mêlée, Daubeny grabbed the frightened horse's reins, the driver lashed out with his whip and Daubeny dragged him to the ground. It was not the most dignified example of the authorities in action.

Again the Riot Act was read three times and again the militia turned up but apart from some jostling and chanting, there was no real conflict and by dusk the crowd dispersed along with the militia, the constables and the magistrates, leaving the bridge unattended and allowing free passage.

It could have been left there, but on the next morning, Monday 30th, as the city was at its busiest, at 9 a.m. a chain was put across the bridge bringing the already congested traffic to a standstill and backing up the chaos throughout the centre of the city. The magistrates and constables arrived and the militia summoned yet again. Daubeny tried – and failed miserably – to improve the situation by lecturing the crowd. When the militia arrived there was still no action and it seems the crowd was confused as to why the soldiers were present and under whose authority they served. The Riot Act was read yet again but apart from some shoving and chanting, the presence of the military did at least allow the tolls to be collected. Daubeny was even collecting them himself but tempers were definitely on the rise.

At dusk the militia was sent back to barracks and some young men started another bonfire, this time breaking into the toll-house and throwing the furniture on the flames. Some of the militia returned and one lieutenant led eight of his soldiers onto the bridge but they were beaten back by the crowd, members of which threw anything they could find. Just after 8 p.m., more soldiers marched from the Council House to the bridge and lined up in the firing position of two ranks, the front rank kneeling. The jeering crowd became quiet as the tension rose and everyone waited to see what would happen.

No-one knows what triggered the events of the next few minutes. Without any warning and no clear order, the soldiers suddenly fired a volley directed straight down St Thomas Street. The crowd panicked and fled, trying to reach safety in doorways, anywhere out of the line of fire, but then the second row of soldiers fired. Amidst the chaos of thousands of people it was a disaster. There were probably only fifty or so actual troublemakers in the crowd and the rest were spectators but the soldiers made no discrimination. As they crossed the south side of the bridge, they broke rank and started to pursue rioters into buildings despite the latters' screams and cries for mercy.

At the end of the evening, eleven had been killed and forty-five wounded; the death-toll was to rise to fourteen as more casualties died of their wounds.

On the next day, the lease of the bridge was bought by four citizens who then opened the bridge for free – tolls would never again be charged on

A late 19th century view of St Nicholas church from the Redcliffe side of Bristol Bridge on the right. To the left is Welsh Back.

Bristol Bridge. The toll-house was eventually knocked down to widen the carriageway and the nineteenth century saw further improvements to the bridge and the carriageway but today's bridge is sitting on essentially the same structure as the 1769 bridge.

And what of The Quay? As Bristol's shipping decreased and its population increased, the Frome became more and more of a hindrance to the traffic flow. It was covered over, beginning in 1857 when culverts were built to carry the river underground, from St John's Bridge to Stone Bridge, the new surface creating what is now Rupert Street.

In 1874 trams were introduced to Bristol and by 1938 the last part of The Quay was covered over in front of the Hippodrome to form the Tramway Centre, or to give its local name, the Centre. The Hippodrome was opened in 1912, so before the final culverting of the Frome, there were ships moored outside the theatre. Eventually the heart of Bristol's trade and shipping became a glorified road-traffic roundabout and although improvements were made in 2000, in celebration of the new millennium, the Centre is still dominated by traffic.

In the 1950s Bristol Bridge was widened and resurfaced, now a seamless continuation of the surrounding streets. It seems soulless compared to the bustle and excitement of the medieval bridge, an understated reminder of the beginnings of the city at the end of Welsh Back and Baldwin Street.

But the story doesn't end there. There is a saying: 'History repeats itself. Has to. Nobody listens.'

In August 2005, in a startling example of déjà vu, the company operating the new bridge across the Severn, the 'Second Severn Crossing', announced that they hadn't realised that they had to pay VAT on the tolls they had collected. These tolls were to contribute to the cost of building the bridge and had been calculated to reach the target income by 2014. But now the company owes the VAT on tolls already collected and consequently motorists will have to continue to pay the current tolls until late 2016. The Government will have clawed back £150 million. By then, of course, the bridge will need repairing and the tolls will be needed to raise the money for its upkeep. As they say, history does indeed repeat itself.

When the river Frome was covered over to create the Tramway Centre, the first trams were horse-drawn, leaving the unfortunate job of clearing up after the horses. The church tower in the background is St Stephen's.

CHAPTER 3

THE CASTLE IN THE PARK

There are castles all over Britain in varying degrees of preservation, from the magnificence of the Tower of London with its eternal stream of tourists to the impressive ruins of Chepstow Castle that dominates the Welsh town. Some castles are classed as heritage sites or preserved by the National Trust, some are still privately owned, such as Berkeley in Gloucestershire, and others, like Corfe Castle in Dorset, are open ruins, exposed to the elements and now part of the countryside. All these castles and more have a real presence in the landscape.

So it is hard to imagine one of the biggest castles in England standing in what is now an attractive green park, sandwiched neatly between the 1990s shopping centre known as The Galleries and the River Avon.

Part of the ruins of Bristol's castle, all that remains of what was once England's second biggest castle.

Castle Park stretches from the corner of High Street and Wine Street, just above Bristol Bridge, to Lower Castle Street, with Newgate and Broad Weir to the north and the Avon to the south.

Criss-crossed with footpaths and dotted with trees, the park contains the ruined shells of the churches of St Mary le Port and St Peter's, as well as a herb garden, some elegant sculptures, a very fine castellated public toilet building and a bandstand donated by the *Bristol Evening Post*. It serves as a shortcut, a dog-walking park, a picnic area and a place to just sit, to escape from the bustling shopping centre.

The southern edge of the park slopes away to the riverside path and the view back up to the park from this path gives an idea of how high the land was between the two rivers. Among the grass, trees and paths of the park are the scattered ruins of the once-great Bristol Castle.

The Saxon town of Brigstowe was protected by the natural formation of the two rivers and most of the wooden buildings of the settlement were clustered on this higher ground, which gave added protection from potential threat of attack.

The arrival of the Normans in 1066 brought major changes to the whole country as well as Bristol. At that time, Bristol was part of the manor of Barton Regis, which was immediately claimed by the new king – William the Conqueror. England now had a new ruling class, one that spoke French instead of English and one that claimed whatever it wanted in terms of land and property.

William then gave this land to one of his allies, Geoffrey de Coutances. Geoffrey was a bishop but was not averse to a battle or two; he had fought beside William at the Battle of Hastings, establishing his loyalty to the King.

One of the most dramatic changes the Normans brought to the country was the building of castles. Within 40 years or so of the Conquest, there were as many as 6,000 new castles in England. In Bristol, Geoffrey set about turning the basic Saxon reinforcements into a castle in order to protect the settlement. Unfortunately, to do so, it seems he demolished some of the housing that was in the way, adopting the typically high-handed approach that was characteristic of the Normans' domination of the country.

Geoffrey built a style of castle popular in the early-Norman period, the motte-and-bailey castle. The motte was an artificially raised mound of earth and stone with a flattened top that could be used as a lookout point with a watch-tower or even temporary accommodation; it was about sixty metres across. The motte was surrounded by a deep 'motte ditch', in places six metres deep and twelve metres wide. Outside that was the bailey, a courtyard that was, in turn, surrounded by a raised embankment topped by a fence of wooden stakes. The 'bailey ditch', about five metres wide, surrounded this embankment and the overall result was a relatively secure and impregnable castle.

As with any claim to the throne, the reigning monarch needed to be confident of a strong, clearly identified heir. William the Conqueror was also Duke of Normandy and had effectively brought England into the Duchy of Normandy but rather than leave everything to one son, he named his eldest son Robert to become Duke of Normandy, and his next living son, known as William Rufus, to succeed him as King of England. Not everyone agreed with this decision and there were many, including Robert, who thought that England should have been left to himself rather than William Rufus. Geoffrey de Coutances sided with Robert, and he and Robert's supporters rose up in rebellion against William Rufus.

It wasn't a good idea. William Rufus' forces quashed the rebellion and those who had supported the uprising were punished. Geoffrey was exiled and his land taken back by the Crown. He died later in exile in France.

William Rufus died in mysterious circumstances, allegedly killed in a hunting accident in the New Forest and, having no children, was succeeded by his brother Henry, who became King Henry I. Henry now took charge of the lands confiscated from the rebels and gave Barton Regis and Bristol to Robert Fitzhamon, one of the barons who had stayed loyal to William Rufus throughout the rebellion. In a time of political intrigue, marriages of alliance and strict lines of inheritance, Fitzhamon had no sons but had been blessed with four daughters. This was convenient for Henry I whose idea of marriage did not stretch to fidelity (he was the father of several illegitimate children). Everyone agreed that his eldest illegitimate son, Robert, should marry Fitzhamon's eldest daughter Mabel, which meant he stood to inherit the estate of Bristol along with Fitzhamon's other estates. Robert was instated as Earl of Gloucester and, with his wife Mabel, made Bristol his home. As a leading figure in the city, one of his first acts was to improve on the castle that had been started by Geoffrey de Coutances.

Only a matter of forty years after Geoffrey's castle had been completed, Robert started further reinforcements and improvements and the most dramatic addition was the great keep, built from stone imported from Caen in France.

Even by the standards of the great Norman castles of the time, the keep was enormous. It was built on the north-east corner of Geoffrey's motte, and was about 100 feet by 95 feet at the base with 25 feet thick walls; it was about 100 feet high with a lead roof. Various written accounts, and later illustrations,

Detail from Millerd's map of Bristol from 1673 showing the castle from the river; its shows the keep and the tops of houses are visible in the Outer Ward.

imply that the keep had four towers with the south-west tower approximately 30 feet higher than the others.

The castle grew into a fortified town. As well as the keep, it had two divisions, an Inner Ward and an Outer Ward. The Outer Ward contained the keep itself, a chapel dedicated to St Martin and lodgings for the constable of the castle. There were apartments for the housing of the castle garrison, stabling for horses and three wells to provide a safe water-supply in times of siege. When one of the wells was later excavated, a human skeleton was

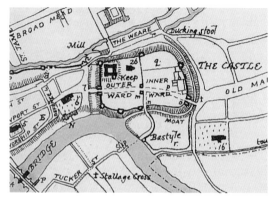

Detail of Bristol Castle from a map of 1480. The keep is in the north west corner of the outer ward.

found – a person probably in their early teens – alongside the arm bones of another adult skeleton.

To the east of the keep, the Inner Ward contained a Royal Chapel, a banquet hall and the Prince's Chambers.

The River Frome was partially diverted to form a moat. By diverting the Frome in a loop around the castle, the moat then joined the Avon at an impressive water gate, and the castle and the remaining town to the west was entirely surrounded by water. The moat is still there – it runs underground and its entrance can still be seen to the south-east of Castle Park where a pedestrian bridge spans a narrow tributary that leads back into the castle complex. It is theoretically possible to navigate the moat by boat following a route underground for about a mile, tracing it back to the Frome and emerging as the Frome joins the Avon at the Watershed media centre. A journey in the dark along Bristol's answer to the River Styx might not be to everyone's taste but access is retained for maintenance and for the collection of debris that inevitably finds its way down into the water.

When Robert was building the castle, he also considered the defence of the whole town. The population was growing and spilling out beyond the

The castle's moat, partially created from the natural course of the river Frome. Today the moat still exists, flowing under Castle Park.

original walls so a new wall was built to the south, crossing the ground between the rivers.

New gates to the city were built, including Redcliffe Gate, Temple Gate and, to the north, Newgate. Weirs that were built to divert the moat and Newgate are remembered in the street names; Newgate joins Broad Weir as a continuous street that separates Castle Park from Broadmead.

Although Robert's priority was to defend the town with its valuable harbour, he also attended to the spiritual needs of the citizens. His father-in-law, Robert Fitzhamon, had already built St Peter's Church close to the castle, and its shell still stands on Castle Green, but Robert, Earl of Gloucester, founded St James' Priory.

St James' is still there, its church and churchyard a haven of tranquillity sandwiched between the north edge of Broadmead shopping centre and the bus station. Local legend has it that Robert gave every tenth stone from building the castle to the building of St James'. He also built the church of St Ewan at the corner of Broad Street and Corn Street; the church still exists, now known as Christchurch, incorporating St Ewan and St George.

Bristol Castle played a crucial role in the events of England. As Earl Robert's stronghold, it was central to the civil war that raged in the twelfth century, the period known as the Anarchy.

The problem arose because Henry I died in 1135 without a legitimate male heir. Henry had sired two sons, and the eldest, William, was named as his successor but, in 1120, a terrible accident occurred whereby the *White Ship*, the newest and fastest ship in the English fleet, sank with all hands as it left the French coast bound for England – carrying Henry's two sons.

This left his only other legitimate heir – a woman. His daughter Matilda (Maud) had been married to the Emperor Henry V of Germany, hence her title Empress Matilda. But Matilda was widowed in 1125 so Henry brought her back and made his barons swear to accept her as his heir if he had no more sons. As a political pawn, she was then married off to a boy aged sixteen, Geoffrey d'Anjou, and the marriage was disastrous.

And what of Bristol's role in all this?

With Henry's death, the throne should have gone to Matilda, as agreed, but the all-powerful barons could not – or would not – entertain the idea of a woman on the throne, especially a woman in a stormy marriage to Geoffrey d'Anjou, who was considered untrustworthy and headstrong. Admittedly, the contemporary chronicle giving the most information on this was written by a sympathiser of Stephen's (Henry I's nephew, Matilda's cousin) so the account might not be entirely objective, but stories were rife of brigands and thieves ranging the countryside, robbing and kidnapping with impunity.

Stephen may have tried to negotiate with the Bristolians but made no progress, so in 1138 he led an army to try to capture the castle, as Earl Robert had sided with Matilda, his half-sister, in the conflict. It didn't work. Robert had built the castle and the town's defences to be impregnable and some historians also think that Stephen didn't have the tenacity for a long siege.

It seems that he simply gave up, and Bristol remained Matilda's and Robert's stronghold. When Stephen was taken prisoner at the Battle of Lincoln in 1141, he was imprisoned at Bristol while his wife continued the struggle. During this period Matilda was temporarily elected as Queen. The situation was brought to a head when Robert was captured by Stephen's wife's forces at Winchester, and to break a crippling stalemate, the prisoners were exchanged.

The whole sorry mess was eventually resolved by the Treaty of Westminster. Stephen's son Eustace, who would have succeeded him, had died so a compromise was reached whereby Stephen would remain on the throne until his death, when Matilda's eldest son Henry would succeed him.

Henry had come to England with Matilda and during the drawn-out years of civil war had spent his time in Bristol, with another prominent citizen, Robert Fitzharding. Here he was tutored and groomed for future kingship. His tutor was 'Master Matthew' but it is likely he also met key scholars of the time, such as Geoffrey of Monmouth (author of *History of the Kings of Britain*) and Adelard of Bath.

When the time came for Henry to become King, as Henry II, he didn't forget Bristol; in 1155 he granted Bristol a charter, freeing the citizens from paying tolls and affirming their rights as freemen. In 1181, he reaffirmed Bristol's rights to hold its own courts rather than travel the full day's journey to Gloucester.

But he was wary of the castle. The experience of Bristol forming a stronghold for rebels against the Crown made Henry want to control it for himself. Earl Robert had left the castle to his son, William of Gloucester, and there was an uneasy truce between him and Henry over its ownership and control. The end of Henry's reign was plagued by squabbles between his sons; Henry and Geoffrey had died and Richard, to be the Lionheart, and John were forever plotting with their mother, Eleanor d'Aquitaine, as to who would take over Henry's throne.

In an attempt to keep some control over the castle, and keep things in the family, Henry had John, his youngest son, betrothed to William of Gloucester's daughter, known as Isabella of Gloucester. When William died in 1173, the estate went to his daughter and hence to John. In 1199, when he succeeded his brother Richard, John had no qualms annulling the marriage and keeping the estate for himself.

The castle, now in the hands of the King, led to a bizarre legal situation; it was outside the jurisdiction of the town. As castles are expensive to maintain, the simplest way for the King to raise the money was to tax the town – not a popular idea with the citizens.

This situation survived for the next 100 years or so, until when, in the early 1300s, tensions came to a head. Edward I died in 1307 and his son Edward II came to the throne, one of England's less effective kings. In 1309, Edward II appointed a new royal constable for the castle, Bartholomew of Badlesmere, with authority over all the residents of Bristol, including the mayor. As if this didn't rankle enough, the task of collecting the taxes due to the Crown fell to him and as long as he delivered the sum of £210 every year, there was no need for detailed accounts or any checks on the collection methods used. This created obvious opportunities for fraud and corruption. As Badlesmere carried out this duty through his deputies, who no doubt also took their own advantage of the situation, the people of Bristol felt they were being fleeced and were not at all happy about such matters.

Resentment simmered under the surface but in January 1312, Edward, reacting to his curtailment by the barons and the banishment of his lover, Piers Gaveston, tried to once more assert his authority. By now he was doubtful of Badlesmere's loyalty so attempted to replace him with someone else – Badlesmere, however, wasn't going anywhere. He was determined to stay where he was in the castle and despite the best efforts of the King, refused to leave. In July, Edward, in a typical display of weakness, gave in and reappointed Badlesmere but the townsfolk had taken advantage of the power vacuum and a rebellion was well under way.

Their wrath had been fuelled by the imposition of demands from the castle; not only were they expected to supply provisions to the castle garrison, they were also to provide military supplies. The muttering and grumbling became a full-scale confrontation when the constable imposed another tax; on behalf of the Crown he demanded a 'tallage', a tax originally employed to raise money for military campaigns. In this case the tax was imposed on fish – and the fishmongers refused to pay.

It didn't help that the town was run by a closed group of fourteen merchants who acted in their own interest and sided with the constable of the castle. So, in September 1312, the people of the town elected their own representative, John Taverner. No ruffian, Taverner was a respectable merchant who had twice been Mayor of Bristol and its Member of Parliament, and he could organise people. This was more than an unruly discontent mob, this was a concerted attack on the castle, and hence the Crown. Wooden barriers and towers were built around the perimeter of the castle, as well as a masonry wall, parallel to the western wall of the castle, complete with battlements to enable the rebels to shoot arrows into the Outer Ward.

Bristol was in a state of internal civil war.

The fourteen merchants that had sided with the constable were driven out and their property seized; in January 1313, their leader, William Randolf tried to appeal to the King for their restoration but despite several orders to the rebels, nothing was forthcoming. The Sheriffs of Gloucestershire, Somerset and Dorset were dragged into the fray, ordered by the King to restore order and get Bristol under control.

Taverner and associates were arrested, taken to London and imprisoned in the Tower. The townspeople were still defiant but with their leader out of action, they lacked focus. The rebellion could have been stopped there and then but for reasons known only to himself, Edward allowed Taverner and his associates to be released on bail.

In June 1313 the Crown conceded that the Bristol merchants might have a case, which sounds more enlightened than it was because when the commission of enquiry was set up, it was headed by Thomas Berkeley. Berkeley was already in dispute with the people of Bristol and consequently this was not the most sensitive of appointments. In addition, the jury was to be made up of people from outside the city and evidence would only be considered from those living outside Bristol or from those who had taken no part in the disturbances. It was a recipe for disaster.

The enquiry was to be held in the upper floor of the Guildhall but the townspeople were already convinced it would be a whitewash. A riot broke out as an incensed crowd stormed the Guildhall armed with sticks and fists; they held the commissioner prisoner and attacked the members of the commission. Some people panicked and jumped out of the windows, breaking limbs on the street below. The whole unpleasant incident left twenty people dead.

Edward then declared the rebels to be outlaws but Taverner set up his own ruling council and the result was a city in stalemate. All through 1314 Bristol was split into two armed camps and although, in June, the Earl of Gloucester was ordered to march on Bristol with 20,000 men, he didn't reach the city. His orders were countermanded – all available troops were needed to travel north, to fight against the Scots at Bannockburn.

The fiasco dragged on into 1315 when the Sheriff of Gloucestershire made three attempts to restore order and arrest Taverner. On his third attempt, he found the city gates closed and barred and the people ready for war. It didn't come to an end until the summer of 1316, when the Earl of Pembroke arrived with siege equipment. He meant business; he closed off the roads, took control of the river and stopped all supplies from reaching the town. The people had no choice but to surrender. The 'Great Insurrection' was over.

Surprisingly, the repercussions were not as bad as they could have been. Bristol was fined just over £1,000 in gold and was forced to pay its back taxes but there was not the mass capital punishment that could have been inflicted. John Taverner, his son and another associate were outlawed but in 1321 they were pardoned; in 1322, Taverner was re-elected as Bristol's representative in Parliament.

The old tower in Castle Street. Part of the old castle wall, this was demolished in the 1920s.

Edward's continuing unhappy relationship with Bristol Castle came to an end in 1329. Conspiracies and plots that had circulated throughout his reign finally culminated in Edward being briefly imprisoned in the castle before being moved on to Berkeley Castle to meet his gruesome death.

Bristol Castle continually suffered from a lack of maintenance and, by the fourteenth century, was already falling into a state of disrepair. Still theoretically owned by the Crown, it was a refuge for criminals who, by hiding in the castle, were immune from prosecution from the civic authorities who could not legally enter the castle and arrest them on Crown property. By 1629 the castle was in ruins and the city wanted to take it back from the Crown. On the 13th of April, the castle was made part of the city and county of Bristol for the fee of £250 but this did not include various rights, which were still charged at £40 per year to the Crown. In October 1630, by paying out yet more money, Bristol took total control of the castle and all the royal properties associated with it. By buying out the lease of the last incumbent constable, the castle was finally part of Bristol.

Castle Street was Bristol's main shopping area until it was demolished in the bombing of World War Two.

By 1640, it was becoming obvious that civil war was again looming on the horizon and the castle was prepared for war. Cottages that had been built in the Outer Ward were demolished to make space for the troops to manoeuvre and guards were put on duty. The Civil War and its effect on Bristol are described elsewhere, but for the castle, 1654 saw Cromwell order its demolition along with many other English castles. The townsfolk were delighted and the demolition was unopposed. The stone was used for other building projects in the city and gradually the land changed use; in time, Castle Street became the main shopping centre of Bristol – a busy, bustling and thriving street.

But, like much of the city, the devastation of the bombing in the 1940s blitz brought Castle Street's central status to an end. The area was laid out as a park in 1978 and updated to its current form in 1993.

Apart from the name of the park and a few ruins that are easy to miss when passing through Castle Park in a hurry, it seems as if Bristol Castle has completely vanished. But it is still part of the city – on the coat of arms. This shows a merchant ship in full sail on the river leaving the safety of the castle's water gate and flanked by two unicorns.

The coat of arms, in various different guises, is seen all over the city – on bridges, public buildings, decoration on the ss *Great Britain* and in the crest of Bristol City Football Club to name but a few. It seems that the combination of the river, the castle and the ship is a powerful reminder of Bristol's origins.

Bristol's coat of arms showing the ship, the river and the castle.

CHAPTER 4

THE TEMPLE

From Bristol Bridge, a wide, rather soulless street runs almost directly to Temple Meads railway station: Victoria Street. Built in 1870 to carry traffic from the gleaming new railway terminus to the ancient southern approach to the city, it cuts through the districts of Temple and St Thomas. In doing so, it passes boarded-up warehouses and shops and then skirts an isolated group of seventeenth-century buildings that include the Shakespeare Inn and heads back towards a church known locally as the Temple Church.

Officially named the Church of the Holy Cross, the building is ruined now, sandwiched between the pub and a uniform grey office block, the

Victoria Street at the end of the 19th century, looking in the direction of Bristol Bridge, showing the square-topped tower of Temple Church.

The Shakespeare inn, a 17th century building that was once part of Temple Street and is now part of the 19th century Victoria Street.

Crescent Centre. Its walls are still standing but there is no interior; it could be one of the several shells of churches that are the legacy of the Blitz, except for its distinguishing feature – its tower, dating from the fourteenth and fifteenth centuries, leans in a disconcerting manner; at thirty-five metres high, the top is one-and-a-half metres off the vertical.

The church has been deconsecrated and is now under the care of English Heritage; there is no access to the interior but it is possible to walk round the exterior. To the west of the church this feels claustrophobic because the surrounding buildings are close and imposing, but to the south-east, the churchyard is now a delightful secluded garden with trees and benches and a sense of space stolen from the surrounding concrete.

Inside the church, glimpsed by peering through the window arches, the ground has been marked by two concentric circular paths that show the ground plan of the original building. The church was circular because it had been built by the Knights Templar and it was for them that the district of Temple was named.

So who were the Knights Templar? Why were they so important that their legacy still haunts a city like Bristol?

Temple Church, formally known as the Church of Holy Cross, and built on the site of the church of the Knights Templar.

To some extent they have become legend, present in popular fiction, Hollywood films and conspiracy theories, all exploiting tales of dark secrets and hidden treasure. But the Knights Templar were real and to establish them in Bristol means separating reality from fantasy.

Their origins lie as far back as the eleventh century when Europe was gripped by the fanatical warmongering known as the Crusades. Pilgrims travelling to the Holy Land were a long way from home and vulnerable to hardships including the unfamiliar land and climate, disease, and marauding gangs of Muslim bandits who saw the Christian pilgrims as an obvious and easy target. The Kingdom of Jerusalem consisted of just a few strongholds and the pilgrims had little means of defending themselves.

In around 1119, a group of eight French knights, led by Hugh de Payens, set up a religious order sworn to protect these pilgrims. The King of Jerusalem, Baldwin II, gave them premises in a part of the temple in the city and the knights became the 'pauvres chevaliers du temple', the 'poor knights of the Temple': the Knights Templar.

The Templars adopted the rule of Bernard, the founder of the Cistercian order. In 1128, Hugh de Payens went to the Council of Troyes (the capital city of Champagne). Here, the Templars formally adopted the Cistercian rule, forming new, hybrid 'warrior monks'. The Cistercians had been established by St Bernard de Clairvaux in response to what he saw as the deterioration in standards of the Benedictines, identified by their dark robes, the 'Blackfriars'. Cistercians wore robes of undyed wool, hence they became known as the white monks or 'Whitefriars'. By adopting the rule of the Cistercians, the Templars swore to obey the rules of obedience, poverty and chastity. They wore the Cistercians' white robes, later adding the distinctive red eight-pointed cross that made them so instantly recognisable.

Despite the austerity of the warrior monks' lifestyle, there was no shortage of recruits, drawn from all levels of society. There were four levels of membership. The knights were each allowed up to three horses and, in a time when the fashion for men was to wear long hair, the knights had to crop their hair and wear full beards; they were the only members of the order to wear the red cross on their white robes. The sergeants were also fighting men, equipped more like a light cavalry when compared to the knights' heavy cavalry, but they were usually from a lower social order than the knights. 'Farmers' administered the property of the order and the chaplains were ordained priests who looked after the spiritual needs of the members.

The Knights Templar became heroes in the eyes of Europe. Their original rule of poverty became less well defined as donations flooded in, from kings, princes, heads of state and wealthy landowners; the Templars were ideal recipients for those who believed that giving money and property could buy credit in the afterlife.

In 1128 Hugh de Payens visited England and met Henry I, who granted him a house in Holborn. By 1129 the London Temple had been established and by the 1130s, Hugh de Payens had returned to the Holy Land and was setting up a chain of 'commanderies', or 'preceptories', across Europe. These would be administrative centres, supply and requisition depots, training and recruiting centres and retirement homes for wounded or elderly brethren.

And so it was that in 1145, Robert of Gloucester gave the Templars an area of marshy ground to the south of Bristol's city walls.

With Robert's help, they set about building a church. The design was based on the traditional Temple churches, such as the one in London, with a circular or elliptical nave. They built themselves a priory and excavations have revealed what could be the remains of a twelfth-century hall.

The area occupied by the Templars became known as the Temple Fee, still reflected in the parish name of 'Temple'. This became the administrative centre of the South West and the port of Bristol was crucial to their administration. Not only did they need to stay in contact with their brethren in

Europe, they also imported goods such as wine from the French preceptories and this cargo was shipped into Bristol. From there, goods could be distributed to other centres in the west of England.

The Templars became an integral part of Bristol's community – with one strange exception. The order was responsible only to the Pope, it owed no allegiance to king or state and paid taxes to no-one other than the Vatican; it seemed to be a 'Church within a Church, a State within a State'.

In practical terms, this meant that the Temple Fee was outside the jurisdiction of the authorities of Bristol. They held their own market, the 'Stallage', which was held in Temple Street and indicated by the ancient Stallage Cross. They raised their own taxes and – crucially – dispensed their own justice. This meant that if a felon, accused of a crime in Bristol, could escape to the Temple Fee he was immune from prosecution. The area became a haven for criminals and ne'er-do-wells, much to the frustration of Bristol's civic authorities.

Yet the Templars brought prosperity to the city. They were shrewd and successful businessmen, managing their resources to the full. By 1185, they had 27 tenants, paying between 3d and 4s a year rent. Among these tenants

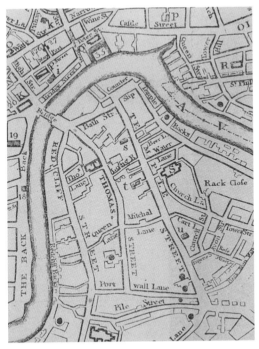

A detail of the Temple area from Mathew's map of 1794, showing the areas of Temple, St Thomas and Redcliffe within the loop of the river Avon.

were three skinners, which implies that there was a tannery on the land. There were also the early activities of the textile industry, which was to become the main employer of the Temple area.

Every knight had to serve in three campaigns on the land and two at sea before being allowed to retire. Crusaders leaving England would first cross the Bay of Biscay to the Portuguese town of Oporto. This was during the period of the Second Crusade and at that time, Portugal was torn by war. Lisbon was held by the Moors, so in a fit of pious enthusiasm the Crusaders joined in with the siege to claim Lisbon back for Christianity. It was at this campaign that some of the Templars from Bristol were reputed to be far more interested in piracy and looting than in the spiritual needs of Portugal. In terms of the Crusades, this Portuguese campaign was counted alongside engagements in the Holy Land as a legitimate operation to reclaim Christian land from the Infidel, so many Crusaders considered they had fulfilled their obligations and, rather than continue the long journey to Jerusalem, they simply went home.

By the thirteenth century, the Templars were so far removed from their original oath of poverty, having accumulated so much wealth and power, that they were making certain heads of state nervous. The Templars were the first international bankers; initially as a way of protecting travellers, they devised a system of accepting a cash deposit in, say, Paris, and issuing a credit note that could be redeemed later in the journey. It was safer than carrying gold around and convenient for both travellers and Templars.

The Templars were prepared to lend money, often to heads of state or rulers, which led to some very powerful people being in their debt. They charged interest on their loans, at the time forbidden by the Church – this was the sin of 'usary', which also made the Church uneasy and the Templars unpopular.

By the twelfth and thirteenth centuries, the Templars had expanded their financial dealings to take on the job of tax collection. For example, in Bristol, in 1238, a mandate from the King to the bailiffs of Bristol demanded they supply good barrels and good carts to John de Plessis, Brother Robert the Templar and a third knight so they could transport the King's revenue – the tax – to the New Temple in London.

In England, the Templars seemed to be well integrated into the local communities and on good terms with the Crown but in Europe, the relationship was much less amiable. Their wealth and power, along with their independent status, led to envious eyes being turned in their direction. Whispers and rumours began to drift around, tentative at first but gaining strength, claiming that the Templars were involved in practices that were at best blasphemous and at worst Satanic. It was the excuse for which Philip IV of France – Philip 'The Fair' – had been waiting. He also happened to be desperately short of money which may have had an influence on his quarrel with the Templars; the rumours also suggested they had amassed a vast treasure, stored in a secret location. Whatever his true motivation, Philip ignored the protests of the somewhat weak and ineffectual Pope, Clement V, and made his move.

At dawn on Friday 13 October 1307, every Templar in France was arrested – the original 'Friday the Thirteenth'.

Philip had no intention of confining his actions to France, however. He had sent out edicts to other heads of state across Europe for them to join him in arresting all the knights. His plan was nothing short of annihilation. He wasted no time in the niceties of justice, instead he arranged for the Templars under arrest to be tortured to extract confessions of their wrongdoings. It was a gruesome affair, the confessions meaningless under such duress, but that did not bother Philip. By 1314, nearly sixty knights had been burned at the stake, including their grand master, Jacques de Molay, and all their property seized.

In England, however, things were slightly different. Edward II had succeeded his omnipotent, domineering father Edward I and had only been on the throne for four months when Philip sent the order to the heads of state in Europe to arrest the Templars. Edward made no immediate move to do so; it seems that he simply did not believe the charges and was prepared to defend the Templars, even writing to the Pope to confirm his opinion. Even though the Pope initially sided with Edward, Philip was too powerful and so the Pope gave in and issued a papal bull against the Templars.

It was not until early 1308 that Edward took action; only under threat of ex-communication from the Pope did he send out orders for the knights to be arrested and imprisoned. It was all very gentlemanly, with an inventory being taken of each preceptory and the knights being allowed to take their own bedding and possessions with them to their imprisonment. In Bristol, the knights were taken to the castle and from the large Somerset preceptory at Templecombe, three knights were taken to the Tower of London. There are various accounts about the fate of the Templars but they did not suffer the fate of their French counterparts. There are several reasons for this.

The justice system in England was very different from that of France and in England, the Inquisition had no jurisdiction. Philip had used the Inquisition to torture and extract confessions from the arrested Templars, but in England, justice was dispensed by a jury of peers and torture was forbidden. Two officers of the Inquisition came to England in 1310 but were not allowed to use torture under English law. Of the knights arrested, only three confessions were extracted.

However, the order was eventually revoked by order of the Pope so the Templars themselves were discretely retired to monasteries where they were to live as monks for the rest of their lives and, again by order of the Pope, their property and lands were passed directly to their brothers, the Knights of St John, the Hospitallers.

The Knights of St John were another order that had been founded in Jerusalem in the eleventh century, this time by Italian merchants from Amalfi who set out to care for the sick and wounded among the pilgrims. When the Crusades came to an end, they moved to Cyprus, then in 1309, acquired the island of Rhodes which they ruled as an independent state for more than 200 years. In a sense, the two orders were rivals but the Knights of St John – also known as the Hospitallers – were less controversial and escaped the persecution endured by the Templars.

When the Templars were disbanded and persecuted, they left behind many a legend and myth but the one that seems to have lasted the longest and most captured the imagination is that of the treasure. The Templars certainly were wealthy but stories abounded that their treasure had been smuggled out of France or hidden out of Philip's reach. This mythical treasure has never been found, although it has spawned some entertaining tales of adventure.

As the Hospitallers took over the Temple Fee, one of the first changes they made was to rebuild the parish church. Fashions come and go in architecture as much as anywhere else and the circular nave of the old Church of the Holy Cross made way for a new, rectangular, aisled nave. But there was a problem. The marshy land donated to the Templars nearly 200 years earlier was just as marshy in the fourteenth century and the Hospitallers did not drain the land properly while building the new church.

The result was the 'leaning tower of Bristol'. The church was built in the Decorated style of the early-fourteenth century and the Perpendicular style of the late-fourteenth century, although this name is an unfortunate one for the tower! The first two stages were completed around 1390 and as the tower started to lean over, the builders rather sensibly decided to stop before it collapsed. Eventually, by around 1460, the tower seemed to have stabilised so a third stage was added, built to what was then the vertical to compensate for the leaning. Unfortunately, the additional weight started the tower leaning again so the builders opted out of adding the planned parapet and pinnacles, leaving a flat-topped tower. It was also said that when the bells rang, the tower swayed alarmingly, although one enterprising individual, in an extreme case of using a sledgehammer to crack nuts, would put nuts into the gaps between the tower and church wall during bell-ringing practise, and use the movement of the tower as a nutcracker!

As the Templars had been granted independence from the state, this feudal condition continued with the Knights of St John, who had established their own independent state in the Mediterranean. It was not resolved until 1535, when Henry VIII ruled that the civic authorities had the power of arrest in the Temple Fee. In any case, the whole matter became irrelevant when, in 1541, the monasteries were dissolved and the property of the Knights Hospitaller was confiscated by the Crown. For 400 years, the Temple Fee had been an independent pocket of Bristol, with its own system of jurisdiction and identity.

Encouraged by the Templars, the Temple Fee had become the centre of the weaving industry in Bristol, and its prosperity was given a further boost when, in 1337, Edward III banned the export of raw wool. English wool was considered the best in Europe, bought by Flemish and Italian weavers to be turned into cloth. Bristol's trade relied on the high-quality wool brought from the Cotswolds. Edward insisted that the cloth was woven in England for export at a higher price. It was a good idea in principle but it meant England was desperately short of experienced weavers and the only answer was to recruit them from abroad.

In Bristol, Flemish weavers set up production in the Temple Fee, including one Thomas Blanket. Local legend would have it that he invented the woollen cloth that bears his name although this is unlikely; his name is simply a variation of 'Blanquette', which means 'white cloth'.

The weavers, similar to many other craftsmen, formed themselves into a guild that regulated standards, prices, wages and so forth and membership was strictly regulated. The Weavers' Guild had its own chapel in the Temple Church, dedicated to St Catherine, the weavers' patron saint.

Most of the cloth industry in the Temple Fee consisted of weaving wool that had already been prepared elsewhere. The weavers would buy the wool in skeins of yarn, which were then loaded onto the loom, the warp onto the loom framework and the weft onto the quills that fitted into the loom shuttle. Once the cloth had been woven, it was scoured, usually in stale urine, to remove oil and size, then cleaned with soap and 'fulled' under water, either by treading or beating, and using fullers' earth. The cloth was then soaking wet and had shrunk; it had to be brushed (often with dried teasel heads) to raise the nap, before it was stretched across 'tenters', a framework of upright wooden poles, to dry. The selvedges of the stretched cloth were held in place by 'tenterhooks', an expression still used today; to be 'on tenterhooks' means a state of nervous waiting under tension.

The street names gave some indication of the processes involved; 'Tucker Street' was named for the 'tucker', the west-country name for a 'fuller'. On older maps of Bristol such as Millerd's map of 1673, the Rack Closes are shown clearly with the racks in place.

Cloth was Bristol's most significant export for centuries, but with the invention of new water-powered mills for fulling the cloth, the industry moved to areas in the countryside with free-flowing streams; the fullers of Temple Fee began to lose their livelihood. Although cloth was still bought and sold at market, it was increasingly cloth brought in from outside the city than that made locally.

The areas of Temple and St Thomas deteriorated into over-populated slums and once Temple Meads railway station had been built, it became obvious that the link from the new station into the city via Bristol Bridge was hopelessly inadequate heading, as it did, through the less savoury areas of the city. Planned in 1845 but not completed until 1872, the new road, Victoria Street, cut a straight line through the area leading from the bridge to the terminus.

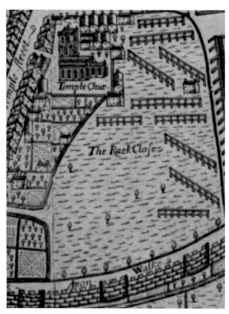

Detail from Millerd's map of 1673 showing the area known as Rack Close, showing the racks used for stretching the manufactured cloth produced in the Temple and St Thomas areas.

In 1940, Bristol suffered a terrible night during the Blitz; part of Victoria Street and the Temple Church were shattered. The shell of the church walls remained standing and the tower remained intact, but the interior was gutted. In the aftermath of the bombing, army engineers came to survey the damage, under orders to make safe or demolish any buildings that had been made unstable. Taking one look at the leaning tower, they started laying charges around the base to bring it down, until it was explained to them that the tower had leaned like that for 500 years and was not going to succumb to the Luftwaffe or the British army!

There are no real physical remains of the Knights Templar other than the marked layout of their original church but their memory is still preserved in local names: the dual carriageway Temple Way, Temple Street, Temple Rose Lane and, of course, Bristol Temple Meads railway station. It's said that the ghost of a Templar haunts the Fire Brigade Headquarters at Temple Back; the Templars were an integral part of the city for 200 years and are still – and always will be – players in the mythology of the city.

CHAPTER 5

MERCHANTS AND MIDDLEMEN

In 1446, the church of St Mary Redcliffe was struck by lightning. A dramatic electrical storm battered the city, a lightning bolt struck the tower and the wreckage crashed onto the church roof, destroying the nave. The church had been worked on for over 200 years and it was just about finished when disaster struck. A church had stood on this site from at least 1115 and the monument of a crusader knight in the north transept is likely to be that of Robert of Berkeley who gave the church the rights to water from a fresh spring two miles away in Knowle.

St Mary Redcliffe in the mid 1800s; the spire was not completed until the end of the century.

St Mary Redcliffe is a parish church and always was a parish church. From the end of the thirteenth century, a rebuilding programme was to take at least a century, with a brief hiatus when the Black Death came to Bristol. St Mary was a community church and in medieval times had at least twenty 'chantry' priests, paid by wealthy families to pray for them. And this is the key to understanding St Mary Redcliffe – it was sponsored and patronised by the merchants of Redcliffe. Today, it is a stunningly beautiful church; so much so, it is occasionally mistaken for Bristol's cathedral. Its spire, completed in the late nineteenth century, can be seen from most of Bristol's centre.

So, back in 1446 when lightning struck, it was a merchant who came to the rescue. William Canynges was five times Mayor of Bristol and twice Member of Parliament and he not only paid for the damaged roof to be rebuilt but made sure the repaired church was even more splendid. He paid for another level of windows to be added and the stone vault to be rebuilt with hundreds of carved bosses. Canynges also paid for a family tomb that carries a monument to his wife, Joanna. On her death, in 1467, he became a priest and so when he died, he was commemorated by a simple alabaster figure rather than made part of the family tomb with his wife.

The design of the church follows a continental style, with its vaulting and an eastern Lady Chapel, rare for a parish church. When rebuilding started in 1340, to renovate the existing church, it was mostly in the Perpendicular style; this was the last of the Gothic styles of architecture of the Middle Ages, and is recognised by its light, high windows and magnificent towers. The building was interrupted by the Black Death of 1347 but this phase of building, finished by the end of century, remains as a symbol of the wealth of the merchants of Redcliffe who built the church.

From the very beginning, Bristol was a trading port and its first overseas trade was with Ireland. In the eleventh century, the major Irish trading ports were Dublin and Cork (Belfast did not become a major port until the eighteenth century). Bristol ships took hides, corn and wool to Ireland and came back with salmon.

By the twelfth century, Bristol had established a trade that would become central to its economy for centuries: wine. Although wine was made in England, much of it in Gloucestershire, demand had outstripped supply and the import of French wine soon overtook domestic supply. And in the middle of the twelfth century, one of Europe's great political alliances dramatically changed the city's trade connections. Before then, Bristol imported most of its wine from Anjou and Poitou, the region around Poitiers, but in 1152, Empress Matilda's son Henry married Eleanor d'Aquitaine and when

*England and France at the time of Henry I showing the principal trading
areas; when Henry II married Eleanor of Aquitaine, a considerable area
of wine producing regions were opened up for trade.*

Henry succeeded Stephen as Henry II, Eleanor brought the great wine-producing region of Gascony as part of her duchy of Aquitaine, making Henry
the most powerful ruler in Europe. Henry's reign brought stability to a country torn apart by the war between Matilda and Stephen, the sort of stability
that was good for trade – and what was good for trade was good for Bristol.

As trade expanded with the great wine-producing region around the
mouth of the Gironde River, which includes Bordeaux, ships had to make the
longer sea voyage across the tempestuous Bay of Biscay. It wasn't good practice to send empty ships on an outgoing voyage, partly for economic reasons
and partly for the stability of the ship. Thus, on the outgoing voyage, ships
carried lead that had been mined in the Mendip Hills, south of Bristol; the
lead could be traded as well as providing welcome stability to the ships.

Trade continued to flourish with Ireland. The relationship with Dublin was strengthened when, in 1171, Henry II took an expedition to Ireland in order to put down a potential rebellion by Richard de Clare (known as 'Strongbow'). Once Henry had firmly established that he was, in fact, their King and de Clare surrendered Dublin to him, Henry then 'granted to his men of Bristol his city of Dublin to be inhabited, together with all the liberties and free customs they had at Bristol and throughout his entire land'. It seems that Henry had made the gesture to acknowledge the economic relationship between the two ports.

When John succeeded his brother, Richard the Lionheart, to the throne, he granted a charter to Bristol in 1188; among other regulations, the charter forbade anyone who was not a burgess or native of Bristol to keep a tavern other than on board a ship. At that point, taverns were the only retail outlet for wine, selling it by the pint, with the wealthy buying their supplies directly from traders. Bristol Castle was used to store wine destined for the Crown. But if wine was such a major import for Bristol, what was being exported?

Bristol's exports at this time were many and varied but were dominated by wool and cloth. Surrounded by the wool-producing region of the Cotswolds to the north and the Mendips to the south, Bristol initially exported this wool to the continent and Ireland. During the thirteenth century, much of this wool was sent to Flanders to be turned into finished cloth but when the tax on raw wool became much higher than that of manufactured cloth more profit could be made if the cloth was made at home. Manufactured cloth could either be exported or sold to the home market; the manufacture of cloth grew both in the surrounding areas and in Bristol itself, as seen in Chapter 4. The trade in finished cloth grew but, when Edward III came to the throne and took the country to war against France (he was trying to claim the French Crown), he needed money; a useful source of income for the Crown was from tariffs charged on the import and export of merchandise. Export to Flanders had been rather disrupted by the war – which would come to be known as the Hundred Years War – so, to enhance the domestic cloth industry, there were brief periods when the export of raw wool was forbidden and people were not allowed to wear foreign cloth. To control all this required administrative centres and in the early 1350s, the Statute of Staples made Bristol one of eleven staple towns. Staple towns had been established at St Omer and Bruges; they were nominated places where merchants and foreigners could meet to do business and acted as compulsory clearing houses for dutiable articles. But, by 1363, Calais became the only staple town for wool and all wool trade had to be channelled through Calais, until it was lost to the French in 1558. Bristol retained certain rights of a staple such as having some legal privileges including borrowing money, the power to settle disputes and having its own mayor and two constables; it was possible to be mayor of staple and town at the same time. In Bristol, the first mayor of the staple was John Spicer in 1353 and the cloth exporter Thomas Blanket came later. In 1381, William Canynges the Elder was mayor of the staple and of Bristol.

It was about this time, with the increasing prosperity of Bristol, that the idea of a council was first mooted. It came from Stephen Goterest (also known as le Spicer) who was mayor, and William Coleford, who held the post of recorder of Bristol. They organised for forty-eight of the city's 'most powerful and discreet' to be elected as Bristol's first council and, so that everyone knew what they were doing, they started to write down the rules, customs and regulations by which the city would be governed. The resulting record was bound in red deer skin and became known as the Little Red Book. It also included copies of the charters of other towns, as well as the rules of all the trade guilds in Bristol.

It seems that there had been various guilds in Bristol from the twelfth century. These associations had something of a religious character, each with their own patron saint; we saw in the previous chapter how the Weavers' Guild was dedicated to St Catherine. They also provided social gatherings with much eating and drinking together, presumably as a bonding experience, yet the guilds also emphasised correct behaviour and, in the craft guilds, set the standards of the industry. Membership of the guild was compulsory for anyone wanting to ply a particular trade and membership was only granted after a formal apprenticeship. An apprenticeship ran for a fixed term, often seven years, and during that time the apprentice lived with the master's family, being fed and clothed and, of course, attending church. Once he had completed this phase, he became a 'journeyman', which meant he was able to work on a sort of freelance basis, paid by the day (hence the name, from the French *jour*, meaning day). To become a full member of a guild, the journeyman had to make a 'master piece' in whatever craft or trade he was employed and this was examined by the guild. If accepted, he became a member and then had to attend meetings and obey the rules of the guild.

By 1450, there were more than twenty craft guilds, each responsible for maintaining the quality of produce and length of training, as well as the standards of behaviour upheld by their members. They acted as mutual benefit societies and represented members' interests to bodies such as the Corporation. The wealthier guilds even gave alms to the poor and endowments to religious houses in the city. Which brings us to the Merchant Venturers.

It generally worked well for merchants to work together, entertaining visiting businessmen, sharing the risk in new ventures and so on, on an informal basis. In 1467, a City Council Act established a Fellowship of Merchants, which has been interpreted as the forerunner of the powerful Merchant Venturers but was basically a part of the council that set prices of certain commodities sold to foreign merchants. It operated for a while but in 1500, a Company of Merchants was established, effectively a guild of merchants, but it does not seem to have been particularly effective. They met in Spicer's Hall, on Welsh Back, holding their religious services in the adjoining chapel. This thirteenth-century building was bequeathed to the mayor and Corporation by Richard le Spycer, who was three-times mayor and Member of Parliament. The Fellowship of Merchants first met there in 1467 but outgrew the hall and in 1561, moved to the new site of St Clement's. The door to Spicer's Hall is preserved today in the City Museum.

Then, in 1552, the Society of Merchant Venturers was created by charter but although it set out to impose a monopoly, it had no real way of enforcing this; it wasn't until 1556 that the charter was reaffirmed by Elizabeth I, which allowed the merchants to confiscate goods from anyone trading outside their society.

This did not go down at all well in Bristol and during the subsequent political upheaval, all the key positions in the city such as mayor, sheriff and aldermen were taken over by those who opposed the monopoly, the result of which was that the 1556 Act that had created the charter was revoked by Parliament. From 1571, the next thirty years or so was the only period in Bristol's history that there were no merchants in positions of power in the city. It wasn't until 1605 that the Merchant Venturers were effectively resurrected; in 1639, Charles I granted them their charter. This is the charter that is celebrated on the 10th of November each year in Bristol Cathedral by the Merchants and their selected guests (followed by a sumptuous dinner in Merchants' Hall in Clifton). The Merchant Venturers will appear again and again in the story of Bristol, as the city developed its maritime trade. They always acted on behalf of the city's wealthy merchants if not the city itself, working together in informal cartels to fix prices and control trade even when not acting in an official capacity.

But, meanwhile, Bristol's trade continued to flourish and by the end of the fourteenth century, one-tenth of England's wine imports were coming through the city. Bristol was also importing dyes for the cloth industry, such as woad from Bordeaux, and madder from Flanders. Woad was derived from the leaves of a plant and used to dye cloth blue, black or purple before the introduction of indigo in the sixteenth century; madder, from the roots of a plant, was a red dye. Fish remained the main import from Ireland. Exports were still dominated by cloth but also included hides, finished leather goods, corn and increasingly, metal goods.

In the fifteenth century, Bristol's trade saw something of a slump during the civil war that is known to us as the Wars of the Roses. The city took its usual attitude to such conflicts, which was to rather pretend it wasn't happening. Ultimately, several prominent merchants, including William Canynges, were supporters of the Yorkist cause.

So what was all the fighting about this time? It is horribly complicated, but the main problem stemmed from Henry VI. His grandfather, Henry IV (Henry Bolingbroke) had seized the throne, some thought illegally, and his heroic father, Henry V had spent most of his reign fighting the French. Henry VI was, in contrast, timid and pious and married to the formidable Margaret d'Anjou, which probably didn't help his self-esteem. When, in 1452, he suffered his first bout of madness, the country was ruled by a Protector, Richard, Duke of York. Richard, a descendent of Edward III, felt he had a rightful claim to the throne so decided to take it but he was opposed by the royal, Lancastrian, party led by Henry's wife Margaret. Poor mad Henry became a pawn in this conflict, as the two sides resorted to bitter violence, and was eventually imprisoned and murdered in the Tower in 1471.

Meanwhile, in 1461, Richard of York was killed, executed by Margaret after the Battle of Wakefield, but his son took his revenge, beating Margaret's forces at the Battle of Towton and claiming the throne as Edward IV in 1461. Bristol men fought at Towton on the Yorkist side under the city's banner of the Ship. Edward, once he was crowned, lost no time in coming to Bristol.

He was keen to consolidate the loyalty of the merchant classes and when in the city, was entertained grandly; his entertainment included the public execution of an outspoken Lancastrian, Sir Baldwin Fulford. In exchange, Edward granted Bristol yet more charters, and he left with a substantial sum of money donated to him by the city. Prominent among the merchants of the time was William Canynges the Younger, the benefactor of St Mary Redcliffe. Canynges was a member of the new emerging class of wealthy merchants and shipowners; he owned 9 ships and over 8 years employed 800 men. It's said that Edward IV stayed at Canynges' house in Redcliffe when he came to Bristol.

Trade with the continent recovered with the stability of the Crown and with wine still the most valuable import. The emphasis, however, was changing from France to Spain. With the loss of Bordeaux in 1451 and Gascony in

1453, merchants turned to Spain and Portugal and by the end of the fifteenth century, when the city was exporting cloth and hides, with some lead and tin, and importing wine and iron, almost a third of Bristol's imports came from Spain.

It should not be forgotten that women played a small but fascinating part in the story of Bristol's trade. Women could occasionally be apprenticed as seamstresses or tailors, but not in weaving. When merchant families traded, there were times when the death of the head of the household left the widow to carry on the business. Perhaps the most well known of these is Alice Chestre who was widowed in 1470. She continued to trade, apparently successfully, as in 1472 she commissioned a fine four-storey house to be built on High Street. She traded cloth, wine, iron and other goods with Spain, Portugal, Ireland and Flanders. A generous benefactor of All Saints Church, she was best remembered for paying £41 to have a crane built on Welsh Back for the unloading of ships.

Bristol's trade with Spain and, later, Portugal, ultimately gave the city its reputation for wine and sherry that is still recognised today. The growth of the wine trade also led to a custom peculiar to Bristol. The honeycomb of storage cellars under the quays meant that instead of wheeled carts, sleds with runners were used to move goods between the quays. Wheeled carts were thought to damage the structure of the cellars whereas the smooth runners of the sleds would be less destructive. In the end, however, the cellars were more secure than originally believed – they still survive intact, even after the damage incurred by the bombing of the Second World War.

At the end of the fifteenth century, the import of wine from Portugal was mostly through Bristol but it wasn't just wine that merchants sought, they also imported cork. And by the sixteenth century, the sweet sherry sack from Andalusia made its first appearance in Bristol. Today, Bristol is most well known for Harvey's Bristol Cream, a heavy, sweet sherry in a distinctive blue bottle that is shipped all over the world. Bristol Cream is one of the more famous products of the firm that began trading at the end of the eighteenth century; John Harvey & Son was one of many small wine merchants in Bristol importing mostly Spanish and Portuguese wine and port. Harvey's originated when William Perry bought premises on Denmark Street, just off St Augustine's Parade, and the site of a thirteenth-century monastery – complete with cellars. As well as sherry and port, he dealt in cheese and leather, and soon took on a partner, Thomas Urch. Urch's sister married Thomas Harvey and their son John joined the firm. His sons, John and Edward followed their father and began the practise of visiting the wine-growing areas

St Augustine's reach – where the ocean going merchant ships were likely to berth while local trading boats berthed at Welsh Back.

of southern Spain, such as Jerez. In 1882, John Harvey II asked a lady guest to taste a sherry known as 'Bristol Milk'; she then tried a fine Coloroso sherry and the story goes that she commented 'if that be Milk, then this is Cream' and the brand was born. Other famous Bristol wine merchants included Avery's, founded in the late-eighteenth century and Phillips & Co., whose cellars under Colston Hall once belonged to the Carmelite friary on that site

It remains to tell the story of an extraordinary trade enterprise that was as dramatic as the great voyages described in the next chapter but is hardly known outside of Bristol. In the fifteenth century, although Bristol was well placed for trade with the Atlantic coast of Europe, the Mediterranean coast was effectively out of bounds to merchant shipping. When the Moors invaded the Iberian Peninsula in AD 711, the Straits of Gibraltar were closed to Christian traders and the Mediterranean coast remained inaccessible from the west until the late-eleventh century when vessels from Genoa began to trade along the Iberian south coast. By the thirteenth century, the Genoese seem to have monopolised this area of trade and when the Straits of Gibraltar were opened, the Genoese were ready to monopolise that route as well.

For the merchants of Bristol, there were some commodities that were particularly difficult – and expensive – to trade, such as spices and, crucially, substances needed for the cloth industry. Because England was at the western end of the chain, these items were more expensive here than in the rest of Europe, as the maximum number of middlemen took their cut. An important part of the process of making cloth involves dyeing the fabric and many of the dyes used in the medieval period needed a substance to fix the dye, to prevent the colour from washing out or fading; this substance was known as a 'mordant' (from the Latin *mordere*, meaning 'to bite'). One of the most useful mordants was alum, a salt of aluminium, which in the fifteenth century, was mined in Italy.

One of Bristol's wealthier merchants, Robert Sturmy had ambitious plans. In 1446, he fitted out a ship, the *Coq Anne*, to sail to Pisa, probably carrying cloth as a cargo and 160 passengers, pilgrims who would travel to Jaffa in their quest to reach the Holy Land. The pilgrims were to make their own way back and the ship was to return with a valuable cargo of spices and goods from the east. The plan was working until the return journey, when his ship was hit by a violent storm off the island of Modon and sunk with all hands, including a crew of 37 Bristolians.

Sturmy continued with his more conventional trading and was Mayor of Bristol in 1453–54. In 1454, he built a ship 'only for war', supporting the Duke of York in his controversial Protectorate, clearly taking the Yorkist side in the coming conflict. Yet, he had every intention of trying again to trade within the Mediterranean, to break into the spice and silk routes.

To do this he needed money and to raise money he needed investors. It was a massive undertaking; this time, he intended sending three ships, again taking cargoes of wool, cloth, tin and lead, and if his plan worked, he expected to make an impressive profit. Stuart Jenks, in his new book, *Robert Sturmy's Commercial Expedition to the Mediterranean*, shows what powerful backers came on board. Apart from the great merchants of Bristol, including William Canynges and Henry Chestre, Jenks argues that Richard, Duke of York, also invested in the project. The total investment was in the region of £6,000, which in today's money approximates to £3 million. Yet Sturmy raised the money – clearly, investors thought the risk was worth the potential gain.

This time he fitted out three ships, again carrying cargoes of wool, cloth, tin and lead and accompanied them himself into the Mediterranean. He successfully traded this cargo, and stopped at Chios in Italy to buy alum. But, again, on the return route, disaster struck. They were intercepted off Malta by several Genoese ships; two of Sturmy's ships were destroyed, over £6,000 of damage was done and it seems Sturmy himself died in the fracas.

Why did the Genoese attack? For the same reason that Sturmy had sent the expedition in the first place – profit. If Sturmy had succeeded in trading for alum to take directly to England, the Genoese would lose a lucrative market. The loss to the investors was disastrous and the outrage in England that the expedition had been attacked led to what amounts to an international incident – the entire Genoese community in London was arrested and their assets seized until compensation had been agreed and paid. And although Sturmy's attempt to break the monopoly of the Genoese and open up trade in the Mediterranean effectively ended in failure, he had shown the potential of such voyages, expanding the international market for England's trade that would eventually lead to the founding of the great trading companies of the next few centuries.

CHAPTER 6

INTO THE WEST

There are not many places in the centre of Bristol where the skyline is not punctuated by the Cabot Tower, which stands on the summit of Brandon Hill. The tower was completed in 1898 to commemorate the 400th anniversary of an astounding voyage – John Cabot's sailing to the New World.

It's a steep climb to the top of Brandon Hill, which stands 260 feet above the river below, and an even steeper climb to the top of the 105-foot-high

The Cabot tower, Brandon Hill, early 20th century. Completed in 1898, the tower is now surrounded by trees and shrubs.

tower but it's worth it for the stunning views across the city. The tower is built of warm, pink sandstone and stands among the greenery of the gardens that form part of the public park, with their paths, streams and waterfalls.

Brandon Hill is Bristol's oldest public space, having been donated to the city by Earl Robert of Gloucester in 1174. It is bounded by Park Street to the east, Berkeley Square and the Triangle to the north and Jacobs Wells Road to the south-west. In the south-west corner of the open space, a nature park is a haven for wildlife, including a pond where frogs, toads and smooth newts breed. There is also a butterfly garden and a woodland walk. In addition, there are the remains of earthworks, some dating from the Civil War and some – possibly – date back much further.

The relationship between the name, Brandon Hill, and John Cabot's voyage is an intriguing one. In medieval times there was a shrine on the top of the hill to St Brendan, the patron saint of navigators. Brendan was an Irish monk who, in the tradition of fifth-century monks, made long sea voyages in a 'curragh', an open boat, which took him around the coast of Ireland and Wales. Of course, even if he had reached South Wales there was no Bristol then to speak of, so it is unlikely there is a direct link between the saint and the hill. However, Brendan's most famous voyage, and the subject of the popular eleventh-century tale, the *Navigatio Sancti Brendani*, could have been the forerunner of Cabot's expedition. The story goes that, aged seventy, Brendan set out with a crew of seventeen other monks to make a journey that had been described to him by a visiting abbot. Brendan sailed west from Ireland, out into the Atlantic. The story goes that his adventures included landing on an island of giant sheep and an island of Latin-speaking birds, passing a huge tower of crystal and a giant hurling fire and stones. But, more dramatically, he was said to have found a Promised Land.

In the mid-1970s, explorer Tim Severin set out to reconstruct Brendan's voyage and took a replica of a curragh on a route that Brendan was thought to have taken. He passed Iceland, which could have explained the fire-throwing giant, if the volcano was erupting, and in the north Atlantic saw icebergs, Brendan's towers of crystal. Events in the *Navigatio* took on extra significance in the light of Severin's voyage because Severin successfully landed on Newfoundland.

Could Brendan have landed in America? No-one knows, but stories of a magical land beyond the western horizon would have been known among mariners, especially in a west-facing port such as Bristol. Certainly as late as the thirteenth century, there were maps showing 'St Brendan's Isle' in the Atlantic.

A mid-19th century view of Bristol from Brandon Hill; to the far right is Bristol Cathedral. Brandon Hill was a public space used for grazing animals as well as for recreation.

The original name of 'Brandon' may well be much older than the tenth century. The word 'don' is an ancient word meaning 'hill' – the name survives in places such as Snowdon ('Snow hill') and Swindon ('Pig hill') – and it's possible that the hill may be named after the Celtic god Bran. The link to St Brendan was more likely to have been made in the eleventh century when the stories of the *Navigatio* became available in written form, rather like a paperback novel of today. Either way, sailors visited Brendan's shrine on top of the hill, to give thanks for a safe voyage or to pray for the next voyage out.

As a public space, Brandon Hill was also used by the washerwomen of Bristol to dry their laundry. On the top lived a lady hermit, as revealed by the anonymous author of *How to See Bristol: A Complete Up-to-date and Profusely Illustrated Guide to Bristol, Clifton and Neighbourhood* (1919), who broke into verse:

Lucy de Newchurch here sat in her cell
A patching her soul, and stopping each hole that the world or the
    devil could enter.
'Twas well
For a woman that knew no better.

But she'd dout the sun with a half-penny squirt,
Or mop up the sea with the tail of her skirt,
Convince all maids 'twas wicked to marry,
Before she could outmanoeuvre Old Harry, or before he alone
    would let her.
Had she handled a broom in some humble room,
Or crooned babe's 'Babel' while rocking her cradle,
Or scalded her hand with the iron ladle
Whilst giving soup to some hungry group,
Or sopped a crust for some toothless gum,
Or kissed the blood from a child's cut thumb,
Or said to some fallen sister, 'O Come!
This way of life abandon!'
Than here by herself on Brandon.

The maritime tradition of sailing west into the Atlantic had been continued by sailors from Scandinavia. At the same time as their raiding parties were instilling terror in coastal communities of the British Isles – and resulting in the payment of Danegeld – the Norse were also sailing west, 500 years after Brendan. Erik the Red had left Norway with his family in AD 963 for Iceland, but did not stay long, having made himself unpopular by his quarrelsome nature, and so moved on to Greenland. From Greenland, legend has it that his son, Eriksson, sailed further west; whether or not it was Eriksson, a Viking expedition landed on what would become Newfoundland, Labrador and Baffin Island.

For Bristol merchants, Iceland presented an interesting trade proposition. Iceland was blessed with generous supplies of cod in its waters and, more importantly, it had the climate to dry it. The cod was hung out in the dry, cold winds of the Icelandic winter, effectively 'freeze drying' the fish, so that it lasted as a convenient food supply for up to a year. The surfeit of cod, however, did not make up for the general deterioration of Iceland's economy. The island was being denuded as timber was used up for building and the soil was unsuitable for large-scale agriculture. However, Iceland needed supplies and England needed dried fish; Bristol merchants were quick to realise a potential market.

By 1436, Bristol ships were already trading with Iceland, bringing back the valuable 'stockfish' – so called because of the way the fish was hung on racks, or 'stocks', to dry. It was also known as 'Poor John'. Dried cod does not sound like the most glamorous of cargoes but in Catholic Europe, with a calendar riddled with Fridays and holy days, it was an acceptable, non-perishable substitute for meat. Stockfish was a welcome addition to the fish-import business; much of England's cured fish came from Ireland but exploiting imports from an additional source made good business sense. Bristol ships established a trade route that included taking provisions such as cloth, wine and metal goods to Iceland, trading them for stockfish and bringing that back to Bristol.

Much has been made in popular literature about this trade between Bristol and Iceland. It was certainly true that the England–Iceland trade became successful enough to attract the attention of the Danish Crown, who also ruled Norway and Iceland, and the Danes wanted all stockfish to be traded through the staple town of Bergen. Meanwhile, England was in competition with the Hanseatic League. Long before the twentieth-century ideas of the Common Market and the European Union, there was a trade alliance among the towns of northern Germany who called themselves the Hanseatic League, from *hanse* meaning fellowship in Middle High German. Formed in the thirteenth century in the north German town of Lübeck, the fellowship spread across Europe. It reached as far as London and also controlled the mouths of major European rivers. By uniting trade, communities could offer protection against piracy and contribute to the maintenance of ports and the building of lighthouses. The Hanseatic League used its own coins, known as 'Easterlings', to distinguish them from the English coins. As the Easterling coins contained a guaranteed amount of silver, the word 'sterling', came to mean 'of assured value'.

The downside of the Hanseatic League began to show when the league started to impose monopolies on trade. It was particularly powerful in Scandinavia where it put restrictions on the trade in stockfish from Iceland.

This restriction in the trade of stockfish has been used by various authors to argue that this was a factor in the exploration of the Atlantic; Bristol merchants desperately needed another supply of cod. A local legend grew to insist that 'Bristol fishermen' discovered Newfoundland, mainland America and the rich fish stocks of the Grand Banks, the relatively shallow seabed around Newfoundland. And this was supposed to be well before Columbus arrived at the Caribbean in 1492. The story then goes that they kept this discovery secret so that no-one would muscle in on their rich fishing grounds.

It's an intriguing idea that, like the best conspiracy theories, is then amplified by feeding in circumstantial evidence that seems to fit the story. However, this particular theory has three initial flaws.

The first is that there were no 'Bristol fishermen'. Bristol has never been a commercial fishing port like, say, Hull or Plymouth, and there is no evidence to show that, apart from hooking fish over the side to feed the crew, ships systematically brought fish back to the quays in Bristol to be unloaded.

The second flaw is the relevance of the Iceland trade. Dr Evan Jones, of the University of Bristol, in his conference paper 'Bristol and the forging of the Atlantic World in the fifteenth and sixteenth centuries' (September 2005) gives some illuminating figures. Although it was a useful source of stockfish, the value of the Iceland trade at its height was rarely more than £1,000 per year and later in the fifteenth century only accounted for £300 or so. Compare this with the trade with Ireland, worth at least £5,000 per year and the continent, worth more than £30,000 per year; this makes the Iceland trade less than 1 per cent of Bristol's total. The loss of the stockfish trade from the local difficulty with the Hanseatic League might have been irksome but not a disaster.

The third flaw is that there is absolutely no evidence at all to confirm that anyone from Europe was fishing the Grand Banks before the arrival of John Cabot in 1497, of whom more later.

Yet, something drove Bristol merchants to send expeditions out into the Atlantic to find new lands. Stories of mythical lands in the west had been circulating even before St Brendan's tale came into the public domain in the tenth century. The story of his discovery of the 'Promised Land of the Saints' and St Brendan's Isle, fuelled speculation that there were real islands in the Atlantic simply waiting to be discovered.

One of these mythic lands was the 'Isle of Brasil', also known as 'Hy Brasil'. The name is a Celtic one, meaning the 'Blessed Isle' but in the tangle of history, myth and legend, it became associated with brasil wood, the red-staining wood that was used as a natural dye.

In July 1480, a ship set out from Bristol under the command of Master Lloyd, an experienced navigator and mariner, and owned, or at least part-owned, by merchant John Jay the Younger. Aughton, quoting from Harvey's (ed.) *William Worcestre – Itineraries,* reveals that according to the medieval chronicler William Worcestre, the ship's mission was to sail to the west to find the 'Isle of Brasil'.

On The 15th day of July, the ship of... and John Jay the younger, of the weight of 80 tons, began a voyage from Kingroad at the port of Bristol, to the island of Brazil to the west of Ireland, sailing over the sea by. . . And... Lloyd was the ship's master, the most knowledgeable man in all England. And news came to Bristol on Monday the 18th day of September that the said ship had sailed the sea for about 9 months, not finding the island but was driven back by storms at sea to the port of... in Ireland for refitting the ship and reorganising the crew.

The 'nine months' is probably an error for 'nine weeks' and although some of Worcestre's writing is hard to decipher, the start of the expedition is clear.

The historical record is silent as to what, if anything, John Jay's ship found; it returned to Bristol in the September. John Jay's wife, Joan, was William Worcestre's sister; William records the death of John Jay but omits to give the year so it is deduced that it was in the 1480s. His death is remembered today because he, his wife and large family are commemorated on a funeral brass in the chancel of St Mary Redcliffe.

The John Jay expedition of 1480 seems to have been covered by a licence issued by Edward IV in the June of that year. The licence names several merchants, including Thomas Croft, Robert Strange, William Spencer and William de la Fount, all merchants of high standing in the city. Thomas Croft had spent some time as a child growing up with the young Prince Edward, now the King, and was the King's Collector of Customs for Bristol, a lucrative role. Spencer, Strange and de la Fount were all shipowners and merchants in their own right, so the fact that they appear to have been part of the next expedition to the west implies that they took the possibility of success seriously.

So if they weren't being driven by the need to find fish, what were they looking for? Again, the answer is more straightforward than the myth. The Bristol merchants were aware of the success of Spain and Portugal in their explorations of the Atlantic; by 1420, Portugal had found and colonised Madeira and by 1460 the Azores had been discovered. Madeira became a source of grapes and, later cane sugar, and the Azores were able to produce fruit and woad for trade.

By 1480, Bristol merchants were trading with Madeira. If Portugal had found profitable islands out in the Atlantic, could Bristol not find lands to claim for England?

In 1481, two ships, the *Trinity* and the *George*, set out again towards the west. The result of this expedition would be as elusive as that of John Jay, except for the report of a Royal Commission sent to Bristol to investigate various shipping activities. Among other things, the commission was interested in an accusation lodged against Thomas Croft; as a Customs Officer, he was banned from trading for personal profit. At issue was the question of the salt carried by the ships, and again, those in favour of the 'fisheries' theory have pounced on this as evidence that *Trinity* and *George* were either fishing or trading for fish somewhere in the Atlantic.

It seems that each ship had been carrying 40 bushels of salt, which is about 320 gallons, or 1,450 litres. It is argued that this is a lot of salt, so its presence implies that Croft and partners were intending to trade – and this trade was something to do with cod. Yet Croft claimed that the expedition itself was not setting out to trade but its purpose was of 'examining and finding a certain island called the "Isle of Brasil"'.

Thomas Croft was cleared of all charges and there is no more evidence to help decide what happened to the expedition or where it had been. But the salt incident does not add anything to the 'fishing' argument because, at that time, an expedition setting out with the specific purpose of fishing would have to carry a lot more than 40 bushels of salt. One bushel would salt about a ton of fish and a ship the size of the *Trinity* would be expected to bring back 100 tons or so had she been fishing. The expedition was setting out to explore and expected to be away from shore for some months. To feed the crew, live animals would be carried on board and if an animal was slaughtered, it was unlikely to be eaten in one sitting. The sensible thing to do was salt the meat to preserve it; the same applied to any fish that they caught, and a large ship like the *Trinity* would be expected to set out with that amount of salt on board.

The push to the west was given more impetus by the voyages of Christopher Columbus. His great discovery of 1492 is the stuff of schoolbooks and general-knowledge quizzes but the background to his voyages has an intriguing aspect. Scholars deciphering his biography, written by his son, Fernando, have found that it includes a note, quoted here from Wilson's *The Columbus Myth*, supposedly from Columbus himself, claiming:

> In the month of February 1477, I sailed one hundred leagues beyond the island of Tile (Thule, another name for Iceland) . . . and to this island, which is as big as England, the English come with their wares, especially from Bristol. When I was there, the sea was not frozen but the tides were so great that in some places they rose fifty feet and fell as much in depth.

It has been argued that for Columbus to have visited Iceland, he was likely to have sailed on a Bristol merchant ship. Any connection with Bristol, or Iceland, would have exposed Columbus to the stories of mysterious lands in the west and possibly answer the question of where Columbus got the idea to sail west, when his previous seafaring experience had been in the Mediterranean.

Whether or not this is true, it is the stuff of history that, after much lobbying, Columbus was blessed by the sponsorship of Isabella and Ferdinand of Spain. Yet it has also been shown that before this, in 1488, Columbus and his brother Bartholomew tried to persuade Henry VII of England to finance them to sail to Cathay (China) and the Orient by setting out westwards. They got nowhere. Henry VII (Henry Tudor) had come to the throne in 1485, consolidating England after the disruptive Wars of the Roses that had torn the country apart. What Henry needed was stability and was busy setting up an alliance with Spain by negotiating a marriage between his eldest son Arthur and Catherine d'Aragon, youngest daughter of Isabella and Ferdinand. He had no intention of upsetting the Spanish at this stage, and besides, he was not known for his financial generosity, so the Columbus brothers were sent away disappointed.

Yet, hearing later of the great success of Columbus' voyages, Henry was ready to think again. This time, he agreed to give permission (but no money) for a Genovese mariner, John Cabot, to explore to the west, but it was on the condition he took a northerly route so as not to impinge on the Spanish. The licence was dated 5 March 1496.

Like Columbus, Cabot was convinced that it was possible to reach the Orient by sailing west. Contrary to popular belief, mariners of the time were perfectly aware that the earth was round and Cabot had worked out that it would be a shorter journey to reach his destination by sailing on latitudes further north, as it is less of a distance 'round the globe'. So, taking advantage of the interest in exploration to the west, Cabot had come to England in about 1494 and settled, with his family, in Bristol.

He chose Bristol for various reasons. Bristol was England's second city and a westward-facing port with a reputation for its shipbuilding and its Atlantic trade. But Cabot needed money and Bristol merchants were quick to see the potential for profit in finding a sea link to the Orient for trade – silk and spices, in particular, were valuable trade goods. Cabot offered a possibility of finding that route.

Cabot's first voyage was something of a non-event. Cabot had received the licence in March 1496 and made his first voyage later that year, so must have used an existing ship chartered for the expedition. There simply would not have been time to build a new one. In summer, he sailed into the west with one ship and a combination of bad weather and low supplies; a less-than-enthusiastic crew made him turn back.

In 1497, better prepared, he made his great voyage. In the *Matthew*, Cabot

The Matthew, *a replica of John Cabot's ship that crossed the Atlantic in 1497.*

left Bristol at the beginning of May; the ship would have left Bristol using the tide to carry her downriver to the Kingroad, the area of water off the coast of what is now Avonmouth, where she would wait for a favourable wind and tide to leave the Bristol Channel. The ship would have sailed against the prevailing westerly winds in the north Atlantic but it eventually made landfall on 24 June 1497. As to where it made landfall, history is not clear and historians are continually absorbed in debate about the possibilities. The consensus seems to be that Cabot arrived somewhere on Newfoundland or Nova Scotia. Once he had landed, however, he took on fresh water and returned to the ship; evidence of a fire and human habitation made him nervous about exploring further. The ship then spent a month exploring along the coast before returning to England, a journey of only fifteen days, probably accelerated by the combination of westerly winds and the Gulf Stream.

He arrived back in Bristol on the 6th of August and by the 10th of August was in London with Henry VII, recounting his adventures and using a globe to explain the route he had taken; he was convinced he had reached the shore of China. The King was delighted and Cabot's proposal to take another expedition to explore further was now met with enthusiasm, as well as the granting of a cash reward and annual pension.

The Cabot family appear in the records for the city after this voyage. A rent book, now in the archives of Gloucester, shows the rent paid on a house in St Nicholas Street for the year 1498–99, from a 'John Cabotto'.

This time, with the enthusiasm of the Bristol merchants and the backing of the King, Cabot set sail in a fleet of five ships, one of which had been provided by the King and the other four by the merchants of Cabot's adopted city.

He left Bristol in May 1498 at the same time that Columbus sailed from Spain in a fleet of six ships – but Cabot was never heard from again.

No-one really knows what happened. Five ships left Bristol, one limped back to Ireland after a storm and the other four seemed to disappear off the face of the earth. For one ship to sink without trace on a voyage is understandable but four ships...

There has been much speculation about Cabot's fate, with different theories accounting for his disappearance. One of the most intriguing is connected to a letter that was found in Simancas, central Spain, in 1955 by researcher Dr Hayward Keniston. It seems to be a letter written by a merchant, John Day, writing to the 'Lord Grand Admiral' who is thought to be Christopher Columbus himself. In *The Columbus Myth* Wilson quotes the letter, apparently dated late 1497 or early 1498, in which Day describes in great detail Cabot's 1497 voyage, including the length of the outward and inbound voyages in days, the description of what he found there and, to the point, explains that, 'it is hoped to push through plans for exploring the said land more thoroughly next year with ten or twelve vessels . . . they want to carry out this new project.'

Even more intriguing, Day also writes: 'It is considered certain that the cape of the said land was found and discovered in the past by the men from Bristol who found 'Brasil' as your Lordship well knows. It was called the Island of Brasil and it is assumed and believed to be the mainland that the men from Bristol found.'

Given that this is a translation from medieval Spanish into contemporary English, it still seems that Day was referring to what was probably local folklore that he overheard – that men from Bristol had already found the island of Brasil, which he interpreted to be the mainland of what would later be called North America, before Columbus. The 'Bristol fishermen' enthusiasts read this as implying that Bristol mariners had already 'discovered' America but Day was likely to be repeating stories that he had heard; it is not hard evidence. The letter also seems to imply that the Spanish knew that Cabot was to lead the next English attempt to claim the new continent for England, which led to the next part of the Cabot disappearance theory.

The notorious Spanish privateer and Admiral, Alonzo de Hojedo had set out from Spain in May 1499 with four ships; his reputation for cruelty preceded him. On board was Amerigo Vespucci, he of the name that was given to the new continent, America. By all accounts, Hojedo behaved like a pirate, raiding and looting ships, and once he had crossed the Atlantic, attacked, robbed and killed any natives he met. The theory goes that he reached the southern continent of the New World near the mouth of the Orinoco River and then sailed west around the coast. Coming the other way was the remains of Cabot's fleet, sailing south from the northern continent, having turned towards the Caribbean and by August were sailing westwards along the Venezuelan coast. Were they slaughtered by Hojedo and his men? Probably not. When Cabot's expedition set out in 1498, the convoy of ships would only have taken provisions for nine months at most and the Spanish did not set out until May 1499; unless Cabot and his crew had over-wintered somewhere, they would not have been sailing around Spanish waters in the summer of 1499.

The simplest explanation is that Cabot himself, possibly with one of his ships, did not make it home, although it's possible that some of the others returned. They had set out to find – and trade with – China and the Orient and instead had found a large, virtually uninhabited landmass and no-one interested in trading. Not a resounding success for the investors. Yet it seems that by 1500, at least one map of the Atlantic was showing the northern coast of the North American continent with English flags, so perhaps some of the expedition, without Cabot, came back with tales of the new continent that stood between them and the riches of the Orient.

There is another aspect of the 'discovery of America' myth that is repeatedly brought up for debate – the naming of America. Locally, it is often claimed, with solemn authority, that America was not named after Amerigo Vespucci, but after one Richard Amerike. Amerike was a Customs Officer in Bristol and had an interest in Cabot's expedition and it is claimed that, as such, the continent was named after him. But Amerike was Welsh and this is only one variation of the spelling of his name; it is equally often recorded as 'ap Meroc' (son of Meroc), 'ap Meric' and 'Ap Meryke'. Given the variability in spelling of written records of the time, the similarity of 'Amerike' and 'America' is by no means infallible evidence.

However, it seems Cabot was the first European to land on what is now North America. Columbus had found the islands of the Caribbean and, on his third voyage, his expedition reached the coast of Venezuela. It is not clear whether Columbus himself went ashore but, on his fourth voyage, he landed at Panama, so he had definitely been to the coast of Central America, whereas the discovery of the North American continent is generally credited to Cabot. Bristol celebrated the 500th anniversary of his great voyage with the building of a replica of the *Matthew*. There was no known plan or drawing of the original ship so designer Colin Mudie used a combination of archeological data and information about other ships of the same period. The *Matthew* was built on a special site on Redcliffe Wharf, not far from St Mary Redcliffe and probably near the site where the original ship was built. Construction began in 1994 and took two years; the *Matthew* sailed under the Clifton Suspension Bridge for the first time in March 1996.

Where possible, she was made from the same type of wood as the original. Unseasoned oak was used for the frames, stern and stern post, although there was a slight hiatus when much of the oak that was destined for the *Matthew* was diverted to be used in repairs at Windsor Castle after the 1992 fire. Douglas pine was used for some of the planking and a single Douglas fir was used for the main mast. There are some modern aspects to the ship by necessity, such as radar, satellite navigation and an engine, which was essential for giving the crew control over the ship in busy shipping lanes.

After sea trials in the English Channel, the *Matthew* crossed the Atlantic in 1997, arriving at Newfoundland to great festivities and a royal welcome as the Queen and Prince Phillip were there to see her sail into the harbour of Bonavista.

The *Matthew* is now back home in Bristol where she is usually moored next to the ss *Great Britain*. Sometimes she is taken out to sea in the summer months, into the Bristol Channel or as far as France. At other times, she takes guests on short cruises around Bristol's docks. As she does so, she passes Stephen Joyce's bronze statue of Cabot on the end of Narrow Quay. He is in a pensive pose, facing west and, perhaps, pondering the 500 years that have passed since he stepped onto the shores of the New World.

On Narrow Quay, outside Bush House, the site of the Arnolfini arts centre, the statue of John Cabot by Stephen Joyce, unveiled in 1985.

CHAPTER 7

SWEET CHARITY

In the summer of 1348, Bristol's role in English history took a sinister turn. The Black Death had arrived. It had come from the continent, first arriving in Constantinople from Asia in 1347, then spreading in all directions via the trade routes and reaching Paris by June 1348. With trade ships arriving in Bristol from so many different ports, it was only a matter of time before the city was infected. There is some debate among historians as to the exact point of entry of the epidemic; some say it came via Melcombe Regis in Dorset, others that it was brought into Southampton first and yet others say that a Bristol sailor was the first to die of the disease.

In *Bristol Observed*, Bettey quotes Henry Knighton, a monk of Leicester, who wrote: 'Then came the dreadful pestilence... came to Bristol, and there died almost all the strength of the town, suddenly overwhelmed by death, for there were few who were sick for more than three days, or two days or half a day. Then this cruel death spread everywhere, following the course of the sun.'

It doesn't really matter how the Black Death entered the British Isles. What does matter is that Bristol was probably the first major town to be affected and the result was truly dreadful. Horrox, in *The Black Death*, quotes a Benedictine monk from Chester, Ralph Higden, who wrote:

> In 1348 there was inordinately heavy rain between Midsummer and Christmas and scarcely a day went by without rain at some time in the day or night... This year around the feast of St John (24 June) the aforesaid pestilence attacked the Bristol area and then travelled to all the other parts of England in turn, and it lasted in England for more than a year. Indeed, it raged so strongly that scarcely a tenth of mankind was left alive. A mortality of animals followed in its footsteps, then rents dwindled, land fell waste for want of the tenants who used to cultivate it, and so much misery ensued that the world will hardly be able to regain its previous condition.

The consensus today is that the Black Death was bubonic plague, spread by the bite of fleas that were carried by black rats. There are some interesting alternative theories that the disease was perhaps an Ebola-like virus, or possibly a variation of anthrax; the discrepancy with the bubonic plague is in the speed of the infection's spread. Bubonic plague, which still exists today in areas such as Asia and Africa, spreads relatively slowly, relying on fleas to transmit the bacteria by biting their victim. So for the disease to spread, the rats carrying the infected fleas have to migrate, which raises questions as to whether they could have moved as quickly across Europe as it is believed the Black Death spread.

Whatever the cause, in Bristol, the plague was quickly out of control, with the general lack of hygiene contributing to the spread of infection. In a desperate attempt to save themselves, the people of Gloucester refused entry to anyone from Bristol but they couldn't keep the disease out for long. And it was said that so many died in Bristol that there was scarcely enough living to bury the dead, and grass grew inches high in the streets. As to the problem of burials – there were so many that normal church burials were out of the question. Bodies were laid in hastily dug plague pits and the area next to St James' Church in Broadmead is said to be one of these sites, now under the House of Fraser building.

Medical care in the time of the plague was an uncertain affair and the rich and the poor were affected alike. The first 'hospitals' had been established in the thirteenth century and, originally, the word meant a charitable institution, providing accommodation and food for the poor, sick, orphaned or elderly. St John's Hospital for the 'sick poor' was in Redcliffe, on land owned by the Berkeleys and nearby St Catherine's was at Brightbow, between Bedminster and Redcliffe.

For the people of the Middle Ages, one of the most terrifying diseases was leprosy and in Bristol a leprosy hospital for men was founded by King John when he was Earl of Mortain. This was St Lawrence's Hospital situated at Lawford's Gate and its name remains with Lawrence Hill; the hospital also owned lands outside the city towards Avonmouth, now the district of Lawrence Weston. When John came to the throne, he granted the hospital its charter in 1208.

At the time, leprosy was an incurable disease, and although it is infectious, probably transmitted by respiratory droplets, in the Middle Ages it was thought to be so highly contagious, that it could even be caught from the glance of a leper, or an unseen leper standing upwind. It was believed that leprosy rotted the flesh, which it doesn't – of course, it wasn't understood then that as the body tries to rid itself of the bacteria causing the disease, the process of tissue destruction and regeneration leads to disfigurement. The fear of lepers led to them being ostracised and in Bristol, in the fourteenth century, local laws were passed to expel lepers from society. A priest, or a 'jury of discreet men' examined a suspected leper, who was 'secluded', the change of status marked by a church service. After this, he – or she – was forbidden to enter a church or any other public place, had to signal his/her approach with a clapper or bell and had to wear distinctive clothes, including a hood or veil.

The hospital of St Bartholomew was a small hospital for a mixed community of men and women and was already established by 1275, intended to minister to the sick and poor. It was dissolved in 1532 in the Reformation when the buildings were handed over to Bristol Grammar School. Some of the buildings are still there at the bottom of Christmas Steps, and a fish and

At the bottom of Christmas Steps, the entrance to what was originally the hospital of St Bartholomew; although the buildings have been restored and rebuilt, some of the original medieval walls have been preserved.

chip shop, said to be one of the first to open in the country, is housed in what is claimed to be one of the thirteenth-century buildings.

The other hospital, perhaps better known, was St Mark's, also known as the Gaunts' Hospital. It was founded in the thirteenth century by Maurice Berkeley de Gaunt, a grandson of Robert Fitzharding, and transformed by Maurice's nephew Robert de Gournay. It was located on the old Fitzharding-owned Billeswick, now College Green, land shared by the abbey of St Augustine. The hospital was originally an almshouse, administered by the abbey and bound to feed 100 poor people a day, but it later became a separate institution, independent of the abbey.

Education in the Middle Ages, if it was given at all, was usually at the hands of the Church or charitable institutions. In some cases, the role of teaching was taken on by a chantry priest, one paid for by an endowment to say mass for the donor and his family. The two original grammar schools in

The chapel of St Marks, the former hospital that was taken over by the city at the dissolution of the monasteries. It is now the Lord Mayor's Chapel.

Bristol were both founded in the sixteenth century. Grammar schools were intended to educate boys who were planning to go into the Church and so mainly taught Latin, hence the name *grammar* school. As paper and books were so expensive, pupils used pieces of horn and a stylus. Discipline was affected by the use of the birch. Boys who did well at grammar school would then go on to Oxford or Cambridge. At the start of the sixteenth century, a small school existed with a schoolroom over the Frome Gate (St John's Gate) headed by schoolmaster Thomas Moffat. In 1532, two prosperous merchants, the Thorne brothers, wanted to establish a school for the education of the sons of merchants and traders in order to prepare them to follow their fathers into business.

They bought the buildings of St Bartholomew's Hospital, near the bottom of Christmas Steps and installed Thomas Moffat and his pupils in the larger premises; Henry VIII issued a charter to the Thornes' new grammar school on 17 March. The school had a chequered history, with some excellent headmasters and teachers and some less enthusiastic, but in 1767 the school had outgrown its premises. The master of the time, Charles Lee, persuaded the Corporation to let his school change places with the other school, Queen Elizabeth's Hospital, and move into the latter's premises on Unity Street. Lee also felt that the school would do much better with fewer pupils and at one stage there was just one. The school revived in the nineteenth century and in 1879 moved to its present site at Tyndall's Park, with new buildings including the Great Hall. By then the school was a successful boys' day school and, like all the ancient boys' schools in Bristol, began to admit girls towards the end of the twentieth century.

The Cathedral School was founded in 1542 by Henry VIII when the abbey church of St Augustine became Bristol Cathedral. He intended it to be modelled on King's Schools such as those at Canterbury, Ely, Rochester and Peterborough. It had a difficult start as the funds allocated by the governors – the Dean and Chapter of the cathedral – never seemed to be enough but it eventually became a choir school, providing singers for the cathedral.

Some of Bristol's first schools originated as 'hospitals' – charitable institutions – and, in this case, the schools were to provide for children who were destitute or orphaned. In 1586, John Carr, a merchant and soap boiler, left money and land in his will for the establishment of a new school modelled on the Christ's Hospital School in London, with the pupils wearing the same style of blue coats. This was to become Queen Elizabeth's Hospital school, and Elizabeth I granted its charter in 1590. It was intended specifically to educate 'poor children and orphans' and Corporation members were to be the school's governors. When it opened, the school only had a dozen pupils but the numbers went up to 40, where they stayed for about 200 years. Initially, it acted as a grammar school, with some of its boys going on to Oxford, but eventually, its role became that of a charity boarding-school, giving a basic elementary education. The distinctive blue-coat uniforms of the pupils made them a popular presence at civic ceremonies and during the seventeenth century the school earned one pound a time when it provided boys as attendants at important funerals. The school was originally situated in buildings in the grounds of St Mark's Hospital, close to the Grammar School; it moved to its current site on the side of Brandon Hill in the middle of the nineteenth century.

Unusually for its time, the next hospital school to be established in Bristol was a girls' school; it was one of the first schools for girls in the country. John Whitson, a wealthy merchant who had been both mayor and MP for Bristol, had no male heirs. So, in 1627, he made a will leaving his estate to the Corporation for charitable use, including starting a girls' school. In 1629, he died after falling off his horse; legal wrangles over the will lasted until 1634 and then, finally, his Red Maids' School was founded; the name comes from the colour of the school uniform, a deep wine red. The initial intake was to be forty daughters of freemen or burgesses of Bristol who were orphaned or destitute. In the 1972 publication *Bristol and Adjoining Counties*, MacInnes and Whittard reveal that the will states there was to be: 'A fit and convenient dwelling house... for the continued abode... of one grave, painful and modest woman of good life and conversation . . . and for forty poor woman children'.

The girls' education was meant to be vocational as well as scholarly, and problems arose because the girls were bound to the mistress as apprentices. She was to have the benefit and profit of their services; the governors gave her and the school such a meagre allowance that she often had to exploit the girls' labour at the expense of their education. The school was originally installed in a house near the newly formed Queen Elizabeth's Hospital and used the chapel at St Mark's for worship. The school crest includes the arms of the Spanish trading company to which Whitson belonged.

The hospital schools were able to care for a small proportion of poor children but the problem of poverty was one that taxed all levels of society. In a city such as Bristol, the very rich and the very poor lived side by side. Wealthy merchants lived by the quay, near their warehouses or shops; the idea of a separate neighbourhood for the well-to-do was more of a Georgian idea, started in the eighteenth century. There was a distinct division between the burgesses, the 'freemen' of the city, and the rest of the population, with a burgeoning gap between them. To become a burgess required either inheriting the title, buying it, being apprenticed to a burgess or his widow, or by marriage to the daughter or widow of a burgess. The advantage of being a burgess included being involved in the politics of the city and being able to trade without restrictions or tolls. Otherwise, even someone born in the city was known as a 'stranger' and could only work in workshops or houses of burgesses, could not be seen trading (officially) and had no say in the political decisions of the city. The poor were seen as the bane of society, and had to live on the streets – and off the streets – as best they could.

For those with a conscience, who couldn't pretend that the poor didn't exist, there were various ways of addressing the situation. There was the simple giving of alms, or 'doles', which could be awarded in the form of money, clothes or food. This was often done through a bequest in a will and administered by the Church. This was known as 'outdoor relief'. The other method was the establishment of almshouses. Such organisations, along with hospitals, were charitable institutions, often becoming residential homes for the elderly. In All Saints' Lane, an almshouse for eight people was founded in 1350 and by 1471 there were no fewer than nine such institutions in the city.

To some extent, Bristol mariners looked after their own. In 1445, they petitioned the mayor; they wanted to establish an almshouse that would house twelve poor sailors. They also wanted a priest to pray for those 'passing and labouring on the sea'. The result was the Fraternity of St Clement, situated in Bartholomew's Hospital. Money was raised by an obligatory payment

The Victorian buildings of Foster's almshouse, originally established in 1483.

collected from each sailor's wages. For a mariner to be accepted as an inmate, he had to have paid his dues for seven years and be prepared to give the Fraternity all his possessions except his own bedding and clothes.

At the top of Christmas Steps, on Colston Street, is Foster's almshouse. John Foster, a salt merchant and mayor of the city, founded it in 1483. Next to the almshouse was the Chapel of the Three Kings of Cologne, and it is thought that this dedication is unique in this country; it refers to a shrine to the three wise men in Cologne Cathedral. John Foster had travelled in Europe and had likely visited Cologne; in his will, he directed that a priest be found to sing in the chapel for his soul. The niches above the door now contain statues of the three kings, made by sculptor Ernest Pascoe in 1962 but the chapel is original, even though it has been heavily restored. The almshouse has been rebuilt several times and today's building is Victorian, coincidentally by an architect also called John Foster. Foster's is still a home for the elderly.

The Merchant Venturers' almshouse was built in 1696 by extending an existing almshouse in Marsh Street so that the new quadrangle opened into King Street. It provided for Bristol's elderly or injured sailors and their widows and daughters and included a free school for mariners' children. The almshouse is still operated today by the Merchant Venturers. Also on King Street, the St Nicholas Almshouse was one of the first buildings to be built

The original 15th century chapel of the Three Kings of Cologne, adjacent to Foster's almshouse. The statues of the kings by Ernest Pascoe were installed in 1962.

when King Street was developed; it was constructed between 1652 and 1656 and backs onto the city wall and a city gate. Again, it still operates as a refuge for the homeless. Edward Colston's Almshouse was built on St Michael's Hill in 1691 to provide housing for twelve men and twelve women who were not to be 'drunkards' or of a 'vicious life'. Every year, each inmate was given 24 sacks of coal and 10s for soap and candles. It, too, is under the administration of the Merchant Venturers.

The alternative to the almshouse, which housed relatively few inmates given the number of poor, was the workhouse, where the able-bodied were made to work for their keep and a small wage. The idea behind the workhouse was that poor relief was centralised under the control of the overseer of the poor, an office created in 1572. This office had the authority to raise money from the local rates, a result of the Poor Law of 1563. After the Reformation, and the dissolution of the monasteries, the responsibility for the poor fell on the parishes rather than the Church.

In 1617, a workhouse was formed for poor boys but did not last long. In 1623, the euphemistically named 'House of Correction' at the Bridewell was enlarged to provide a workhouse for the unemployed. A House of Correction was a sort of workhouse where able-bodied vagrants were set

St Peter's Hospital, formerly the site of the Bristol mint and used as a work-house in the 19th century. It was destroyed by bombing in World War Two.

to work, to stop them receiving outdoor relief: alms as a charitable handout. A master was appointed and to give the inmates work, he was allocated £200 to buy flax and hemp for them to make nets, but this enterprise didn't last.

The year 1695 saw another workhouse established, this time in St Peter's Hospital on the bank of the Avon, between St Peter's Church and the river. It was built in 1402 as a private house, but was later rebuilt to accommodate a sugar refinery; in the 1690s it operated as Bristol's mint, the name 'The Mint' staying with the building, but in 1698 it was adapted as a workhouse.

When Sir Frederick Morton Eden investigated the workhouse as part of his late-eighteenth-century survey of the conditions of the poor, he found the food and accommodation 'basic and lacking'. This was probably something of an understatement. The workhouse housed 350 inmates with the numbers sometimes as high as 390 and this mixture of unfortunates hailed from across Bristol society. Many were sick, some with infectious diseases of which 63 were kept separate in a pest-house; some were mad, some were elderly and infirm, some blind and disabled, some just children. Those that could work were given menial tasks and often the only work available involved making 'oakum'. When hemp ropes reached the end of their useful life, they were unpicked to separate the fibres, which created the oakum, to be used in shipyards. Oakum fibres were packed into the gaps between planks and sealed with hot pitch, a process known as 'caulking', which made a ship waterproof. As the inmates were paid a meagre wage for this, it's possible this is the origin of the phrase 'money for old rope' although there are alternative explanations.

For those who fell foul of the social code of conduct, which may have been through as minor an offence as stealing a loaf of bread, there was the horror of the prison system. Prison was not the end result of a sentence, it was somewhere to hold felons, debtors and dissidents until the authorities decided what to do with them. Prisoners were not segregated; hardened criminals were held with debtors or young offenders and hygiene was non-existent. Punishment itself ranged from execution, usually in public at the gallows on St Michael's Hill, to the stocks and pillory, or a public whipping.

The Bridewell prison originally stood on the site of the Central Fire Station. It was hell on earth. When, in 1664, the Quakers were being prosecuted, fifty-five women were imprisoned in a facility with five beds and two died simply from the appalling conditions. It was demolished and rebuilt in 1771 but without much improvement in conditions and was burned down in the notorious 1831 riots; it was rebuilt again but closed in the 1860s. Similarly, Lawford's Gate prison was destroyed in 1831, but was then restored. This only lasted until the 1860s. The most infamous of Bristol's prisons was the Newgate, situated where The Galleries now stands. It was established in the middle of the fifteenth century, in the fortified gateway at the town end of the castle's drawbridge across the north-west corner of the moat. In 1761, John Wesley compared the conditions in Bristol's Newgate prison to that of the London prison of the same name, Newgate, as Bettey quotes: 'Of all the seats of woe on this side of hell, few, I suppose, exceed or even equal London Newgate. If any region of horror could exceed it a few years ago, Newgate in Bristol did; so great was the filth, the stench, the misery and wickedness which shocked all who had a spart of humanity left.'

In 1777, prison reformer John Howard visited Bristol to collect evidence for his report into the state of the nation's prisons. He found small, ill-ventilated rooms and tiny passages; the prison contained thirty-eight felons and fifty-eight debtors with no separation between men and women or between debtors and felons. Sanitation consisted of open sewers and at the centre of prison was a dungeon, or 'night room', used for male prisoners. It was seventeen feet in diameter and eight-and-a-half feet high with no bedding or straw and one small window. Disease was rife and in 1720, many of the prisoners were killed by a 'raging distemper'.

One of the Newgate's more famous inmates was the architect Francis Howard Greenway who designed the Hotel and Assembly Rooms in the Mall at Clifton. The story of how such an esteemed personage came to be languishing in Bristol's notorious prison is one of bankruptcy and forgery. Financially ruined by the outbreak of war with France in 1809, he forged a document claiming that he was owed £1,300 for the completion of a house in Cornwallis Crescent. He was discovered, sent for trial and sentenced to hang. While he was in Newgate prison the sentence was commuted to transportation to Australia. When he arrived in Sydney in 1814, he carried a letter of introduction to the governor, who realised that Greenway was a talented architect. He was allowed to practise and within two years was made civil architect to the government; he built a lighthouse, churches, a hostel for women convicts and designed a mansion-house for the governor based on Thornbury Castle; this last was vetoed in London as too grand for what was still a colony for convicts. He was finally commemorated with the inclusion of his image on the Australian ten-dollar note and two plaques in Bristol; one is outside the Clifton Club and the other, outside The Galleries, marks the site of his stay in the Newgate.

The New Gaol, the last of Bristol's 'old prisons' was built in 1816 and opened to inmates in 1820; the ruined remains of the gatehouse still intimidate Cumberland Road. It was to replace the Newgate and although conditions did

A view, labelled 'Old Jail', of the complex of the New Gaol on Spike Island.
All that remains today is the ruin of the gatehouse, seen here just right
of centre.

seem better at the New Gaol – prisoners at least had individual cells – it soon deteriorated and was closed in 1883, replaced by Horfield Gaol which is still used. The gatehouse not only acted as an entrance to the gaol but served as a platform for hangings, with a trapdoor to allow the victim to drop. The New Gaol was the site of the last execution in Bristol. In 1849, a 17-year-old servant girl, Harriet Thomas, was found guilty of murdering her elderly employer by bludgeoning her to death and was hung, having been dragged to the gallows screaming to the last.

The story of Bristol's care of its poor, sick and outcast is one that has no ending. There are those who gave their lives to the cause, such as George Muller who built the orphanage, to name but one of many, and there are those who organised the alleviation of the slum conditions that grew with Bristol's rise as an industrial city. It is a story that needs a telling of its own, without the space here to do it, yet it can be said that Bristol has a long relationship with its charities that attempted to alleviate at least some of the problems. Perhaps the last word should remain with Sir Frederick Morton Eden, quoted by Bettey, who wrote, in his report of 1797:

Few cities possess such a number of public charities as Bristol. There are 30 almshouses in which 83 men and 230 women reside, with an allowance nearly sufficient for their support. There are several charity schools in which about 960 children are educated and most of them clothed and maintained. The donations to the Poor are considerable but the exact amount could not be ascertained.

CHAPTER 8

CIVIL WAR

It's possible to walk right past without noticing it – a simple plaque, easily missed, on the wall outside the City Museum and Art Gallery, which marks the site of 'Washington's Breach'. The plaque was installed in 1932 to commemorate an event that completely changed Bristol's position in the first Civil War of 1642–45. The 'Washington' named on the plaque was one Colonel Henry Washington, part of the family who, four generations later, produced a rather more famous Washington, called George. The 'breach' refers to the relatively uneventful breakthrough of the city's defences by a small band of dragoons led by Colonel Washington while the rest of the Royalist forces were attempting to take the Parliamentarian city by storm.

The plaque on the wall outside the City Museum on Queens Road, marking the position of Washington's breach.

Washington and his men were part of Colonel Wentforth's force trying to take the city from the north-east; once the city had fallen, Bristol changed from Parliamentarian to Royalist. The good folk of the city were between a rock and a hard place, victims of an ugly war that, in the words of Parliamentarian general Sir William Waller, was 'a warr without an Enemie', a war that no-one wanted.

Throughout its history, Bristol had wanted no part of any war. Put simply, war was bad for business. Even in Elizabeth's war with Spain, Bristol had grudgingly supplied four ships to fight the Armada, as demanded by the Crown, but was far more concerned with the way the war might threaten its wine trade with Spain and Portugal. The idea that a squabble between the King and Parliament, which was mostly about taxation and partly about the niceties of religion, could develop into armed conflict sent shivers down the spine of every Bristolian; the easiest way to deal with it was to pretend it wasn't happening.

So, through 1642, as the two sides grew more and more entrenched, Bristol did its best to stay neutral and it wasn't an easy balancing act. On the one hand was the king; Charles I was convinced of his divine right to rule as he saw fit, which included raising taxes to pay for his war with Scotland. On the other hand, Parliament was outraged by Charles' behaviour.

Charles had dragged an unwilling England into his war with Scotland. The 'Bishops' Wars' referred to two campaigns fought in 1639 and 1640. Charles was trying to impose Anglican religious practices on the Scots, who were having none of it. War is expensive and Charles had to resort to summoning Parliament, without whom he had reigned for eleven years. Parliament, called in April 1640, became known as the Short Parliament because it only lasted for three weeks, preferring to use the opportunity to complain about the king than grant him the funds he needed. Charles, in a huff, dissolved Parliament and continued the war, which wasn't going at all well. In November 1640, he once more summoned Parliament. This became known as the Long Parliament because, as events overtook him, it was not officially dissolved for thirteen years. However, Parliament was still not prepared to grant the king what he wanted and instead forced him to agree that Parliament could not be dissolved without consent. It also condemned Charles' high-handed style of government and demanded that he give up control of the army – which he refused.

At the end of 1641, as communications further deteriorated, the petulant king set out to arrest a member of the House of Lords and 5 members of the House of Commons for treason, personally leading 400 men to make the arrests. But the men escaped, the king retreated from London and, on 20 November 1642, he raised his standard at Nottingham. He had declared war on his own people.

Bristol had two MPs in the Long Parliament but they were more interested in local issues than the more noble principles at stake at national level. And for the citizens of Bristol, the idea of losing life or property for these principles was incomprehensible. The thorny issue of religion was raising tempers; at the risk of over-simplifying the situation, the king and the Royalists were mostly Anglicans, with a leaning towards a 'high church' and Archbishop Laud's influence that was 'Catholic' in its approach to ritual and Church organisation. In contrast to this, many of the Parliamentarians were Puritans. Yet, at this stage, Bristol was not a hotbed of religious dissent and didn't really want to get involved.

As Bristol dithered, the storm was gathering. On 23 October 1642, the first blows were struck at the Battle of Edgehill, near Warwick; England's Civil War had begun. However much Bristol wanted to stay out of it, such an important port would be a crucial prize for either side. An Association had been formed between the counties of Somerset, Gloucestershire and Wiltshire to defend the region against 'all forces sent without the consent of parliament' and, in October, the Association wrote to the council in Bristol, asking for the city's support. The council still didn't want to be seen making an obvious alliance with Parliament – they didn't want to make an alliance with anyone – so the members agreed to consider the idea and did nothing about it.

In December 1642, word arrived that Parliamentarian forces were gathering outside the city; Colonel Thomas Essex was planning to march on Bristol with two regiments. The council made a half-hearted attempt to hold the city for the king but by many accounts it was the women of Bristol who made the decision. They dreaded the implications of an armed resistance and probably realised that, in the long run, the city could not win, so persuaded the council to open the gates, letting Colonel Essex lead his troops with little resistance through New Gate and into the city.

So, almost by default, Bristol had not so much taken sides but had been bounced off the fence and was officially Parliamentarian. Essex, as a military leader, had what can be described as a 'positive' style. He had started to organise the defence of the city, which was not easy. The castle was no real use. Ruined and crumbling by the 1600s it was hardly a model of military strength; there had been a move by the council to improve the castle's defences by negotiating with owners of houses inside the castle to demolish them and make space for training troops but the city had grown and the population certainly could not be contained inside the castle walls in a crisis. Until the 1600s it had been assumed – assumption not being the best military strategy – that an attack on the city would probably come from the river. But the Civil War changed that – whoever was going to hold Bristol needed to defend it from all directions and it suddenly became crucial to strengthen the city walls. To the south, the wall from Redcliffe Gate via Temple Gate to Tower Harratz, created during the great building works of the thirteenth century, was a substantial deterrent and access was only through the three gates. But, to the north of the city the defences were virtually nonexistent. A new wall and ditch system with strategically placed forts would be built in a huge loop.

Some of these defences can be seen today; at the bottom of Brandon Hill, on the river side, the remains of the water fort and the wall and ditch to the top of the hill can be seen. Brandon Hill has a complex system of earthworks,

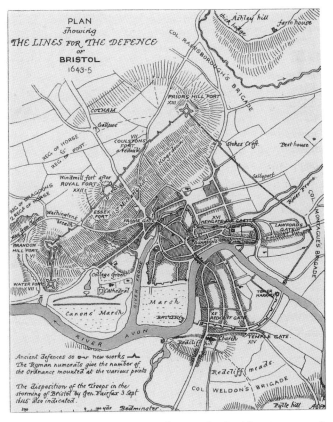

Map of the city's defences in the Civil War; the fortifications are shown surrounding the city and the annotations show the positions of troops as Bristol was stormed by Fairfax in 1645.

grown over but obvious from the shape of the ground. A fort was built on the summit then a wall and ditch followed a line to what was then known as Windmill Hill but today is better known as the site of Royal Fort House. At the summit of the hill at Kingsdown, Priors Hill Fort was built (now Fremantle Square) and the line continued, with smaller forts in places, to the south-east of the city, via Stokes Croft, Lawford's Gate (near Old Market), to Tower Harratz. Bristol was to provide the labour and pay for the materials and, despite the best intentions, progress was painfully slow.

No-one in Bristol was really happy. To have 2,000 troops billeted on people who had no choice in the matter was bad enough but the troops were getting more and more disgruntled as they hadn't been paid. Eventually, in January 1643, a group of soldiers asked to see Colonel Essex to discuss their lack of pay. It went badly wrong. Essex, who was more often than not either drunk or hung over, flew into a rage and refused to listen. When one brave soldier, William Kendall, tried to argue his case, Essex drew his pistol and shot and killed him. That, together with doubts and rumours about his friendships with known Royalists, led to Essex's swift replacement by Colonel Nathaniel Fiennes.

Fiennes was not so experienced in military matters but did know how to organise people. He galvanised the workforce into action, getting more done in a matter of days than Essex had achieved in as many weeks. But it was hard work, particularly as, when working on the line between Brandon Hill and Windmill Hill Fort, the labourers found bedrock just below the surface rather than the more manageable soil and did not complete the defensive line. This, ultimately, would have far-reaching consequences – Washington's breach.

While Fiennes tried to prepare the city for war, there were many in Bristol who still sympathised with the king. Charles' nephew, Prince Rupert, had joined the King and was leading the cavalry and it was obvious that Bristol was on his list of conquests. The Royalist sympathisers wanted to bring Rupert into the city, so hatched a plot, although it was hardly a fiendishly clever plot as plots go. The idea was to co-ordinate the arrival of Prince Rupert with opening one of the city gates to let him in. The ringleaders were Robert Yeamans and George Butcher, both Merchant Venturers, with support from other merchants, as well as some of Fiennes' own officers.

The conspiracy grew to include more than 100 people. The plan was that Rupert would wait outside the city at the top of Cotham Hill, near where the gallows were and Cotham parish church is now, and on a given signal, the conspirators would take over the guardhouse and gate of St John's Gate (Frome Gate) and let Rupert's troops into the city.

St John's arch, the city gate that was the scene of the women of Bristol's spirited resistance to the Royalist attack.

The conspirators were to recognise each other by wearing white tape 'upon their breasts before and their hats behind' and they came up with a suitably cryptic password – 'Charles'. The idea was that two of the officers who were in on the plot and were on duty in the guardhouse on Wine Street, would leave at midnight to inspect the sentries and with soldiers who were also part of the conspiracy, would overcome the guards at the outer gatehouse. In the meantime, George Butcher's house on Christmas Street and Robert Yeamans' house in St Michael's would be the assembly points for the groups of armed men. Once the guardhouse and gates were secured, the church bells would be rung to let Rupert know the city was his.

Fiennes, of course, knew everything. At around ten o'clock, he sent some of his more loyal troops to each location and all the conspirators, more than 100 of them, were arrested. Rupert, frustrated and embarrassed, on hearing the message that the plot had unravelled, led his troops back to the Royalist stronghold of Oxford. It isn't clear how Fiennes had discovered the plot but with so many people involved it would be more of a surprise if they had kept it secret. Some accounts blame 'tattling women', with gossip from alehouses and brothels spreading the word, but it was also likely that the officers involved in the plot could have gone along with it simply to feed the information back to Fiennes. Certainly none of them suffered the repercussions expected for what could have been considered mutiny.

Four of the conspirators were sentenced to death. The king tried to save them by threatening reprisals but it didn't work. Yeamans and Butcher, as prisoners in the castle, had been denied access to their own clergymen and Fiennes had sent in two Puritan preachers, Cradock and Fowler, to explain the error of their ways. And on the 30th of May, Yeamans and Butcher were hanged in Wine Street.

The Royalist plot had failed but, throughout the nation, Charles' forces were gathering strength: and they were determined to take Bristol. In a less-than-brilliant stroke, William Waller, the Parliamentarian general in the west, withdrew troops from Bristol to strengthen his army. In the beginning of July he fought two battles against the Royalists and was beaten. Disastrously.

This left Bristol with only 2,000 infantry and 300 cavalry to defend a city of about 15,000 people. Rupert once more advanced on the city, this time at the head of 20,000 men and took up his position at Westbury-on-Trym. Meanwhile, the Royalist Western, or 'Cornish' Army was approaching from the south. Between the two armies, the city was surrounded.

The first siege of Bristol began on Monday 24 July 1643 but the early days were frustrating for the Royalists; both sides fired cannon at each other but no ground was gained or lost. Rupert then decided to try a concerted attack to storm the city; the attack should have been co-ordinated to start at dawn on the Wednesday but the Western Army took matters into their own hands and started firing at about 3 a.m. Rupert had no choice but to order the attack. It wasn't ideal as much of the preparations weren't finished, and it's never a good military strategy to be firing weapons in the dark from several directions.

It was to Fiennes' credit that the siege did not break through earlier and as time went on, the Royalists were becoming more and more frustrated. As the Western Army pounded away at the city from the south, Colonel Wentworth and his men, including Henry Washington's dragoons, attacked from the north-west. As his troops waited where the Victoria Rooms stand today, Washington discovered the weakness in the defences; he led his men through the poorly defended and unfinished city wall and into Bristol. He had to get past a small fort, Essex's Fort, at the top of today's Park Street, but by the afternoon, the Royalists were at College Green. Fiennes tried to rally his troops to defend against this attack but they were exhausted and Rupert, taking advantage of Washington's breach, led his army towards St John's Gate.

At this point, the irrepressible women of Bristol intervened once more. When they heard the news of Washington's breach, about 200 women rushed to St John's Gate to help the men block the portal with woolsacks and soil, then offered to face down the approaching enemy with their children in their arms. But, to Fiennes' credit, he surrendered. Faced with 20,000 troops trying to get into the city and aware that if they did not get their own way, they might start to burn their way in, with hindsight it seems the sensible thing to have done. He was court-martialled for his role in all this, and sentenced to death, although later pardoned, yet had obtained what seemed like reasonable terms from Rupert for the surrender. The Parliamentary garrison was to be allowed to leave Bristol for Warminster and, in theory, there was to be no looting or damage by the incoming Royalist troops.

It was a nice idea but had no chance of working. Fiennes' troops were insulted and robbed as they left, and the city's shops and homes were looted, with families being evicted to make billets for the Royalist troops. The Corporation tried bribing Rupert to get his troops to behave but he could not – or would not – control them.

Bristol was now a Royalist stronghold and for two years, the city suffered untold misery, with troops imposed on a sullen population and, just when the citizens thought it couldn't get any worse, another visitor to the city – the plague – took 3,000 victims in 1644 alone. Rupert had strengthened the Windmill Hill Fort, renaming it the Royal Fort, and reassured his uncle, Charles, that Bristol could be held for months. It seemed so secure that the young Prince of Wales, who would eventually become Charles II, visited Bristol in March 1645.

Yet the Royalist cause was not going so well. In June 1645, the Battle of Naseby saw a swing in power to Parliament and throughout the summer, Parliamentarian forces were advancing through the west towards Bristol. Led by Sir Thomas Fairfax, they took Bridgwater in July, Bath surrendered at the end of July and Sherborne Castle fell in August. Yet Bristol was the prize – Fairfax needed to take the city to stop it becoming a rallying point and centre for regrouping Royalists, with reinforcements from Wales.

Detail from Millerd's map of 1673 showing a plan of the Royal Fort built by Prince Rupert during the Royalist possession of Bristol.

The situation had completely reversed – there was about to be another seige at Bristol. Rupert, inside the city, contemplated breaking out with the cavalry and leaving the city to its fate but decided against it as such a plan was neither safe nor honourable. As August drew to an end, Fairfax and his talented second-in-command, one Oliver Cromwell, were close enough to be examining the city's defences. By the 28th of August, the fort at Portishead had been taken, which gave Fairfax's army access to the river and the navy, which could bring ships up to the entrance to the Avon at Kingroad. But Fairfax had to decide, as Rupert had two years earlier, whether to besiege the city or storm it. While he and his commanders contemplated the best way forward, Rupert, with 1,000 cavalry and 600 foot soldiers, sallied out to attack the besieging army but did little damage, probably because Fairfax's men were spread too thinly around the city for a sudden onslaught to have much effect.

Fairfax decided to attack, and planned to do so on the 10th of September. There was an added complication – the weather. It had been pouring with rain for days and days, with men and horses sickening, as they could not shelter from the wet. As the time neared for the attack, the weather began to improve and Fairfax summoned Rupert for talks, demanding he surrender the city. Initially, Rupert was stalling for time but Fairfax's patience was running out and an attack was becoming the only way forward for him.

The strategy was not dissimilar from the Royalist attack that took place two years earlier. Fairfax's troops surrounded the city and at two in the morning, started firing on Priors Hill Fort. It was not an easy target, partly as it was well defended and partly because whoever had done the reconnaissance for Fairfax had misjudged the height, so their ladders were too short. The attack from the south did not break through the wall and ditch, as in 1643, and an attempt to take the water fort from the river also failed because the tide had been misjudged.

And yet – Rupert surrendered. He was concerned because fires had broken out in the city. It isn't clear whether this was accidental or deliberate but morale in the city and among his troops was at rock bottom. He and Fairfax agreed terms, and on the 11th of September, Rupert was allowed to leave the city with full honours, as McGrath quotes in *Bristol and the Civil War*: 'The Prince was clad in scarlet, very richly laid with silver lace, mounted upon a very gallant black Barbury horse...'

He was accompanied by Fairfax's men over Durdham Down. But, however grand the procession, Rupert was in disgrace. Charles would not listen to him; he claimed that Rupert had assured him he could hold Bristol for at least four months but had surrendered after less than four days. Furious, Charles banished his nephew, and although Rupert made a point of publicly defending his action, he and his supporters deemed it prudent to leave England.

So Bristol was Parliamentarian once more and would remain so for the rest of the war. Gradually, it became less of a garrison town as troops were slowly withdrawn, and despite the lingering plague, life began to return to normal. Although it seemed that issues had been resolved on a national level, things are never that simple. With the king as prisoner, both sides tried to use him as a pawn in their negotiations and Charles was not above trying to scheme and plot with the Scots. Cromwell, now running Parliament – and hence the country – decided enough was enough, and put the King on trial. Charles was executed on 30 January 1649.

Bristol was busy re-establishing itself as a trading port and Britain was now a republic. But being a republic wasn't much fun; Lord Protector Cromwell was a Puritan and the Puritans set about cancelling religious festivals, games, the theatre – and Christmas. It's interesting to wonder whether Britain would have stayed a republic if the Puritans hadn't been such killjoys and been more laid back. However, the city did not seem too perturbed when, in December 1654, Cromwell ordered the castle to be dismantled; it had become more of a liability than an asset.

As it was, Bristol had a role to play, however indirect, in the restoration of the monarchy. In January 1651, the Prince of Wales, who would become Charles II, had been crowned as King of Scots and had to flee for his life to escape the wrath of Cromwell. Travelling in disguise as the servant of a friend, Jane Lane, they made for the south, riding pillion on the same horse. They planned to find a ship to take him to the continent and his journey brought him to Bristol in September 1651. He and Jane Lane made for her friend's house in Abbots Leigh, but when they arrived, Charles recognised his old chaplain. He could not risk being recognised himself, so as part of his disguise as a manservant, went straight to the stables. However, Charles had been recognised by the chaplain and several others, but they were loyal to him and maintained their silence. They tried to find Charles passage on a ship out of Bristol and when that proved impossible, they helped him continue his journey, he and Jane slipping through the streets of Bristol undetected and on to Brighton, from where Charles sailed for freedom across the Channel.

When Charles was crowned as Charles II of England in 1661, Bristol had already returned to some sort of stability and trading had resumed as normal. Yet, in the aftermath of the disruption of the Civil War, it became obvious that Bristol's landscape of belief – of religious conviction and loyalty to Church and God, which were not always the same thing – had changed for ever.

CHAPTER 9

IN GOD WE TRUST

It was said that in the Middle Ages, there were so many churches in Bristol that if everyone went to worship at the same time, there would still be plenty of standing-room. Certainly, by the mid-sixteenth century, there were nineteen parish churches. It wasn't that Bristol was a particularly pious or God-fearing city, it was more that wealthy merchants needed to be seen spending money on the Church, with the possible motive of gaining credit in the afterlife.

The architecture of Bristol's churches is well described in specialist books and architecture guides – this is the story of the religious life of the

St James Priory was established by Robert of Gloucester in the 12th century; the west front is mostly from this period.

people who filled those churches and their responses to the changes that swept through the country.

As soon as a settlement began to form on the banks of the Avon and Frome, places of worship grew with it. Many of Bristol's medieval churches were probably built on sites of earlier Saxon worship. The first religious house in the city was the Benedictine priory of St James; its church, now sandwiched between the bus station and Broadmead shopping centre, was established in the early-twelfth century by Robert, Earl of Gloucester, as a cell of the Benedictine Abbey of Tewkesbury. However, by the end of the twelfth century, many of the churches that are well known today had been founded, including All Saints on Corn Street, Temple Church on Temple Street, St Nicholas' Church close to Bristol Bridge, SS Phillip and Jacob Church ('Pip n Jay's') on Narrow Plain (in its time on the outskirts of the city), St John straddling the city gate of the same name and St Thomas' Church south of the Avon.

The abbey of St Augustine was founded in 1140 when Robert Fitzharding gave land overlooking the Avon to the Augustine canons; when he became Lord of Berkeley after the civil war between Stephen and Matilda, he donated further land and wealth to his abbey. During the war, when Matilda's son, the young prince Henry, was in Bristol he knew Fitzharding well and, on coming to the throne as Henry II, also donated generously to the abbey. The reason for the name of St Augustine, however, is not clear. The Augustine canons took their rule from the fifth-century St Augustine of Hippo and were known for wearing black robes, hence their alternative name, Black Canons. Yet it's thought that the land given to the abbey was already the site of an earlier chapel or shrine. Local legend has it that St Augustine of Canterbury, the first archbishop, stayed here on his way to his meeting with the Celtic Bishops; tradition gives the site of that meeting as Aust, on the Bristol Channel, just north of the city.

The story goes that Augustine stopped at this site, close to Bristol Bridge, which would have been en route from the east of England to the meeting place. Accompanying him was a monk named Jordan, who died and was buried there. In the later Middle Ages, a chapel existed on College Green dedicated to St Jordan, known as a 'disciple of St Augustine, the apostle of England'; its remains are under the site of today's Council House.

There is a fascinating piece of evidence that could further imply that there was a holy shrine on the site of St Augustine's before the Norman period. It is the carving known as the 'Harrowing of Hell'. Two metres high, it is now in the south transept of the cathedral but it lay undiscovered until

Bristol Cathedral was originally the church of the Augustinian abbey founded by Robert Fitzharding.

1831, when it was found under the floor of the Chapter House after a fire. It is believed that it was used as a coffin lid but is dated to around AD 1000 and as such is a superb example of its kind. The image depicted in the carving symbolises the story of Christ descending into hell to assert himself over the powers of evil.

The abbey's founder Robert Fitzharding, as Lord of Berkeley, started a long relationship between St Augustine's and the Berkeleys, which included generous donations of cash to the abbey. Indeed, when Edward II met his undignified end in Berkeley Castle in 1327, Abbot Knowle refused to bury Edward in St Augustine's, in the interest of diplomacy. Edward, incidentally, was laid to rest at St Peter's, now Gloucester Cathedral.

Like all great abbeys, St Augustine's went though phases of enthusiastic building – and hence spending – and phases of slightly less worthy and noble activity. During the twelfth and thirteenth centuries, building included the Lady Chapel and the Chapter House. All this needed money and although the abbey had its benefactors, another source of income was to appropriate a local parish church and take income from that church's tithes. In 1311, for example, the canons of the abbey appropriated the parish church of Wotton-Under-Edge. Yet, there were times when life in the abbey did not match up to the exacting standards of the Church, which precipitated the occasional reprimand from the Bishop of Worcester for the mismanagement of the estate or neglect of services. Joseph Bettey, in his booklet 'St Augustine's Abbey, Bristol', tells how, in 1278, one instruction for reform insists: 'The canons were not "to fly out of the choir like bees" as soon as the services were ended but remain to pray and thank God for their benefactors.'

College Green in the mid-nineteenth century. The cathedral is just visible behind the trees.

There was a long-running squabble between the abbey and the people and officials of Bristol that involved the use of the open land that would become College Green. At the time it lay between the abbey and St Mark's Hospital (now the Lord Mayor's Chapel at the bottom of Park Street). The problem was over who had what access to the green and whether patients from St Mark's could be buried there. The Bishop of Worcester had to arbitrate; the arguments had started in the early-thirteenth century, when St Mark's was built, and flared up at regular intervals for the next few hundred years. There was also controversy around the sanctuary offered by the abbey to fugitives escaping from the civil authorities.

A small nunnery, St Mary Magdalene, was founded by Robert Fitzharding's wife, Eva, at the bottom of St Michael's Hill, now only the ghost of its memory appearing in the names Upper Maudlin Street and Lower Maudlin Street. Eva founded the nunnery when she was widowed and was probably its first prioress.

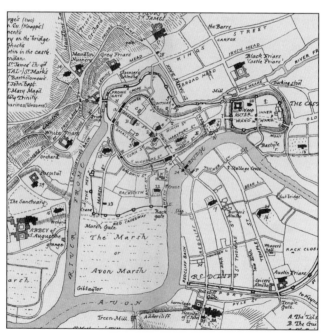

Map from 1480 showing the distribution of friaries around the city.

As well as parish churches and the monasteries, by the thirteenth century, a new type of religious house began to appear – the friary. A friary was not unlike a monastery but the brothers, or friars, depended solely on donations and charity for their livelihood. Because of this, they became known as the 'mendicant' orders, from the Latin *mendicus* meaning a beggar. Another difference between friars and monks was that friars were out and about in the world, more than the secluded monks, preaching and teaching. In Bristol, the four main orders of friars were well established by the middle of the thirteenth century. The Dominicans, known also as the Black Friars because they wore a black mantle over a white habit, were set up within the existing parish of St James in 1227 or 1228 by Maurice Gaunt who was a grandson of Robert Fitzharding. Henry III was a benefactor, providing timber for the building from the royal forest and granting the friary a licence to extend the burial-ground. Successive kings also donated generously, including gifts of oak for fuel from Edward I and money from Edward II. The garden of their friary was the site for the building of the first meeting-house for the Quakers in 1669, now known as Quakers Friars and today serving as Bristol's Registry Office. Apart from teaching and looking after the moral welfare of its citizens, the friaries made a major contribution to the city itself by the building and management of water-pipes.

In 1234 the Franciscans, the Grey Friars, were founded; their house was at Lewins Mead, now under the site of the Dental Hospital. It was built on land that was originally marshy, but was drained after the diversion of the Frome. They had a conduit from St Michael's Hill to the friary and the pipes are still intact. In addition, a Carmelite friary was founded on a site near to today's Colston Hall, with a garden that extended to the site of the Red Lodge. They were known as the White Friars, and their water-supply ran from Brandon Hill, down Park Street; an offshoot of the conduit crosses the Frome and still emerges at the tap at St John's Church. There was a time during the Second World War when this was the only fresh water-supply to the city.

South of the River Avon, the friary of the Austin Friars, or Augustinians (not to be confused with St Augustine's abbey), was founded close to Temple Gate.

Two major differences between the four orders and the monasteries became more pronounced with time, making the friars more popular among the citizens. The first was that the monasteries were not above accumulating wealth, contrasting somewhat with their teachings, while the friaries were usually impoverished and poorly furnished. The second was that the friars were much more part of the community than the closed orders; they often preached outdoors, and the population found it easier to identify with their humility and poverty. People often chose to be buried in a friary graveyard such as St James' rather than in their parish church.

The mendicant orders were paving the way for new ideas to come to

Bristol that would eventually surface with the Reformation. Indeed, Bristol had already something of a reputation for unconventional ideas and free thinking. There were two reasons for this. The first was its activity as a thriving port, where a continuous stream of people, tradesmen and mariners came from far and wide, sharing new ideas with anyone who would listen. The other was its geographical position. Although, in 1373, the city had become a county and therefore a centre for its own administration, its religious houses were split across two dioceses. Everywhere north of Bristol Bridge was under the jurisdiction of the Bishop of Worcester, making Bristol one of his more far-flung outposts, and the city to the south of the Avon was part of the diocese of Bath and Wells. Bristol was on the edge of both dioceses so was much harder to control when unconventional ideas were raised and discussed.

The end of the fourteenth century saw the first outspoken protests that the Church was not practising what it preached. A certain element of hypocrisy was being noticed in an institution that taught the merits of poverty yet wallowed in unashamed wealth. An Oxford theologian, John Wycliffe, was prepared to speak out against the Popes (this was during the period when political squabbling had produced two of them, one at Rome and one at Avignon) and claimed that the communion did not produce the body and blood of Christ from the bread and wine. This did not go down at all well with the Church but did find a ready audience in Bristol. John Purvey, one of Wycliffe's followers, stayed in the city and, at the invitation of the vicar, another follower, William Taylor preached at Christ Church. Taylor would later be burned at the stake in Smithfield. Wycliffe and his followers became known as Lollards, from the Dutch word *lollaert*, meaning 'mumbler' and they were, essentially, forerunners of the Protestant movement.

Isolated lone voices speaking out against the Church were silenced (usually burned at the stake for heresy) but however much the Church protested, these ideas would not go away. In Germany, Martin Luther (1483–1546), an Augustinian monk, was disturbed by the practice of selling indulgences for cash; these were a sort of 'bypass purgatory card' issued by the Pope, which in reality translated as a profitable sideline condoned by the Church. In rethinking the whole meaning of the Catholic faith, Luther came up with some radical ideas: priests did not have special powers and everything anyone needed to get to Heaven was in the Bible. This was serious heresy that should have sent him to the stake but Luther had powerful political allies in Germany who protested against the treatment he and his followers received from the Pope – hence the name Protestant.

Meanwhile, in Switzerland, John Calvin was also speaking out against the Church; again, he claimed priests did not have special powers and there should be no ornamentation or icons in a church. The idea of an alternative to the existing order of the Catholic Church was spreading across Europe like wildfire.

In 1533, the controversial preacher Hugh Latimer came to Bristol to preach three Lenten sermons. Along with William Tyndale, who also preached in the city, he claimed, among other things, that the Bible should be available in English. Latimer did not hold with ideas such as purgatory, and openly questioned the authority of the Pope. He was opposed by other preachers such as William Hubberdyne and the resulting furore in the pulpits attracted the attention of Henry VIII's henchman, Thomas Cromwell. He set up a Royal Commission to see what all the fuss was about, the conclusion of which blamed the preachers for stirring up controversy; they were told in no uncertain terms to desist. Latimer went on to eventually become Bishop of Worcester and hence supervised Bristol, but when Henry's Catholic daughter Mary came to the throne in 1553, his position was no longer secure. He was burned at the stake for heresy in 1555.

Yet, despite the new ideas that were circulating in the early 1500s, no-one really believed that that the presence, authority and financial stability of the Church were in any real danger. Even so, the comfortable existence of the clergy and churches all came to an abrupt end with Henry VIII's break from Rome. Before the crisis over his desperate need for a male heir and his passion for Anne Boleyn, Henry had been aware of the ideas of preachers such as Luther and opposed them. He even wrote his own book that supported the position of the Church, which earned him the title Defender of the Faith from the Pope. But when the Pope refused him a divorce from Catherine d'Aragon, Henry set up his own Church, the Church of England, which immediately granted him the divorce he needed.

So how did this affect Bristol?

Initially, a series of edicts insisted on an English bible in every church, that births, deaths and marriages were to be recorded systematically and that images of saints should be removed. The people of Bristol did not seem to be too perturbed by this and followed the new instructions.

But Henry was on a roll. He decided that he would not tolerate a shrine to Thomas à Becket, who had been murdered in Canterbury Cathedral by Henry II's men, so set about dismantling the shrine at Canterbury. In Bristol, St Thomas' Church, dedicated to St Thomas à Becket, prudently changed its dedication to St Thomas the Apostle.

Matters took a turn for the dramatic when, in 1535, Henry decided he was short of money and Thomas Cromwell had an idea to get some for him; monasteries were sitting on an impressive amount of wealth, much of it as land. If it could be shown that the monks (and nuns) were living a life of sin and debauchery then Henry would have good reason to intervene and confiscate their property. Cromwell's commissioners set out to dig the dirt and, disappointingly, could not really find much to complain about in the Bristol houses. The only example that came to light was that of a canon at St Augustine's with a gambling habit. But as Cromwell's men gathered evidence throughout the country, he was able to persuade Parliament to agree that initially, he and his men could go after the smaller houses, with an income of less than £200 per year. This affected three of the Bristol houses. Of these, the convent of St Mary Magdalene at the bottom of St Michael's Hill was the only one disbanded. St Mark's was left alone because it was regarded as a hospital and St James' was a cell of the larger, more powerful Tewkesbury Abbey. There is no record of what happened to the two nuns from St Mary Magdalene but the building was leased back from the Crown to become a private dwelling.

It was inevitable that Cromwell would turn to the larger, wealthier houses. St Augustine's, St James' and St Mark's held out until 1539; St Mark's and St Augustine's were suppressed in the December. The abbot of St Augustine's and eleven of his canons were pensioned off and all the property of any value, together with the abbey's lands, was seized by the Crown. Likewise, at St Mark's, also known as the Gaunts' Hospital, the abbot and the canons were pensioned off and the patients and servants given some money and evicted. In 1541, however, the Crown sold St Mark's and its lands back to the city of Bristol. It meant the city gained a considerable amount of land and, as the church was taken over by the Corporation of Bristol, it became – and has remained – the Lord Mayor's Chapel.

In 1542 Henry VIII, in his new role of Supreme Head of the Church of England, created the diocese of Bristol and the church of St Augustine's was chosen to be the new cathedral. For reasons unknown, this new diocese consisted of Bristol itself, some nearby parishes – and Dorset. This strange and wondrous administration system lasted until 1836 when Dorset became part of the diocese of Salisbury.

Henry's sickly son, Edward, succeeded him in 1537 as Edward VI. A staunch Protestant, he enforced the destruction of all ornamentation in churches and introduced the first Book of Common Prayer in 1549. But Edward only reigned for six years and was succeeded by his sister, Mary. And to Mary, Protestants were heretics of the worst kind. The burning started in

1555, and martyrs were executed at Bristol. Edward Sharp, a sixty-year-old man from Wiltshire was burned on 8 September 1556. William Saxton, a weaver, was condemned to be executed on 18 September 1556 and the fire was prepared with green wood to prolong his suffering but a John Pikes took pity on him and fetched dry wood from Redland that would burn more quickly. Richard Sharpe, also a weaver, had not helped his case by interrupting the service at Temple Church, shouting that the altar was 'the most abominable thing there ever was'. He was arrested and condemned to death, dying on 7 May 1558, with Thomas Hale, a shoemaker. The two were bound back to back and burned to death on the top of St Michael's Hill and Thomas Banion, yet another weaver, was executed in the same way on 27 August 1558.

Two martyrs being burned at the stake for heresy; as they are shown tied back to back it is likely the image, from Foxe's Book of Martyrs, shows Richard Sharpe and Thomas Hale.

There is a church on the site of the former gallows and the site of the executions by burning; this was formerly the Highbury Chapel and is now Cotham parish church. On the north wall is a plaque to the five martyrs that died under Mary's reign, although the names and dates are not wholly accurate.

Elizabeth succeeded her sister and tried to steer a more moderate middle course between the extremes of her siblings as she modified the Church of England. But the genie was out of the bottle. Edward's fanatical Protestantism and Bloody Mary's rabid anti-Protestant campaign had forced people to consider where they stood on matters religious. During Elizabeth's reign, a movement peopled by Puritans was gathering strength, pressing for a further purification of the English Church.

The term Puritan was a general term, not necessarily complimentary, used for Protestants who criticised the Church of England. There were many and varied groups who considered themselves true Protestants and throughout the turbulent seventeenth century, when England was effectively a republic, their numbers and commitment grew. But in the early part of the century, Nonconformists met in the grounds of Bristol Castle; the castle was, legally, still a small piece of Gloucestershire in the centre of the city and so Bristol's magistrates could not prosecute them. Among these Nonconformists, was the redoubtable Dorothy Hazard. She had been married to Anthony Kelly, a grocer and one of the first to meet in the castle precincts. When he died, she continued the business, defying Holy Order by keeping her shop open on holy days. She then met Matthew Hazard, a minister, and married him; they opened their house to Puritans needing a last lodging before leaving for the New World.

In 1640 Dorothy and her four other members formed the first open, public, Independent congregation, and this church survives today as Broadmead Baptist Church. It was not Baptist in the seventeenth century but, gradually, the idea that baptism was an essential part of the covenant between a person and God grew in popularity. The church is still in Broadmead, now part of the shopping centre, in a building opened in 1969 and known as 'the church over the shops'. Another group of Independents, who also met in the castle grounds around 1650, still exists as the Castle Green United Reform Church, now in Greenbank, near Easton.

As England lurched through the Civil War of the 1640s, it seemed that the various Nonconformists were becoming accepted and the situation was growing more stable. But then everything was disrupted again by the arrival of the Quakers. The Quakers took a completely self-contained, spiritual approach to their religion, rejecting the established Church and insisting that communion with God was personal and direct and needed none of the trappings of church services. They called themselves the Society of Friends; the name Quaker was originally a term of derision used by their enemies, referring to the extreme emotional responses experienced in their meetings.

Their founder, George Fox, came to Bristol in 1656 but two of his followers had visited the city in 1654 and it wasn't long before they attracted an enthusiastic following, disillusioned by the authority of the Church. So many attended their meetings that there was nowhere big enough to hold them all and meetings were held in the open. The authorities, both civil and ecclesiastical, were not best pleased with their impulsive and emotional approach to their services. Admittedly, the Quakers didn't always help themselves; they were given to disrupting church services to make their point, even causing mayhem in the cathedral.

There is a saying that any publicity is good publicity but the Bristol Quakers were caught up in the strange incident of James Naylor, which did not help their cause. Naylor had claimed to hear the voice of God speaking to him directly and, having met George Fox in 1652, decided that his calling was to be a Quaker. He became a charismatic, evangelical, itinerant preacher and gathered a loyal following, all encouraging him to cultivate his image of beard and hairstyle that resembled the contemporary images of Christ. Things went badly wrong, however, when he staged a re-enactment of Jesus' entry into Jerusalem by riding into Bristol on a mule with his adoring followers strewing cloaks and other garments in his path. The effect was rather spoiled by the pouring rain but he had attracted the attention of the authorities and was arrested for blasphemy. It was only the intervention of Oliver Cromwell, by then Lord Protector, that spared him from execution; he was punished by floggings, branded with a 'B' on his forehead, his tongue was pierced and he was sentenced to two years' hard labour.

The Bristol Quakers couldn't disown him quickly enough but the incident provided fuel for their enemies. It seemed that neither side was prepared to compromise; the Quakers insisted on public displays of their convictions and the authorities insisted on sending them to prison. They suffered the squalid conditions of the Newgate gaol (where The Galleries now stands) and many of them died of fever. Yet, in 1669, they purchased the site of the Dominican friary in Broadmead and set up the first of several meeting houses in Bristol.

By 1689, and the Act of Toleration, the Quakers began to be tolerated, if not accepted. Banned from attending university, as they were not members of the Church of England, Quakers became leading merchants and industrialists in the city. Perhaps the most well known of the Quakers of the time was

The Quakers' Friars Meeting House, part of which was built in 1749 on the site of the medieval Dominican friary of Blackfriars.

William Penn, son of Sir Admiral William Penn, who had been born in Bristol in 1621. Father and son were to both make their marks on history for different reasons.

Admiral Sir William (senior) seemed to tread a delicate line between the two sides that took the country to Civil War. He fought for Parliament yet offered to send the fleet to the exiled Charles II; he commanded the expedition sent by Cromwell to the West Indies and captured Jamaica for Britain yet, at the Restoration, was knighted. Crucially, he loaned a large sum of money, possibly £16,000, to Charles II and he died in 1670 without the loan being repaid. There is a memorial to him in St Mary Redcliffe.

William (junior) was initially something of a trial to his father. From the early days of his education, William became a Nonconformist and by 1666, had decided to join the Quakers, much to his father's disapproval. He suffered prosecution and imprisonment for stating his beliefs in public but in 1670, his father died – reconciled to his son's religion. Penn junior inherited his family's estates and began to move in more auspicious circles, becoming a friend of Charles II and his brother James, Duke of York, who later became James II. He had also become friends with George Fox and accompanied him to Bristol, the first of several visits that, later, included his first wife Gulielma. In 1681, Penn asked the King for repayment of his father's loan; Charles II, being short of cash, gave him 40,000 square miles of land in the north-east of the American continent, to be named Pennsylvania, or 'Penn's Forest', after his father.

Penn, with investments from several Bristol Quakers, established Pennsylvania as a colony. These included Edmond Bennett, a tobacco cutter, John Barnes, who later moved to Pennsylvania, a soap maker, James Peters and Robert Vickis, who would later become a master of the Merchant Venturers. By 1682, they had started to develop Philadelphia (meaning 'brotherly love'). So far, this doesn't seem like a major connection with Bristol but in 1696, having lost his first wife two years earlier, Penn was in Bristol and married Hannah Callowhill. Hannah was the daughter of Thomas Callowhill and Hannah Hollister. Hannah (senior) was the daughter of merchant Dennis Hollister, one of Bristol's founding Quakers.

William and Hannah lived in Bristol for the next two years, attending meetings, and they had eight children over the next twelve years. Penn was twenty-seven years older than her and, when his health was failing, she nursed him and managed his business affairs, acting as executor for his interests in Pennsylvania when he died.

John Wesley's chapel at Kingswood that later became the Kingswood Reformatory for boys.

By the middle of the eighteenth century, another new religious awakening reached Bristol. John Wesley came to the city on 31 March 1739 and from this visit came Bristol's leading role in the Methodist Church. Wesley had been part of the Holy Club while at Oxford in 1726 and because of the precise, methodical, regularity of their way of life, they became known as Methodists. When he came to Bristol, approximately a fifth of the population was Nonconformist, namely Quaker, Baptist, Presbyterian or Independent. Wesley had come at the invitation of George Whitefield and, with his encouragement, preached in the open air and visited the poor house at Lawford's Gate and Newgate, the city gaol.

Much of Wesley and Whitefield's preaching, however, was in Kingswood, in the open air, and addressed the miners and their families who had always been somewhat marginalised from Bristol life. Whitefield had started a school for the colliers' children and Wesley established his own boarding-school for boys in Kingswood in 1748, insisting on strict discipline and Christian teaching. The school survives, now relocated to Bath, as Kingswood School, a Methodist Independent School.

John Wesley was influenced by another sect that he had met while on a

John Wesley, a statue by C A Walker, shows him with prayer book in hand and on horseback, symbolising his long journeys across the country as he preached his ministry.

missionary trip to the American colony of Georgia – the Moravians. They had originated in Europe, rebelling against the Catholic Church, and in the 1700s found sanctuary in Germany on the estates of Count Nicholas von Zinzendorf. They attempted to set up a community in the American colony of Georgia and it was here that John Wesley met them. One of Wesley's early companions, John Cennick, set up a Moravian church in Bristol in 1742; the congregation grew and included Central European immigrants. Their church, now amalgamated with the United Reform Church, is still in Kingswood.

John Wesley's younger brother, Charles, was just as influential in the early days of Methodism, particularly in Bristol. Charles married and lived in Bristol between 1766 and 1771, where he worked as a pastor to Methodists. Famous as a writer of hymns, he is responsible for such classics as 'Hark the Herald

The interior of St Mary le Port; the building was destroyed by bombing and the empty shell now stands next to Castle Park.

Angels Sing', 'Gentle Jesus Meek and Mild' and 'Rejoice the Lord is King' to name but a few from the 6,000 or so he wrote.

Initially, John Welsey preached in various existing religious societies but with the growing interest in his sermons, he needed more space of his own. He acquired some land between St James' churchyard and the river and in 1739, built the New Room, the first Methodist meeting house, on the Horsefair in the centre of Bristol. Today, the New Room is open to visitors and contains many artefacts from Wesley's time, including the original communion table and the clock given by Wesley. In the forecourt, stands a statue of John Wesley on horseback. The location of the New Room, in the middle of the 1960s shopping development of Broadmead, seems incongruous. Also in Broadmead, a few hundred yards from the New Room, is Quakers Friars, now Bristol's Registry Office and the site for weddings. Starting in 2005, the whole of Broadmead is being redeveloped as a new shopping centre, to be named the Merchants Quarter. It will include the development of a new square based around Quakers Friars yet maintain the New Room as it is today, symbols of Bristol's diverse Christian background set within the city's commercial heart.

CHAPTER 10
A BOTTLE OF RUM

In Robert Louis Stevenson's magnificent novel *Treasure Island*, young Jim Hawkins is brought to Bristol to join Squire Trelawney and Dr Livesey for the start of his adventure:

The Llandoger Trow on King Street, the legendary haunt of pirates and smugglers.

Mr Trewlawney had taken up residence at an inn far down the docks to superintend the work upon the schooner. Thither we now had to walk, and our way to my great delight, lay along the quays and beside the great multitude of ships of all sizes and rigs and nations. In one, sailors were singing at their work, in another there were men aloft, high over my head, hanging to threads that seemed no thicker than a spider's. Though I had lived by the shore all my life, I seemed never to have been near the sea till then. The smell of tar and salt was something new. I saw the most wonderful figure-heads that had all been far over the ocean. I saw, besides, many old sailors with rings in their ears and whiskers curled in ringlets and tarry pigtails, and their swaggering, clumsy sea-walk.

Local legend has it that Robert Louis Stevenson came to Bristol to get inspiration for the novel and stayed at the seventeenth-century inn, the Llandoger Trow, on King Street. The legend goes on to claim that he used the pub as a model for the Admiral Benbow inn that appears at the start of his book.

It is very hard to find any evidence that Stevenson actually came to Bristol at all. He wrote *Treasure Island* in Scotland, having drawn a treasure map to entertain his stepson during the rainy summer of 1881. He based the character of Long John Silver, the ship's cook, on his friend, the Gloucester-born poet W.E Henley, who had lost a leg to tuberculosis and had something of an overbearing personality; the book was originally entitled *The Sea Cook* as Long John Silver is one of the main characters.

There *are* connections with Bristol, however, as Stevenson had read *The Journal of Llewellin Penrose*, an autobiographical novel by the writer and painter William Williams. Williams had been a painter in America but came back to England in about 1780 and spent his last days in a Bristol almshouse; his novel was published in 1815. It is also likely that Stevenson had gleaned material about Bristol from his friend John Addington Symonds, a poet and writer who was born in Bristol and, although educated at Harrow and Oxford, maintained links with Bristol all his life. He was involved with Clifton College and the establishment that was to become the university. After a serious riding accident on the Downs, his slow recovery was compounded by tuberculosis and he moved to Davos, in Switzerland, where Stevenson was also convalescing (having suffered from tuberculosis throughout his life). They met and became friends and no doubt Symonds' passion for his home town would have influenced their conversations.

The Llandoger Trow, however, would have been a popular haunt of Bristol's seafaring community from the seventeenth century. Built in 1664, it was one of a group of five gabled houses and the original Llandoger Trow was the right-hand building when facing the group. The name comes from the flat-bottomed boat, the 'trow' that traded in the Bristol Channel and brought trade goods in and out of Welsh Back. In this case, the trade was with Llandogo in the Wye Valley and at some point the name was transferred to the pub. The building suffered bomb damage during the Second World War and only three of the group of houses survived. In 1962, the Berni group bought all three and extended the pub to include a restaurant and several bars. It seems that it was around this time that the link to Stevenson and *Treasure Island* was born, adding an atmosphere to the pub that appealed to tourists. Part of the refurbishment involved reinforcing the whole interior of the building with a steel frame before restoring some of the original fireplaces and staircases.

The other pub that is said to feature in *Treasure Island* is the Hole in the Wall on The Grove, also a previous Berni inn but now owned by the Beefeater chain. To *Treasure Island* fans, this is said to be the inspiration for the Spyglass Inn:

> When I had done breakfasting the squire gave me a note addressed to John Silver, at the sign of the Spy-glass, and told me I should easily find the place by following the line of the docks and keeping a bright lookout for a little tavern with a large brass telescope for a sign. I set off, overjoyed at this opportunity to see some more of the ships and seamen, and picked my way among a great crowd of people and carts and bales, for the dock was now at its busiest, until I found the tavern in question.

> It was a bright enough little place of entertainment. The sign was newly painted; the windows had neat red curtains; the floor was cleanly sanded. There was a street on each side and an open door on both, which made the large, low room pretty clear to see in, in spite of clouds of tobacco smoke. The customers were mostly seafaring men, and they talked so loudly that I hung at the door, almost afraid to enter.

Although the direct link with Stevenson is tenuous at best, it is a popular Bristol myth, and the Hole in the Wall was certainly another favourite drinking haunt of seamen. It was once called the Coach and Horses but for some time in the eighteenth century was known by both names, just to confuse everyone. Its claim to notoriety is the little spyhouse on the dockside of the pub with small windows through which a lookout would be kept for the law, rival pirates or, much worse, the dreaded press gangs. In the eighteenth century, during wartime, it was legal to 'press' recruits – to kidnap them, as long as they had willingly accepted the Queen's or King's Shilling. Devious means were used to trick the hapless victim into accepting the coin, including dropping it into a tankard of beer, hence the invention of the glass-bottomed tankard so that by holding it aloft, a coin lurking in the bottom could be seen before the beer was drunk.

It was inevitable that a busy port such as Bristol would attract the darker side of maritime activities including smuggling and piracy. Yet there was a very fine line between out-and-out piracy and 'privateering' and this distinction had, initially, been blurred by Queen Elizabeth I in her campaign against the Spanish. As soon as Columbus had discovered and claimed the New World for Spain, the Spanish Pope, Alexander VI, divided this new land between Spain and Portugal; not surprisingly, other European states did not wholly agree with this arrangement. When, in 1518, Hernando Cortés led an expedition to Mexico to find and claim the Aztec empire, gold became a prize that was bound to attract the attention of others and started a practice that was to last for 200 years. Famous names such as Sir Francis Drake and Sir Walter Raleigh were privateers and many others operated out of Bristol.

'Privateering' was a respectable career condoned, even tacitly encouraged, by the monarch. A letter from the Admiralty gave the bearer permission to recoup losses sustained from engagement with foreigners and proof had to be shown of the loss incurred. These letters of 'marque, mart or reprisal' were later used in times of war, when the bearer could take reprisals against the enemy but in such circumstances it was often less clear exactly what had sparked the reprisal. The word 'privateer' can refer to the ship or the captain and by the end of the seventeenth century they would set sail specifically to capture and claim the cargoes of foreign ships, the possibility of Spanish gold being a great incentive to finance such a voyage. During the War of Spanish Succession (1702–13), when Britain was at war with both France and Spain, the conflict inevitably spilt over onto the seas. Letters of marque were issued to numerous ships; it was a cheap way of raising a fighting fleet as, unlike the Navy, the ships were self-funded. Financial backers were all too keen to sponsor a ship in exchange for a share in the spoils; all the Admiralty had to do was provide the paperwork.

Among these letters of marque was one allocated to Captain James Woodes Rogers for an expedition sponsored by a group of Bristol merchants, including Thomas Goldney, a Quaker not above investing in privateering. Woodes Rogers lived in Bristol, in Queen Square, with his wife Sarah, the daughter of Admiral Sir William Whetstone. It seems that Rogers, despite the fashionable address, was short of funds so the opportunity to take on a privateering voyage must have seemed one not to be missed. In overall charge of the expedition, he was to take two newly built ships, the *Duke* and *Duchess*, both fully armed with cannon.

The pilot, or navigator, for the expedition was one William Dampier, who joined the enterprise with a history that would come back to haunt him. He was an experienced mariner and skilled navigator with knowledge of the South Seas but at the time of the preparations for Rogers' voyage, he was facing legal action. From 1703–06 he had commanded an expedition to the South Seas during which he had lost two ships, the *Cinque Ports* and the *St George*. The owners were justifiably upset and were planning to sue him for their loss – a situation that spurred Dampier on to find a place on a new expedition.

There was no doubt about the intentions of the Woodes Rogers voyage; in his publication *Captain Woodes Rogers' Voyage Round the World,* Donald Jones quotes John Parker, a midshipman on the *Duke,* who confirmed that: '. . . we went out as Private Men of War and *not* as trading ships, And that no sort of Merchandise was shipped on board said Ships to trade withal. . . ' In other words, they planned to raid Spanish ships for treasure.

The expedition set out in June 1708 and the two ships were rowed out to Kingroad; they then set off in August via Cork. Within a few weeks they had intercepted a Swedish frigate. Rogers realised there wasn't much contraband on board but the crew thought differently and when Rogers ordered them to move on they attempted to mutiny, which was dealt with firmly by Rogers and his officers. His plan was to go for the big prizes by waylaying the Spanish on the Pacific side of South America where they would not be expecting the English. However, to get there the expedition had to sail across the Atlantic then round Cape Horn. As they did so, they sailed further south than anyone had been so far, reaching a latitude of 61° 53' S. They survived the violent gales of the Cape and sailed north along the Chile coast, making for the islands of Juan Fernandez, to anchor and take on water. The *Duke* and *Duchess* arrived on 2 February 1709 and it was here that they found Alexander Selkirk.

Selkirk had been on the same earlier, fateful expedition as Dampier. He was master of the ship *Cinque Ports*, at the time captained by Thomas Stradling, while Dampier had captained the accompanying *St George*. Selkirk and Stradling fell out because Selkirk was convinced the *Cinque Ports* was riddled with ship worm and he asked to be put ashore rather than risk going down with the ship. He was right – the *Cinque Ports* was later lost with most of her crew. But Selkirk had badly misjudged the timing. He had assumed that another ship would be along in a few months and he'd be rescued but when the *Duke* and *Duchess* arrived he had been on the island for more than four years. He had lived on shellfish, then feral goats that had been introduced by earlier expeditions to provide meat and milk. Selkirk had befriended the feral cats, also refugees from earlier ships, to give him protection from the inevitable rats.

Two ships had appeared during his exile but they were Spanish and it seemed prudent to hide rather than risk being taken prisoner by the enemy. The irony was that when rescue did arrive in the form of Rogers and his expedition, Dampier was on board. As Dampier had been on the expedition that had stranded Selkirk, they recognised each other; Dampier vouched for Selkirk and Rogers took him on board. The expedition moved on, capturing treasure and eventually, Rogers gave Selkirk command of one of the captured prize ships.

All this seems a long way from Bristol but Rogers' expedition had another claim to fame. Leaving the Juan Fernandez islands and continuing his harassment of the Spanish, he decided not to return via Cape Horn, and the storms that would threaten the safety of his ships and the prizes. Instead, they returned across the Pacific and around the Cape of Good Hope, making Rogers only the third English commander to circumnavigate the globe after Francis Drake and Thomas Cavendish. The expedition was a success for the investors – by the time the ships reached home in 1709, they had amassed nearly £200,000 worth of treasure but for Rogers and the crew, legal tangles resulted in delays in the crew actually getting their share. Dampier died before receiving anything and Rogers himself went bankrupt.

After returning from their expedition in 1711, Woodes Rogers and Selkirk came back to Bristol. Selkirk appears in the local records as having been served court papers for being 'rowdy' in the Naval Volunteer, another King Street pub. Which brings us to another famous Bristol literary connection – *Robinson Crusoe*. Local legend again has it that Daniel Defoe met Alexander Selkirk in the Llandoger Trow and heard his story, hence adapting it for his famous novel. Yet again, this is not entirely true, although Defoe came to Bristol several times, including a period in the 1690s when he was facing bankruptcy and had fled to a debtors' sanctuary in the city. It was then that he earned the label the 'Sunday Gentleman' as Sunday was the only day he could appear in public without being arrested. But this had been a decade earlier than the arrival of Woodes Rogers and Selkirk in Bristol and even if Defoe was in the city at the same time he is very unlikely to have stayed at the Llandoger Trow which, at that time, occupied just one of the group of houses. A later biography suggests he met Selkirk in a Mrs Daniel's house in St James' Square but this is not substantiated. Indeed, he need not have actually met Selkirk to hear his story; Woodes Rogers had published an account of the whole voyage, including Selkirk's experiences, in 1712, under the title *A Cruising Voyage Round the World*.

Defoe wrote *Robinson Crusoe* in his later years; he was 59 when it was published and although convention gives his inspiration as Selkirk's story, a recent theory was put forward by explorer Tim Severin that the story was actually based on that of Henry Pitman, a surgeon who had been marooned by pirates on an island off the coast of Venezuela. And Mark Steeds, of the Long John Silver Trust of Bristol has made the interesting suggestion that Robert Louis Stevenson could have based the character of Ben Gunn on Selkirk.

And what of Woodes Rogers? He was appointed Governor of the Bahamas, arriving there in 1718. He was a man with a mission – to rid the Caribbean of the scourge of the pirates who had been terrorising the islands and the local shipping in an orgy of lawlessness. It was a depressing prospect; the Bahamas were in a state of social decay and pirates were free to use the local harbours in exchange for a share in their booty. As well as the other pirates in the region, it was here that Woodes Rogers had to take on one of his more formidable opponents – also from Bristol, the notorious pirate Edward Teach, or Blackbeard. Thought to have been born in Bristol around 1680, his origins are as much a part of legend as historical fact; some accounts give his family name as Drummond but he was calling himself 'Teach' by the time he took up his career on the sea. He was initially a crewman aboard a Jamaican sloop commanded by the pirate Benjamin Hornigold who was raiding ships around the West Indies. Teach was obviously a 'natural' and adapted to the lifestyle of the pirate well enough for Hornigold to give him command of one of their captured vessels. Between them, they brought their own brand of greed and terror to the West Indies.

One of their great prizes was a richly laden French ship, the *Concorde*, with twenty-six guns, but it was about now that Woodes Rogers had reached the Bahamas and offered amnesty to pirates. Hornigold decided to accept. Teach, however, declined the pardon and set about converting the *Concorde* into his flagship. He brought her armament up to forty guns and renamed her the *Queen Anne's Revenge*, taking her on raids around the Caribbean, instilling terror under his name of Blackbeard and carefully cultivating his image. He had a huge, thick black beard that covered most of his face and wore a red coat; when going into battle he wove fuses into his hair, set alight like fireworks, and wore a collection of pistols and cutlasses, all of which added to his fearsome image. The *Queen Anne's Revenge* met another pirate ship, the *Revenge*, commanded by the 'gentleman pirate' Stede Bonnet and initially the two of them sailed as a partnership. But Blackbeard decided that Bonnet was a poor sailor and an even worse pirate so appointed one of his crew to command the *Revenge* and brought Bonnet on board the *Queen Anne's Revenge* as his 'guest'.

All through the winter of 1717–18, the *Queen Anne's Revenge* and the *Revenge* scoured the Caribbean raiding ships, helping themselves to treasure and occasionally commandeering ships.

A popular image of Blackbeard the pirate; with fireworks in his hair and guns at the ready he was a terrifying sight to his victims.

And it seems that Blackbeard was responsible for another part of pirate lore – the pirates' song from *Treasure Island*:

Fifteen men on a dead man's chest
Yo ho ho and a bottle of rum
Drink and the devil had done for the rest
Yo ho ho and a bottle of rum.

'Dead Man's Chest' or 'Dead Chest' is a tiny island in the southern part of the British Virgin Island group of Caribbean islands. Now an uninhabited national park, it was said to be the island where Blackbeard marooned some of his crew who had mutinied. There was no water on the island and he left each pirate with a cutlass and a bottle of rum, thinking they would kill each other; when he came back some time later, he found that fifteen had survived and 'drink and the devil had done for the rest'.

Having refused Woodes Rogers' offer of amnesty to all pirates in 1718, Blackbeard left the Caribbean and sailed up the coast of North America, in command of four ships and 300 pirates. In an audacious attack he blockaded Charleston, South Carolina, for a week, intercepting and plundering shipping and holding the town to ransom. In return for the release of the town he demanded a chest of medicines and such was his reputation that not only was he given the chest but he also received an additional payment of between £1,000 and £1,500 in gold and silver.

It is an irony that should not be underestimated that, for a brief two-year period, a Bristolian was America's 'public enemy number one' according to the first regular newspaper, the *Boston News-Letter*. But Blackbeard was not infallible and in the June of 1718 the *Queen Anne's Revenge* ran aground in what is now Beaufort Inlet near Charleston. Blackbeard transferred his loot to another ship, effectively downsizing his crew by marooning some of them, and set sail for Ocracoke in North Carolina to take 'retirement'. He went so far as to build a house and struck up an amiable relationship with Charles Eden, the Governor of North Carolina. It didn't last. The temptation of ships leaving Virginia laden with tobacco led Blackbeard back into his old ways, causing financial hardship for wealthy Virginians. Their governor, Alexander Spottiswood, realising that Eden was not going to intervene, arranged for the Royal Navy to solve the problem.

Which it did. In an inspired tactic, Lieutenant Robert Maynard, in charge of the operation, set a trap by ordering his men to hide below deck leaving only himself and two other officers on deck. As Maynard had planned, Blackbeard assumed the rest of the crew had been killed or wounded so came aboard intending to finish off the remainder. In hand-to-hand combat, Maynard's crew emerged, took on Blackbeard's crew and in a bloody and dramatic exchange, ended the career of the most notorious pirate the seas had known for some time. Succumbing to five musket-ball shots and several sword cuts, Blackbeard's head was eventually cut off and his body thrown overboard. Maynard kept the head and hung it on the bowsprit, partly to warn off other pirates and partly to claim the substantial reward offered for Blackbeard's life.

Closer to home, piracy was a problem in the Bristol Channel, with the island of Lundy used as a stronghold and refuge for pirates. And the Channel's countless inlets and creeks, together with the ever-changing sand bars and treacherous currents, allowed another activity to flourish without too much fear of hindrance from the authorities: smuggling.

The big merchant ships that had to wait at Hungroad for the incoming tide were in contact with the pilots who were to bring the ship into the port; it was here that the 'tide-waiters' – the customs officials – boarded the ship to stay on board until all the goods had been unloaded. If the price was right, the official could be accidentally 'looking the other way' when certain goods were unloaded.

The geography of the Avon around Bristol did not add to its security. The river, between Kingroad and Bristol has all sorts of places along the bank that make ideal hiding places; for customs officials trying to keep a grip on smuggling in the Channel, local knowledge gave smugglers the edge. And the port of Bristol itself was inevitably ripe for smuggling. Most ports such as London, Liverpool, Glasgow and Plymouth all have docks that are self-contained, in their own districts away from the centre and generally secured with walls and security officers. Bristol, on the other hand, has its quays in the centre of the city without any such security to speak of and once a ship's cargo had been unloaded, it was easy to spirit it away into the labyrinth of streets and alleyways around the quays.

Smuggling is as old as the introduction of 'customs' – the tax levied on goods being imported or exported. There were various attempts to collect this tax in some form dating back to King John, who established a system of 'Ancient and Rightful Customs' in 1203 but it was Edward I, in 1275, who imposed an export tax on wool and hides such as fleeces and leather. English wool was very much in demand in Europe and Edward saw this as way of raising money for his ongoing war with France. So the first instances of smuggling were attempts to avoid this tax when exporting wool.

Where the Crown had imposed customs duties, they had to provide a means to collect it, so the office of customs collector was introduced and his lot was not always a happy one. Bristol was designated one of thirteen Great Ports and, as Graham Smith shows in *Smuggling in the Bristol Channel*, in 1387 the collector received an order from the Exchequer to '. . . clear the Severn Sea of pyrates and diverse persons who make large frauds on the King's Revenue.'

A few years later, the collector William Canynges the Elder, whose family was to come to prominence later in Bristol's history, received a sharp order that if he didn't stop the smuggling on the coast of the Bristol Channel he would be liable for the losses. It wasn't until 1429 that a customs boat was provided, stationed in Bristol, but apart from taking the tide-waiters out to the incoming vessels, it isn't clear whether it was used to capture smugglers or their goods.

Smuggling, like piracy, has an element of romance about it but, in reality, it could be dangerous. And it wasn't just isolated boatmen trying to land their

With Bristol's busy harbour in the centre of the city, the potential for spiriting contraband goods away into the surrounding streets made enforcing customs regulations almost impossible.

precious contraband on a secluded beach or inlet that risked being caught, it seems that smuggling went though the upper echelons of society. Some of Bristol's most eminent citizens were involved in a form of 'white ruff' crime. For them to be caught meant a hefty fine and confiscation of goods so, for smuggling to be worth the risk, it had to be profitable. This meant the higher the duty on something, the more likely it was to be smuggled. Dr Evan Jones of the University of Bristol has adopted techniques normally used in fraud investigations to examine records of shipping and cargo in sixteenth-century Bristol. He found that smuggling was an integral part of Bristol's economy, with merchants keeping sets of well-organised books that showed accounts to be presented to the customs officials as well as their own records of transactions. It might seem risky to us to keep such records, but it was only relatively recently that account books were of interest to customs officials and became admissible in court.

Dr Jones studied the records of William and Robert Tyndall from 1544–45 and of John Smyth for 1538–50, all eminent Bristol merchants. He found that their illicit exports were mainly of grain and leather; not particularly glamorous but compared to other cargo, they incurred a higher duty, with leather up to 10 per cent. The other problem was that to export these materials required a licence issued by the Crown as their export was normally prohibited. Once issued, the licences could be bought and sold, with the cost of a legitimate licence adding to the expenses of export.

Profit was everything. When England was at war with Spain, culminating in the Spanish Armada, Bristol merchants had a ready market for guns made in the Forest of Dean – the Spanish themselves. If the guns could be spirited away and sold abroad, the merchants made money and the Spanish acquired arms; whether the merchants involved actually slept at night is not recorded.

In the middle of the seventeenth century, the new tax of excise was introduced. This was a tax on goods sold within the country rather than for import or export; the first commodity to be taxed was salt but quickly included alcohol, as it does today. But as international trade grew with the growth of the American colonies, the import of tobacco attracted massive smuggling operations. Tobacco was supposed to be imported to Bristol to be re-exported to the continent but was simply 'exported' further along the coast of the Bristol Channel, often to Wales, and then brought back into Bristol by market boats. Another scam was to land the tobacco bales at the mouth of the Avon so it did not have to be brought into the harbour to be made subject to customs charges. Bribery was rife and the hapless customs officials, if they did try to recover a stash of contraband, such as one discovered along the bank of the river near Bedminster in the 1660s, were subject to abuse and possibly violence from local people.

Excise officers tried their best to enforce the collection of excise duties and regularly inspected the shops and bars in the centre of Bristol, seizing goods that were not shown to have been subject to the correct duty. In 1738, the Kingswood miners were openly selling their own home-made ale and cider, as well as smuggling brandy and rum. An attempt by the excise officers to seize the goods and/or the duty owed resulted in a riot and the army had to be brought in to bring the situation under control. Smugglers were not above using violence to resist the customs officers; in 1725, a gang was caught landing brandy and tobacco near Portishead but the officers were helpless to do anything in the face of threats of violence. The navy was no help; relations between customs and the navy were strained at best and openly hostile at worst. The navy crews were old hands at smuggling and the customs interfered with navy ships whenever they had a chance, creating resentment and distrust.

It seemed that customs and excise officials were fighting a losing battle and every time a tax was put on another commodity, a new way to smuggle it would be invented. By the late eighteenth century, vinegar, starch and candles were smuggled alongside alcohol and tobacco. Yet smugglers did, occasionally, make mistakes. By 1748, even Irish sailcloth was liable to import duty. This affected Bristol as so much of its trade was with Ireland. Graham Smith, in

The Custom House in Queen Square, the centre of operations for collecting customs revenues from trading ships. Built in 1711, the original Custom House was destroyed in the 1831 riots, so was later rebuilt.

his *Smuggling in the Bristol Channel 1700–1850* describes an ingenious attempt to avoid paying duty on sailcloth. The enterprising master of the *Catherine Lacey,* arriving at Bristol from Cork, had folded the new sails and attached them to the outside of the hull below the water line so that they could not be seen, either by anyone on board or by anyone looking at the ship from the quay. As ideas go, it was quite a good one, except that as the legitimate cargo was unloaded, the ship became lighter and started riding higher in the water. . .

CHAPTER 11

THE SPA

One of the main trunk roads into Bristol runs along the bank of the Avon, from the port of Avonmouth where it connects to the M5 motorway, all the way into the city centre. The Portway is a busy road – dual carriageway in places – and carries much of the traffic from the south-west into the city; there is little opportunity for sightseeing as drivers are more intent on getting somewhere in a hurry than enjoying the local attractions.

Yet, driving into Bristol, having gone under the Clifton Suspension Bridge, the traffic passes an unusual building on the left, set back from the road with a slightly apologetic air to it. This is the Colonnade, one of the few visible reminders of Bristol's role as a health spa. The district of Hotwells, between the river and the heights of Clifton, is now a residential suburb but

The Colonnade, built in 1786 to complement the Pump Room of the Hot Well;
it contained shops and a lending library.

was once a centre of healing, where the wealthy and not-so-wealthy came to take the waters in the hope of curing what ailed them.

The geology of Bristol is nothing if not complex; it is mostly built on carboniferous limestone, a feature of which is the presence of freshwater springs. Much of Bristol's water-supply came from these springs; at the heart of the old Saxon city was St Edith's well or St Edywell, which supplied water until 1887. This well was between St Peter's Church in Castle Park and St Mary le Port and the only reminder of its presence is a slab stone that looks a lighter colour than its surroundings. Other wells included one at the Pithay, and Beggar's Well in what is now the St Paul's district. There was a spring on Brandon Hill, on the west side, which became known as Jacob's Well – the origin of the name Jacob's Wells Road. It was essential to the ancient Jewish community, who lived outside the city walls and built a synagogue and a ritual bath, or Mikvah, using the spring water. Their burial-ground was under what is now Queen Elizabeth's Hospital. By 1290, a combination of resentment against the Jewish practice of money lending and Christian bigotry amplified by the Crusades, led Edward I to expel all the Jews from England, giving them a subsidy from Parliament and a promise of safe passage as they left.

In Bristol, when the Jews left, the spring reverted to the Crown, and access was granted to the monks at St Augustine. A century later, Edward III gave the spring to the city of Bristol and, although less well known than the Hot Well spring, it was also believed to have healing properties, attracting pilgrims from the Middle Ages through to the eighteenth century.

But all these other healing springs were eclipsed by the spring that gave the district of Hotwells its name. It was the source of the fabled, miraculous, healing water that emerged from the rock of the Avon Gorge at a point just below today's suspension bridge, known as St Vincent's Rocks. The spring was only accessible during low tide; it is nine metres below the high-water mark and three metres above low water. To describe it as 'hot' is perhaps a bit misleading, but it is warm, at a steady temperature of twenty-four degrees centigrade. It was known by William Worcestre in 1480, who, as Vincent Waite reveals in *The Bristol Hotwell*, wrote about its existence: ' . . . there is a spring . . . and it is as warm as milk or the water at Bath. . .'

It is warmer than the surrounding river water because it comes from the same source deep underground as the water in the more famous neighbouring Bath spa. Water that has seeped down through porous limestone is heated by passing over the hot rocks of the earth's crust and emerges through a fracture in the hard limestone as a hot spring. In the case of the Hot Wells, mixing with cooler water on its way to the surface means, contrary to

Worcestre's observation, the water is not as warm as that at Bath (which is about forty-six degrees).

What is so special about this water? It is effervescent, the tiny bubbles giving it a milky-white appearance, and it contains minerals such as salt, iron and magnesium chloride among others. In 1912 analysis showed it was also radioactive, with a reading more than 100 times higher than the normal water-supply. It was a continual, reliable source of water, with the dramatic exception of 1 November 1755, when, as Reid quotes in *Chronicle of Clifton and Hotwells*, the water suddenly turned as red as blood, which sent good God-fearing men into a panic: '. . . the consternation it created, being considered an omen of the world's final slaughter. All flew to the churches where incessant prayers were offered to avert the apparent approach of their destruction and to appease the rage of heaven.'

It wasn't the end of the world, or the rage of heaven. It was a result of a devastating earthquake, with the epicentre in the north Atlantic, which had annihilated the city of Lisbon. The effects had been felt as far away as Finland and affected wells and springs across Europe but until this was understood, the symbol of the blood-red spring caused panic and confusion.

The spring was notoriously difficult to reach on the slippery rocks at low tide and it seems that the first people to use its medicinal qualities were sailors who could access the water from the river. They believed it cured scurvy. By the start of the seventeenth century, the spring's reputation as a cure-all had spread far and wide and in 1630, John Bruckshaw was granted a lease to turn it into a commercial venture. He built a brick wall around the spring in the first of many attempts to solve a fundamental problem with the quality of water. During high tide the spring was submerged by the river (which at that time was Bristol's natural sewer), so the spring water was polluted at high tide and for some time afterwards. The addition of river water may have added a certain piquancy to the taste but probably didn't do a lot for its medicinal qualities. The brick surround went some way to improving the situation but it was a problem that successive leaseholders of the spring struggled to solve.

Yet, for whatever reason, the spring water's reputation for healing flourished. In 1680, a baker, Mr Abel Gagg, dreamed he should drink the spring water as a cure for his advanced diabetes. The dream turned out to be prophetic because he drank the water, no doubt quenching the terrible thirst that comes with diabetes and, by all accounts, after a few days stopped losing weight. He claimed he was completely cured. Other claims of cures followed, particularly of diabetes, as well as other more vague

Detail from Millerd's map of 1673 showing the steps built into the rock as access to the Hot Well.

complaints. As Waite illustrates in *The Bristol Hotwell*, often quoted by various doctors in descriptions about the water's healing properties were ailments such as 'hot livers, feeble brains and red pimply faces' and it was considered as 'much commended for affections of the kidneys, taken inwardly and for old sores, applied outwardly.'

It is possible that the water had a mild diuretic effect, and the minerals might have made up for dietary deficiencies but the effect would have been minimal. Cures were claimed for eye and skin problems, scurvy and the palsy. Faith, it seems, played a big part in any cures the water brought.

In 1677, Charles II's queen, Catherine of Braganza, came to take the waters. She came on a daytrip from Bath, normal for a visit to the Hot Well; at that time there was no accommodation and the access to the spring was still difficult even though steps had been cut into the rock. But her royal patronage further enhanced the reputation of Hotwells as a healing spa and the Merchant Venturers, who owned the land, realised that there was serious money to be made. They granted another lease in 1695 to Charles Jones and Thomas Callow Hill, charging them an annual fee of £5 but imposing the condition that they spent a further £500 on improvements to the spring. Jones and Hill built a pump room, with a more sophisticated system for stopping river pollution, along with lodgings to house the visitors. The great and good came to the spa to see and to be seen, to mingle, gossip and discuss the latest scandal.

The smart set brought prosperity to the Hotwells area and by the middle of the eighteenth century, it was flourishing. The lodgings on the upper floor of the pump house were by no means sufficient to meet the demands of visitors so new houses were built to offer apartments for rent. Dowry Square – still an elegant square passed by the traffic coming off the Cumberland Basin and Portway into the centre – and Dowry Parade were built at the start of the century and a tree-lined promenade was constructed along the river bank to encourage the taking of fresh air and exercise, probably more effective as a cure than the spring water itself.

A pleasure garden, the New Vauxhall Garden, was opened in 1743. It is thought to have stood where the Cumberland Basin flyover is now and on opening attracted 2,000 visitors. The whole scene was thriving in the mid-1700s, with parties, public breakfasts, dances, balls and games. It seemed to be as fashionable as Bath and made the district of Hotwells as much of a visitor attraction.

In 1729 there was even a little theatre built to entertain the visitors. It was on a site about halfway down Jacob's Wells Road and was built next to a pub; the buildings shared a wall and with the simple expedient of a hole in that wall, drinks could be passed to the actors and those of the audience that were seated on the stage. It was not the most wholesome place to visit, as the area was a haunt of pickpockets and ne'er-do-wells, and with the opening of the Theatre Royal in King Street, the theatre lost money and eventually had to close in 1771.

A lesser-known spring, the 'New Hotwell', was a kilometre or so further downstream than its more famous rival and by most accounts produced water from the same source; its isolation, however, was a problem and access was difficult. Its most famous visitor was John Wesley, who claimed its water had cured 'a greedy consumption' but even this endorsement did not keep it viable as a spa, and by 1792 the buildings were lived in by workmen who were quarrying Avon Gorge.

Water from the Hot Well had a major advantage over Bath water – it could be bottled and not lose its properties. As its reputation for healing grew, an industry to bottle and sell the water grew with it, with Bristol's glass-makers prospering as a result. The water was regularly shipped to London and in the beginning of the seventeenth century, a Cambridge don, Dr Samuel Ward, had his own supply shipped to him personally.

Several factors came together to bring an end to this prosperity and when it started to decline, it happened relatively quickly. War with France affected all of Bristol; for the Hot Well there was the advantage that travel to Europe had been curtailed so those in need of spa cures came to the English spas – good for business. But the war needed money and the recent prosperity of Bristol had been built on lines of credit. Once those lines of credit had been broken, the last decade of the eighteenth century saw a massive financial crash and building slump – bad for business. The merchant classes became more preoccupied with solvency than with parties.

It didn't help that the medical profession still had a touching faith in the Hot Well's healing properties. This endorsement might seem to be a good thing but it backfired. Doctors recommended the treatment for 'consumption', the slow and fatal disease of tuberculosis, and so patients came to the Hot Well in a last desperate search for a cure. It didn't work, of course, although the combination of rest and fresh air might have slowed down the advance of the disease, and many of these patients came to the area of Hotwells simply to die. The presence of the terminally ill was not good for tourism and some of the lodgings where they stayed became known locally as Death Row.

In 1784, the Merchant Venturers were once again looking for a tenant and whoever was prepared to take on the lease needed to spend yet more money. They specified that the Hot Well needed more work done on repairs to the pump room, more money spent on protecting the spring water from the river tides – at least £500 – and a quay wall built along the river at a cost of £1,000. Not surprisingly, there was no rush to take on a lease needing this sort of expenditure.

It was about this time that the Colonnade was built, and it was finished in 1787. The ground floor contained a Georgian shopping mall and it also contained a library, the end result of a stormy collaboration between two remarkable women. One was the writer and campaigner Hannah More, who had been born in Fishponds, now a suburb of Bristol, and became a member of literary and political circles, a passionate social reformer and educationalist. The other was Ann Yearsley, a working-class mother of six who had taken up writing in what little spare time she had. While the members of high society were spending their money and leisure at the Hot Well, the poorer citizens of Bristol were struggling to make a living. Ann, born Ann Cromartie, had married John Yearsley, a yeoman farmer, and ran the farm alongside caring for her children. She would go to Hannah More's home to collect pigswill and at this time got to know More, who, discovering Ann's writing ability, encouraged her.

Hannah More organised for Ann Yearsley's poetry to be published, to great critical and commercial acclaim. Known as the 'Bristol Milkmaid', or 'Latilla', her poems sold well, making a profit of over £350, but this money set off an acrimonious quarrel. Hannah More invested the money in a trust fund whereas Ann Yearsley wanted to control it herself and accused More of fraud, of not trusting her with the money. Eventually, with the intervention of a Bristol merchant, the money went to Yearsley and she used some of it to set up a circulating library at the Colonnade but the two women sustained their quarrel until Yearsley died in 1806, followed by More in 1833.

In 1790, a second spring, known as Sion Spring or the Upper Hot Well was created when a local solicitor, Morgan, sunk a well from his house on Sion Hill to find water; he found it at a depth of 245 feet, from the same source as the Hot Well itself. Not to miss out on a business opportunity, he built a pump room with facilities for bathing, as well as providing water to local domestic houses.

The Merchant Venturers' problem of finding a tenant for the Hot Well was solved in 1790, when Samuel Powell took on the task. The economics were a disaster waiting to happen, as it seemed that the only way for Powell to recoup his expenses was to increase the rent. Before this, a family would pay 10s a sea-

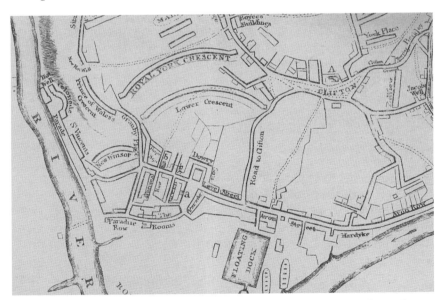

Detail from Mathew's map of 1794, showing the Hot Well and Colonnade on the left, Dowry Square just left of centre and the Jacobs Well on the right.

son for them all to drink from the well but with the new prices, it cost 26s per person, a 260 per cent price rise and a substantial deterrent to visitors.

The presence of so many patients terminally ill with tuberculosis attracted the attention of Thomas Beddoes, a doctor and philanthropist who had become fascinated by a discovery made in 1772; this was the identification of the gas nitrous oxide by the chemist Joseph Priestley.

Beddoes reasoned that the breathing of gases such as pure oxygen or nitrous oxide would cure many diseases, but in particular, tuberculosis. In 1793 he came to Bristol, to Hotwells, where he could develop his cure by trying it out on the terminally ill consumptives, of which there was no shortage. But, as he had dismissed the medicinal property of the spa water in favour of his method of inhaling gases, he contributed to the failure of the spa itself. He set up a laboratory in the basement of a house in 11 Hope Square, where he worked on various dubious experiments involving animals and oxygen. But he was so convinced his methods worked, particularly with tuberculosis, he set up the Pneumatic Institute, at 6 Dowry Square, for the consumptive patients that had come to be cured by drinking the Hot Well spring water and were desperate enough to try anything.

The Institute was set up in 1798 and Beddoes employed as its director a young but brilliant chemist from Cornwall, Humphry Davy. An advertisement in the *Bristol Gazette and Public Advertiser* of 21 March 1799 announced:

New medical institution.
Upper end of Dowry-Square, Hotwells, corner house.
Treating incurable diseases.
Medical professors at Edinburgh.
Many Physicians in England.
Consumption, Asthma, Palsy, Dropsy, obstinate Venereal Complaints, Scrophula or King's Evil. Other incurable diseases. Patients treated gratis.
Expectation: Considerable portion of cases will be permanently cured. Methods are not hazardous or painful.
Attendance will be given from 11 till 1 o'clock by Thomas Beddoes or Humphrey Davy. Subscriptions for support of Institution received by John Savery, Esq., Narrow Wine Street, Bristol.

Humphrey Davy was born in Penzance in 1778, the son of a poor Cornish woodcarver. But he was apprenticed to a surgeon-apothecary and showed a precocious ability, even when young. He was only 19 when he came to Bristol and took on Beddoes' ideas with enthusiasm. In the spirit of true scientific enquiry, he experimented on himself, breathing in pure nitrous oxide and observing the results. Later in 1799, Davy announced that nitrous oxide could be inhaled safely by humans; the effects, of creating a 'high' accompanied by much giggling and laughter, inspired Davy to name the new recreational drug 'laughing gas'.

It became the height of fashion to attend social gatherings where Mr Davy and his friends would indulge in this laughing gas. And Mr Davy's friends included some illustrious figures. His colleague at the Pneumatic Institute was another doctor, who had qualified in Edinburgh. This was Peter Roget who went on to practise medicine most of his life before coming to fame in his seventies with the publication of his invaluable *Thesaurus*.

Literary figures came to the parties; Robert Southey and Samuel Taylor Coleridge became friends of Davy who, among his many other talents, considered himself something of a poet. Davy's notebooks, archived at the Royal Institution and quoted at http://oufcnt2.open.ac.uk/˜gill_stoker/davy.htm, reveal he even wrote lines *On breathing the Nitrous Oxide:*

Not in the ideal dreams of wild desire
Have I beheld a rapture-waking form;
My bosom burns with no unhallowed fire
Yet it is my cheek with rosy blushes warm.
Yet are my eyes with sparkling lustre filled
Yet is my mouth replete with murmuring sound;
Yet are my limbs with inward transports thrill'd
And clad with new-born mightiness around.

Some of his most heart-felt poems, however, were those written to Beddoes' young wife, Anna Edgeworth Beddoes. When Davy first arrived in Bristol, she introduced him to the area and they took long walks around the heights of Clifton and along the River Avon. It was not a relationship that could blossom but it seemed from Davy's poetry that their friendship stayed in his heart all his life.

And while all this society life was going on, based around Hotwells, there were still people hanging onto the futile hope that treatment from the Pneumatic Institute would cure their tuberculosis, which, of course, it didn't. It became obvious very quickly that while nitrous oxide provided an entertaining way to spend a few hours, it was not a miracle cure. Ironically, Davy had noted that while inhaling the gas, it had numbed the pain of his toothache but the idea of using nitrous oxide as an anaesthetic would take another forty years to come to fruition.

Davy moved on in 1801 to the newly formed Royal Institution. He married the widow Jane Apreece, his passport into high society, and proved himself to be a brilliant chemist; he was only the second 'natural philosopher' – scientist – to be knighted after Isaac Newton. He went on to isolate the elements sodium and potassium, studied electro-chemistry and invented the first miners' safety lamp, thus rescuing countless canaries from a miserable existence in the coal mines.

Beddoes, on the other hand, had a less illustrious career; the Institute closed in 1802 and he moved to Clifton, where he died in 1808, frustrated and disappointed. He is buried in the Strangers' Graveyard (at the bottom of Lower Clifton Hill and York Place/Meridian Vale in Clifton), alongside many of his patients who had lost their struggle with the wasting disease. It had been a brief but, literally, heady three years.

Just as the Pneumatic Institute had closed, another new attempt at a medical initiative arrived in Bristol when Jacob Schweppe's company set up a factory and shop in Hotwells selling soda water. Jacob Schweppe, a Swiss, had also investigated Priestley's and others' ideas about gases as a medical treatment and had set out to make carbonated mineral water. From its development in Switzerland, Jacob came to London in 1792 to set up his factory to sell mineral water; in Geneva, the medical profession had supported Schweppe's work and in England, eminent figures such as Erasmus Darwin, grandfather of Charles, and Josiah Wedgwood, who had supported the

A mid 19th century impression of the Hot Well.

Pneumatic Institute, all endorsed Schweppe's water. When the company was set to expand out of London, the first city they came to was Bristol. Initially, they opened on Philadelphia Street but further advertisements show that by 1814, they were manufacturing soda water at Upper Hot Well Spring and Sion Spring, with new company premises in Clifton.

None of this enterprise helped the flagging fortunes of the Hotwells spa itself.

Even when the war against France ended in 1815 those with money to visit spas went to the great spas of Europe. And George, who had become Prince Regent in 1810 as his poor mad father, George III, was finally locked up, created a new fashion for sea bathing. Coastal resorts such as Brighton became the places to be seen in the notoriously fickle world of high society.

Like its patients in terminal decline, the Hot Well had the occasional remission. In 1822, a new attempt to revive the spa led John Bolton to build a new spa house, the Royal Clifton Spa; at the same time, the last remains of the Hot Well, the old Hotwell House, was demolished so that a new road up the side of the gorge, that would become Bridge Valley Road, could be built. The new spa, under the enterprising Bolton, included the sale of items found in most tourist shops today – guidebooks, postcards, stationery, lavender soap, fossils – as well as the spa water. But it didn't work. By 1867, the new venture had failed and the new pump room had to go, demolished in its turn to make room for widening the river for shipping.

This was the end of the original spring, although some time later, in 1877, a new pump was installed in a grotto at the base of the gorge to supply free

The prestigious district of Clifton, rival to Hotwells, as seen in this mid 19th century view.

water from a different spring that arose further downstream than the original. It even had an attendant paid for by the Bristol Docks committee and, despite analysis by a local doctor showing that this water was not from the original Hot Well spring, the pump provided water until 1913. It was finally conceded that pollution from the river made the water dangerous and the pump was closed. The entrance to the cave can still be seen, blocked off but still visible, close to the bottom of the Suspension Bridge.

One last gasp for the spa came in 1890 when the Merchant Venturers gave permission to Sir George Newnes to build a cliff railway that would take passengers from the riverside at the Hot Well up the hill to Clifton; they had agreed on condition that Newnes build another hydropathic institution and pump room at the same time. To comply with this condition, he built the Clifton Grand Spa Hydro, which opened in 1898, but as a pump room it went the way of the spa's patients. The building is now the Avon Gorge Hotel and the remains of the pump room are closed off, next to the hotel terrace.

But Newnes' original idea, the Clifton Rocks Railway, was more successful. Until then, the only way from Hotwells up to Clifton was by the steep hills of either the Zig Zag, a path directly up the side of the gorge, or via Granby Hill. A funicular railway is not, in itself, that unusual – but this one went through solid rock, giving access to Clifton but avoiding the inevitable eyesore of a rail system on the side of the gorge. A 500-foot tunnel led from the Lower Station near the base of the Suspension Bridge to the Upper Station, next to the Avon Gorge Hotel. The tunnel was blasted through the rock, which was a nerve-wracking operation as the limestone was subject to faults and veins of other sorts of rock – rock falls were a real and present danger. Building the railway took two years, but when it opened, in 1893, it was the widest tunnel of its kind in the world, over twenty-seven feet wide and lined with two feet of brick throughout its length.

There were four passenger cars, linked in pairs to operate a counterweight system known as 'water balance', whereby the descending car carrying water and passengers was heavier than the ascending car; the brakesmen on the two cars were in contact with each other by the new electrical telegraph system.

Yet, by 1908, the venture was no longer viable and a receiver was appointed; the railway was finally closed for good in 1934. It had a brief revival during the Second World War when the tunnel was used by the BBC as their emergency headquarters but after the war the railway lay untouched and ignored. The closed entrance to the Lower Station can still be seen from the Portway, but the Upper Station, next to the Avon Gorge Hotel was re-opened in May 2005 by Sir George White to show the work in progress by the Clifton Rocks Refurbishment Group who have been working tirelessly to restore the station. The system can never be fully restored, the tunnel would need a massive investment to make it stable, but the enthusiasts of the Refurbishment Group have been able to give Bristolians a glimpse of the system as it might have once been. A penny fare to go up and a halfpenny to go down, a forty-second ride and no traffic jams; a nostalgic dream for those stuck in Bristol's traffic today.

Most of the remains of the Hot Well in its prime have also gone, mostly to make way for the Portway, opened in 1926. Much of the gorge has been quarried on the north side of the river, the splendour of the scenery that so inspired the landscape artists of the eighteenth century, having also been lost to today's Bristol.

The lower station of the Clifton Rocks Railway, the remains of which are still visible from the Portway.

CHAPTER 12

QUEEN SQUARE

Queen Square is one of several Georgian squares in Bristol but commands respect as the biggest and most well known. The others have their share of elegance and interesting architecture, with intimate gardens or interesting quirks of history but Queen Square has a central role in Bristol's past.

Rysbrack's 1736 statue of a somewhat idealised William III at the centre of Queen Square.

To emerge onto Queen Square is something of a surprise, even for someone used to the city. It is big, elegant and open, bounded by King Street to the north, Welsh Back to the east, the Grove to the south and Prince Street to the west. Rows of tall terraced Georgian houses only allow access to the square via the corners and three lanes in the centre of the terraces, which enhances the effect of the square being a world apart. Trees, grass and paths leading to the centre of the square where the statue of William III gazes down from his horse, add to the openness which is a marked contrast from the busy surrounding city centre.

Queen Square is at the end of the spur of land created when the Frome was diverted in 1245. For centuries this was public land known as the Marsh, enigmatically named, as it was once a soggy piece of wetland. But by the sixteenth century it had been drained and was a place for popular entertainment, such as bull baiting and wrestling – it was a large, open space ideal for gathering crowds. Livestock were grazed there and in 1622 a bowling-green was laid out.

Bristol was graced by a visit from Queen Elizabeth in 1574 and the city laid on the full works. She entered the city from the east, through Lawford's Gate where she was met by the mayor's entourage. Symbolic of her sovereignty, she was presented with the ceremonial mace by the mayor and having accepted it, she graciously presented it back to him. Of a more practical nature, the city recorder presented her with a silk purse containing gold coins to the value of £100. A long enthusiastic procession accompanied her through the streets past the cheering crowd, led by the mayor and followed by the council, the nobility and hundreds of liveried soldiers.

She was accommodated at the Great House (now the site of Colston Hall), which was owned by a John Young; she must have been reasonably comfortable for she later knighted him for his hospitality. And over her four-day visit she was treated to an extravagant pageant. The Marsh was dominated by a wooden viewing platform built for her majesty to watch the performance, which was a live-action mock battle. Two forts had been built specially and the battle raged for days, interspersed with long-winded declarations of loyalty from various officials. No doubt the occasion cost the city a small fortune but the Queen seemed suitably impressed and grateful so it was considered a good investment.

By the 1600s, the site of the Marsh was maintained by labourers, the costs covered by rent from butchers who were grazing their cattle on the land, as well as by interest on a sum of money donated for the purpose. Despite its role as a public space, the Corporation did not seem unduly bothered by the citizens dumping their rubbish there.

The Civil War saw the Marsh requisitioned again, this time for the building of a battery on the bowling-green to defend The Quay in the siege of 1643. The Marsh was not reinstated as a public space until 1656. It was still used for the training of soldiers and as a gathering point for elections but by the late 1600s trees had been planted and, crucial to a shipbuilding city such as Bristol, rope manufacturers used the space for rope-walks, where ropes were hung between the trees to dry.

The first stirring of the Marsh's transformation into a residential district came with the development of King Street on the north of the space. King Street was built mainly in the mid-1600s and, by then, there was building to the west of the Marsh on what was then called Wood Quay, now known as Narrow Quay. Then, in 1669, a proposal was made to the common council to build on the Marsh but apart from the council instructing the city surveyors to consider the idea, nothing happened for the next thirty years.

London was already setting the trend for building squares and the first one, at Covent Garden, was finished in the 1660s. The biggest square in England and the one that inspired the design of Queen Square is Lincoln's Inn Fields, laid out in part by Inigo Jones as part of fashionable London and now consisting mainly of solicitors' and barristers' offices.

In Bristol, several factors came together for the construction of Queen Square after a period of procrastination. Firstly – and probably most urgently – the council was short of money, so they proposed selling leaseholds on lots from the Marsh, for a period of 'five lives', as building plots. No rent would be charged for the first two years as long as a house of a suitable standard was built on the site. The second factor was Bristol's ambition to be seen as comparable to London in terms of status, fashion and architecture and the plots sold well, mostly to the gentry of Bristol. When, in 1699, a Dr John Reade petitioned the council to be allowed to build a house on the south side of the Marsh, the lease was granted within three days.

There was a slight technical problem – the ground level of the Marsh needed raising; although it had been drained, such low-lying land had potential for flooding. A landfill site was created, which did not take long to fill with industrial and domestic waste and so raised the ground level by two metres. Once building had started, the Corporation dictated that the houses should have the back and sides made of stone and the front wall of brick, with a brick walled courtyard at the front, but otherwise, the design of each house was left to the leaseholder. By 1703, twenty-five houses had been built and in 1711 the new Customs House was finished and leased to the Crown.

The Customs House building was bigger than the adjoining houses; it was in the centre of the north side of the square and is still there, although it has lost its original fine appearance.

By the end of 1716, the central space was used to create a formal garden, with lime trees planted for shade and gravel paths crossing the square diagonally. And twenty years later, at the centre of the square where the paths crossed, a new statue was installed, that of William III, William of Orange.

T.L.S Rowbotham's 1827 view of Queen Square, looking east.

The statue was commissioned by the Corporation and the Merchant Venturers. Two leading sculptors, both Flemish-born, John Michael Rysbrack and Peter Scheemakers, were asked to compete for the commission. They were rivals, both having a reputation for other sculpture in England and they both submitted maquettes; Rysbrack's was chosen and he was paid £1,800 while Scheemakers received £50 for the work he had done for the commission. Rysbrack created a clay model that was then cast in brass, rather than bronze, by Van Oost; the statue arrived in Bristol by boat in 1735 but it took another year before it was finally installed on its stone plinth, with lamps and railings to complete the centrepiece of the square.

The square was still referred to as 'the Marsh' until 1702 when Queen Anne visited the city and the mayor and aldermen announced that the new square was to be called Queen Square. It became *the* place to live.

The start of the nineteenth century saw the beginnings of a turbulent few decades. Politically, the idea of a democracy was nothing more than a sham and with the Industrial Revolution in its infancy the population was growing rapidly in the Midlands and the North. Yet the distribution of MPs to represent the people seemed almost random.

It is best explained by the wonderfully scheming Edmund Blackadder, in Curtis and Elton's comedy, *Blackadder III*. Explaining to Mrs Miggins

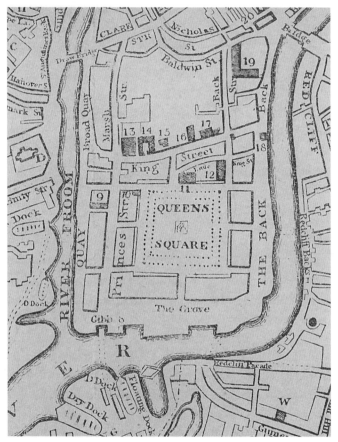

A detail from Mathew's map of Bristol of 1794, showing the layout of streets around the square much as it is today.

about the farcical nature of democracy, Blackadder gives the example of 'Manchester – population 60,000, electoral role, 3'. In a plot to avoid Prince George being struck off the Civil List for spending too much money on socks, Blackadder needs one more vote in the Commons so takes advantage of a rotten borough – 'a constituency where the landowner controls the voters and the MP'. They discover that a rotten borough, 'Dunny-on-the-Wold', has one voter and one MP and in a superb display of cynicism, when the incumbent MP dies before he can be bribed, Blackadder puts forward Baldrick as the next MP and, with Blackadder himself conveniently becoming the only voter, elects him to the Commons.

In reality, even more ridiculous than the comedy, was the rotten borough of Old Sarum in Wiltshire, which had no inhabitants, no voters and two MPs... In contrast, cities like Manchester, Birmingham and Leeds had no representation in Parliament. The situation was a farce.

Bristol was not as badly off as some, but with a population of over 100,000, only 6,000 were eligible to vote. To resolve this, in 1830, Earl Grey – he of the tea and the Whig party – proposed to King William IV, that the balance should be redressed, the rotten boroughs dissolved and proper representation given to the growing industrial communities in the north.

The Whig party was generally in favour of 'Reform', as it became known, but didn't have a sufficient majority in the Commons to bring it about. Grey asked the King to dissolve Parliament, trusting that an election would give the Whigs the majority it needed to pass the bill. It worked, they won and the Act of Reform was passed in 1831, to the delight of the general public. But – a big but – the House of Lords was dominated by the Tories and the Tories blocked the Bill. This did not go down at all well with the public, to such an extent that in many cities, they took to the street in riots.

The most dramatic and infamous of the riots was in Queen Square, Bristol. Yet, although the Bristol riots of 1831 are often referred to as the 'Reform Riots', they do not quite fit the pattern of the other riots in Nottingham, Derby, Bath and Worcester. With two MPs, Bristol had less to lose than the other cities with the failure of the bill. And when Bristol did flare up into a full-blown riot, it was three weeks after the bill had been rejected.

Riots were nothing new to Bristol; the good citizens seemed prepared to take to the streets at the slightest provocation. Apart from the altercation between the people and the castle in 1312 (Chapter 3) and the Bristol Bridge riot of 1793 (Chapter 2) there had been riots in 1659, when the apprentices protested, demanding the restoration of the monarchy; in 1709, when miners from Kingswood rioted against the crippling increase of food prices; in 1714 a celebration of the coronation of George I got out of hand, and in 1729 the weaving community released pent-up frustration at their low earnings. The introduction of turnpikes in 1727 set off more trouble and the failure of the harvest of 1752 forced the prices of meat and bread out of the reach of many, who then took their grievances to the streets.

It doesn't seem to fit the pattern of the other Reform Riots, that when the Reform Act failed in September 1831 Bristol was quiet for a few weeks. So what set off the most destructive riot – both in terms of loss of life and loss of property – in Bristol's history?

The catalyst was a Sir Charles Wetherell. He stood in the Commons and announced that the people of Bristol were against Reform – but Wetherell didn't actually represent Bristol. He was an MP, but MP for Boroughbridge in Yorkshire and he stood to lose his seat if Reform went ahead. His relationship with Bristol was that of Recorder, a barrister from London who was appointed as part-time judge and therefore responsible for presiding over the Assize Courts that were held at regular intervals in the major cities of England and Wales. When word of his speech reached Bristol, the people were incensed that someone who had no right to speak on their behalf had proclaimed their city to be against Reform.

Wetherell was due to arrive in Bristol on Saturday 29 October, to hold the Court of Assize and the people were determined to show him their disapproval. The general mood of the city meant that the time of his arrival was changed in an attempt to avoid the crowd but the news soon leaked out and his carriage was subject to general abuse and stone-throwing as it made its way from Totterdown into the city. He managed to open the Assize Courts and then left for the Mansion House in Queen Square where he was due to have dinner with the mayor, Charles Pinney.

Given the ugly mood of the crowd, which was no surprise to the authorities, the security arrangements were a shambles. The Corporation only had access to 100 regular constables to keep order so had thought that they could control the crowd by recruiting another 300 special constables. The problem was that these should have been drawn from the middle classes, the 'respectable' citizens but they wanted no part of it, so in their wisdom the Corporation hired 100 men with fewer sensibilities and probably spoiling for a fight.

The crowd followed Wetherell and his retinue to Queen Square and although, by then, troops had been called in, no-one tried to disperse the mob; crowd control was hampered by antagonism between the troops and the special constables who were heavy handed and aggressive. By the end of the afternoon, some of the crowd had gone so the special constables were allowed to go home as long as they returned in the evening. This proved to be an unwise move because as soon the rioters realised there were no constables, they came back and started to tear up the railings outside the Mansion House, throwing stones to break the windows of the ground floor.

The mayor read out the Riot Act, which was received with more verbal abuse from those in the crowd who could actually hear him and the mob then set about using the railings to bludgeon their way into the Mansion House, breaking furniture, and anything fragile, and making their way to the kitchens where the dinner for the civic reception was being prepared. The rioters were about to set fire to the kitchens when reinforcements of troops arrived and the situation was brought back under control. Meanwhile, the catalyst for all this chaos, Sir Charles Wetherell, had donned a change of clothes and made an undignified exit by climbing out of a window and over the roofs to safety, unceremoniously leaving the city the following morning.

As it was his arrival that had sparked the trouble, it would seem that his departure would end the affair but by now the genie was out of the bottle. On the Sunday, the Mansion House windows where boarded up and Queen Square seemed quiet so the soldiers on guard were sent away. Another bad move. Word got round that the Mansion House was unguarded so some of the rioters came back, broke in again and this time raided the mayor's well-stocked cellars of fine wine.

A belligerent crowd, drunk and with their blood up, then broke into the Custom House and started on the other houses on the north side of the square. Control was complicated by the fact that there were two different regiments involved to control the crowds; two troops of the 14th Light Dragoons, in their distinctive blue uniforms were already known for their heavy-handed methods of crowd control, which gave them the reputation as the 'Bloody Blues'. A troop of 3rd Dragoon Guards were more popular with the crowd, seen as more sympathetic to their cause and were cheered on their arrival. All the troops were under the control of Lieutenant Colonel Brereton, who had lived in Bristol for some time and claimed to be for Reform.

The troops from the 3rd Dragoon Guards had been used to clear Queen Square the day before, and the Bloody Blues kept out of sight in case they inflamed the crowd further. But by the Sunday afternoon, the drunken mob was out of control; Lieutenant Colonel Brereton should have been able to order the troops to charge and fire but he did not have the authority. He needed clear instructions from the civic authorities and after the fiasco on Bristol Bridge only forty years earlier, no-one was prepared to take this responsibility; without the official order, Brereton could do nothing.

By the end of the Sunday, the Mansion House, Customs House and many of the other buildings in the square were on fire, as well as warehouses around the square. Some of the mob had broken into the Bridewell, the gaol where some of their compatriots had been held, broke down the gates and freed all the prisoners. They then did the same for the New Gaol. Even the cathedral wasn't spared – the Bishop of Bristol was known to have voted against Reform and the mob turned their attention to the Bishop's Palace, which was looted and set on fire.

At the height of the riots, the fire could be seen from as far away as Wales. As Queen Square burned, looters were inside houses as rioters set them ablaze, some trying to escape by jumping out of upper-floor windows and others having no chance to escape the inferno. There was no liaison between the military and the civic authorities; they did not even have a central command post. Brereton had set up headquarters at the recruitment office on College Green while Mayor Charles Pinney and the magistrates scuttled between Queen Square, College Green and Berkeley Square. Brereton couldn't even find a magistrate to issue the orders he needed, let alone persuade one of them to make a decision.

On the Monday morning, Bristol was on the verge of total lawlessness. As word had got out, it was drawing yet more looters in from outside the city to share in the spoils. The situation within the city was out of control. The magistrates, who were under pressure to ride into the city at the head of the troops to establish their authority, claimed they could not ride but it was also thought they were afraid to be seen and recognised by the mob, in case the rioters turned to burning and looting their warehouses and property.

Even when the mayor, Charles Pinney, finally gave the order to Brereton to use 'the most vigorous, effective and decisive measures to quell the riot', Brereton was not entirely convinced that he and his men would not be subject to criminal charges if there was bloodshed; he needed a direct order to fire. In the end, it was a junior officer, Major Beckwith together with Major Mackworth, a member of the Horseguards, who took the initiative and restored order, giving the order for the troops to charge the crowd and take control of the situation. There were fatalities – different accounts give different numbers, depending how sensationalist the report; at least twelve people were officially identified as having died but there were many more who were too badly burned to be identified so the death-toll could never be finalised. Many more were injured and Queen Square was left in ruins, with twenty-nine houses destroyed.

There were, of course, repercussions. There were trials, of both the mayor – he was acquitted – and 100 or so of the rioters. Five rioters were hung and over eighty either imprisoned or shipped off to Botany Bay but the real tragedy occurred over the court-martial of Brereton. It was never concluded because, Brereton, seeing the inevitability of the verdict, shot himself.

Queen Square was rebuilt but it took several years, delayed by wrangling over financial responsibility. Over time, it lost its reputation as the desirable residence of the upper classes, who moved to the cleaner area of Clifton away from the river; by the 1860s it was mostly an area of offices and lodgings and, by the 1890s, used as lodgings by workers on the adjacent docks.

It seemed that Queen Square was lost for good when, in the 1930s, Bristol's inner circuit road was created and the route took a dual carriageway diagonally across the square; it was no longer an elegant Georgian square but a set of buildings either side of a dual carriageway carrying the worst of Bristol's traffic. King William was relocated to the centre of the carriageway like an uncomfortable traffic warden watching over the traffic and despairing of the parking that was clogging up the square.

In later decades of the twentieth century, however, a concerted effort between the restored Bristol City Council (after the demise of the county of Avon), the Queen Square Association and the National Heritage Lottery Fund brought a long, complicated planning phase to completion. The square needed a lot of work but, together, they removed the dual carriageway, restored the gravel paths, filled in the gaps in the trees, restored the statue of

An early 20th century echo of the days when the Marsh was a public space with grazing rights – Queen Square with sheep grazing in enclosed pens.

King William and installed new artwork, with local artists commissioned to make bird boxes to be placed in the trees. A growing sense of community amongst the office workers who appreciate it simply as a place 'to be' was reflected in the attitude of the whole city; in September 2000, the square was officially re-opened as a public space suitable for hosting occasional concerts and festivals. It has once more become a focus for Bristol's heritage.

CHAPTER 13

VIRTUE AND INDUSTRY

Redcliffe caves attract some of the more romantic legends about Bristol. They are described as being used to imprison slaves (which they weren't), to imprison French prisoners of war (which they might have been) and to hide contraband goods during Bristol's thriving smuggling trade (which is unlikely). There are wonderful stories, such as King Alfred sheltering in the caves when hiding from the Danes, or that the caves can be accessed from inside St Mary Redcliffe but there is no evidence for this. A small cave, an offshoot of the main system, does appear in medieval records; it was home to a hermit called John Sparkes who was 'sponsored' by Lord Thomas of Berkeley in 1346 to pray for him. Several hermits succeeded Sparkes in the cave through to the seventeenth century.

The entrance to the old hermitage in Redcliffe.

The caves are reached from the entrance on Redcliffe Wharf but are not usually accessible to the general public – for good reason. They form a labyrinth of caverns, interspersed with columns that look like stone tree trunks and stretch for over an acre under the built-up area of Redcliffe. No-one knows how far they go, as some of them are blocked with rubble and rubbish and in places a wall from an overhead building or a root from a tree block the way. The Axbridge Caving Group has taken on the role of exploring and mapping the caverns and occasionally opens them up to the public on events such as Open Doors Day.

Despite the mystique of the caves, they are technically mines, which have been dug entirely by human hand. An obvious question might be – why? The reason is the type of rock; a soft, red sandstone that gives Redcliffe its name. It was mined for the sand itself, which was used in two of Bristol's main industries: glass and pottery. There were probably small natural caves that had been formed by the action of the river and there may have been some excavation to enlarge these in medieval times but the main phase of excavation was done in the seventeenth century, as the fine, high-quality sand was mined.

There was a time when Bristol was one of the county's leading glass-making towns. There were small-scale glass works from the thirteenth and fourteenth centuries but it was the sixteenth century that saw the beginnings of the craft that was to become a major industry for the city. The burgess books have entries referring to glaziers; one Hugh Conwaie became a freeman because he married the daughter of a glazier. In the fifteenth century the glass made was probably window glass but that changed in the sixteenth century with the visit of a glass-maker from Italy. Edward Dagney, or Dagnia, came to England to meet the ironmasters of the Forest of Dean and advise them on their smelting process and brought his considerable glass-making knowledge with him.

Glass is made when silica, or sand, is heated with soda and lime and melted; it is then cooled quickly so that it does not form visible crystals and remains transparent. It is a sort of 'super-cooled liquid' – another example of which can be seen by heating table sugar so that it melts and then cooling it suddenly by dropping it onto a cold surface; the result is a smooth amorphous lump that shows none of the crystal structure of the original sugar grains. The process of making glass requires very high temperatures and before the seventeenth century, glass manufacture needed masses of wood as fuel for the furnaces. Because of this, glass-makers were situated outside towns and cities; wood was a limited resource and the glass-makers often had to decamp and move on to a new area just because they had stripped out all the trees and wood supplies. This did not endear them to the locals. In 1615, legislation was passed to force glass-makers to use coal-fired furnaces instead of wood. This move made Bristol a natural site for the industry – because Bristol had plenty of coal.

By a happy accident of geology, Bristol is at least partially situated on carboniferous limestone. Some 300 million years ago, the area consisted of vast swampy forests, which, as they broke down and decayed, created a form of peat. As sea levels rose and the area was covered by deep water, this peat was compressed and changed to form coal. In the sea above, the shells of microscopic marine organisms that died and sank to the bottom created lime-stone, which today covers the coal seams that characterise so much of South Wales and England.

The coalfield under Bristol is huge. It stretches from the Mendips in the south to Wickwar in the north and from Frome in the east to Clevedon in the west. In the early days of Bristol's coal industry, the seams were easy to reach as they appeared in outcrops at the surface. There is evidence of coal being used as fuel as early as 1223 and for centuries it was collected and used to heat homes and blacksmiths' furnaces. It was this access to local coal that gave Bristol an advantage in the development of industry that led up to the Industrial Revolution; the coal was readily available and didn't incur large transportation costs. In the sixteenth century, there was more demand for coal as industry grew and the coal seams began to be mined more systemat-ically in pits. Much of this coal came from the district of Kingswood; this was once a Royal Forest, or hunting-ground, but was reduced in status in 1228 to a Royal Chase. It was essentially an area of scrubby heathland to the east of Bristol but, with easy access to coal on or just below the surface, became home to a community of miners that were, effectively, squatters. They lived a primitive existence in scattered cottages, and could be unruly trouble-makers. The authorities of Bristol tended to leave them well alone and most travellers would not risk passing through the area.

The coal was hacked out of bell-shaped open pits, carried away in baskets and transported on packhorses; when Celia Fiennes visited Bristol in 1698, Keith Ramsey records in *The Bristol Coal Industry* that she bravely passed through Kingswood and noted, '. . . a great many horses passing and return-ing loaden with coals dug just thereabout; they give twelve pence a horse load which carries two bushels. . . '

The eighteenth century saw both a rise in population and a rise in indus-try, including glass-making, which created a demand for local coal. Between 1670 and 1750, the number of coal pits doubled, mostly in Kingswood. Coal mines had developed in other areas, such as what is now Soundwell, and Bedminster. In the middle of the eighteenth century, Bedminster was a market town with brickworks and rope-walks and some opencast mining but in 1748, the first shafts were sunk and by the end of the century, there were eighteen coal pits in operation. In Kingswood, by 1779, more technically advanced deep mines were being worked alongside the shallow pits and additional coal mines were being operated in the north-east and south-west of the city.

It was this coal, then, that led to the expansion of the glass industry. By the end of the seventeenth century there were ten glasshouses in Bristol, six of which produced bottles and four produced 'flint glass', a clear, strong type of glass that had been invented in 1676 and was more suitable for windows and domestic glassware. All the glasshouses were the distinctive tall, cone-shaped buildings that became a familiar site on the city's skyline; the tall cone was needed to create the draft necessary for the coal furnaces. This was a practical, utilitarian industry, making functional glass, either as bottles or as window glass; there was not much decorative glassware being produced at this time. Towards the end of the eighteenth century, a building boom in Bristol and Bath created a market for windows. There were glasshouses in Redcliffe, St Philip's and Crew's Hole but the Redcliffe glasshouse, in Prewett Street, is the only survivor of the industry; the cone was once ninety feet high but only the base of the cone has been preserved and is now a restaurant.

A view of the glass house in Prewett Street from the churchyard of St Mary Redcliffe.

As well as providing windows for the building industry, Bristol's glasshouses were producing bottles, in great demand for both the wine industry and the bottled-water trade from the Hot Well spring. In *Bristol Observed*, Bettey quotes Daniel Defoe, who commented on glass-making in Bristol in the 1720s:

> There are no less than fifteen glasshouses in Bristol, which is more than are in the city of London. They have indeed a very great expense of glass bottles by sending them fill'd with beer, cider and wine to the West Indies, much more than goes from London; also great are the number of bottles, even such as is almost incredible, are now used for sending the waters of St Vincent's Rock away, which are now carry'd, not all over England only, but, we may say, all over the world.

The bottle-making industry received a blow in 1728, when the government tried to reduce the amount of wine that was smuggled into the country. The import of wine in small casks or bottles was forbidden, which was a disaster – a major part of Bristol's industry was to export new, empty bottles to be filled with wine, which would be imported back. It got worse, when, in 1795, the American bottle trade was hit by a 10 per cent tax on all bottles, and wine merchants began to rely totally on casks – another blow to Bristol's glass

Hugh O'Neill's watercolour of 1821, 'Glasshouses in St Philips', shows the distinctive shape of the glasshouse cones.

industry that never really recovered its former glory.

There is one distinctive type of glass that is still made in the city – Bristol Blue Glass. It originated in the eighteenth century, probably when a consignment of high-quality cobalt was imported from Germany and was used to colour glass a deep blue. The firm of Isaac and Lazarus Jacobs became well known for the high quality of its decorative glass. Other coloured glass followed but the blue glass is still popular and known for its distinctive colour well beyond the realm of Bristol.

Bristol was also a centre for soap making from early medieval times; in 1192, the monk Richard of Devizes referred to the number of soap makers in Bristol – and the unpleasant smells their activities produced. By the sixteenth century, the minutes of the Bristol Company of Soapmakers for the years 1562–1642 show a list of 180 individuals who were engaged in soap making, many of them from the same families who had been in the trade for several generations.

Soap is made by boiling fat with an alkali; in the early days this was ash and the fat was tallow from beef or mutton. The products of this are soap and glycerine and the quality and type of soap depends on the original materials; the Spanish were the first to use olive oil as the fat element with ash produced by burning a local plant, producing the white, hard Castile soap. Bristol soap makers began to use imported Spanish olive oil to make their soap; this created a black soft soap that was known, cryptically, as Bristol Soap, as well as a harder soap known as Bristol Grey Soap.

The disruption in the relationship with Spain in the sixteenth century made the import of olive oil less reliable and expeditions to the west had, by then, opened up the fisheries of the Grand Banks, off Newfoundland. This led to the utilisation of a by-product of the new whaling industry – whale oil or, as it became known, train oil. The term 'train oil' comes from High German, meaning 'tear' or 'drop', describing how the oil was squeezed out of the whale blubber drop by drop. The soap makers reasoned that if they could adapt their process to use train oil instead of olive oil they would be less dependent on Spain for their olive oil and that had to be a good thing. It was a brilliant idea in theory, but it all went horribly wrong – the smell of the soap-making process was unbearable, even to the good citizens of Bristol who were already used to a more 'industrial' flavour to the smell of their city. And besides, a quarrel with Spain rarely lasted very long and when peace was restored, it was made compulsory for soap makers to use olive oil rather than train oil.

The Bristol soap makers were prospering at the start of the seventeenth century; they had their own company and had even built themselves a new hall in 1610. But they became embroiled in a bitter battle with London at the start of what would become the Civil War. Charles I was wont to give out charters to his favourites and these resulted in trade monopolies that could financially cripple those not so favoured. In 1633, Charles granted a monopoly on soap making to the London manufacturers and Bristol was limited by law to making only 600 tons of manufactured soap; to add insult to injury, they were subject to a tax of 3s 4d a ton (about 17p for those who don't remember the good old days before decimalisation) and were obliged to sell their soap for 31/2d (about 2p) a pound. The Bristol soap makers were continually harassed by London, made to produce weekly accounts and the unfortunate thirty or so who produced more than their allotted quota were summoned to London, imprisoned and heavily fined.

This did not go down at all well and although Bristol officially tried to remain neutral at the start the Civil War, it is not difficult to see why manufacturers such as the soap makers were on the side of Parliament.

By 1722, there were sixty-two freemen in Bristol listed as soap makers or soap boilers and by the end of the eighteenth century Bristol was the third largest soap-making area in the country. Various prominent businessmen were involved in the industry, including Joseph Fry of chocolate fame, who we shall meet in the next chapter. The soap-making factories needed to be close to the river for the transport of coal, wood ash, tallow and alkali, all used in the burning of kelp and quicklime.

The soap industry prospered in the nineteenth century and by the 1870s, the firm of Christopher Thomas & Brothers was producing 8 per cent of the country's total; the firm was taken over by Lever Brothers in 1910 and in the 1950s, the production ceased completely.

Bristol pottery dates back to the thirteenth century but the first tin-glazed earthenware, known as Bristol Delft, was made in Brislington in the early 1650s. A commercial pottery had started in 1683 at Temple Back and by the early-eighteenth century there were potteries at Limekiln Lane and Redcliffe Back as well as several other smaller potteries. The Temple Back pottery became known as Pountney's Bristol Pottery when it was taken over by J.D. Pountney; it was moved to St Philip's Marsh in 1884 and to Fishponds in 1905. The pottery at Limekiln Lane had, as a partner, Woodes Rogers who we met in Chapter 10.

Stoneware was made from the late-seventeenth century, and in the nineteenth century, William Powell improved the glaze used. Stoneware was used for the mass production of stone bottles as well as ointment and drug pots, needed by apothecaries. From 1617, Bristol also produced clay pipes for

The Pountney's potteries in Fishponds, with their smaller but still distinctive-shaped chimney cones.

smoking tobacco, a business that lasted until the 1920s.

The first manufacture of porcelain from Cornish china clay – kaolin, found in the granite deposits of Cornwall – began in 1750. Two Bristolians, Benjamin Lund and William Miller made a type of porcelain called 'soft paste' in their factory, which was probably in St Philip's, but two years later the method was taken over by Josiah Wedgwood. In 1768, William Cookworthy made a type of 'hard paste' porcelain in Plymouth but needed more investment and expertise. He transferred the whole business to Bristol around 1770 and went into partnership with Richard Champion, who was also experimenting with ceramics. Their Bristol enterprise was under pressure from the start, however. Although it made an elegant range of fine china, they had a direct competitor in Josiah Wedgwood. Champion ran into financial difficulties and the factory had to close in 1781.

The Bristol coalfields also fuelled the development of Bristol's metal-based industries. Iron foundries in St Philip's made cannons for ships and, nearer the shipyards, the firm of Acram's made chains and anchors. Brass wire was used to make pins by the early seventeenth century when the Tilsley brothers employed eighty 'boys and wenches' but this was probably as much to offer employment to pauper children as make a profit. Brass is an alloy of copper and zinc so, by the eighteenth century, Bristol's brass industry could take advantage of the availability of coal for the furnaces, calamine from the Mendips to provide the zinc and copper ore from Cornwall. The Bristol

Watt's shot tower on Redcliffe Hill produced lead shot until the 1960s.

Brass & Wire Company was established in 1702 at Baptist Mills, where the River Frome provided water-power. At least three of the partners were Quakers, including Abraham Darby, who, in 1707, developed a method of casting iron to make pots. The story goes that his apprentice, John Thomas, found a way to cast the pots in sand and agreed with Darby to keep the method secret for three years. Unfortunately by then, it was apparent that Bristol coal was not of a high enough quality for their method and Darby moved away to Shropshire. The methods of making and working brass were new to England so workers arrived from Holland and Germany to bring the expertise needed. The Warmley Brass Company was started in 1746 by William Champion. He was the first person to successfully smelt zinc in the country and was followed by James Emerson who refined the technique; their factories were based at Crew's Hole, near the coal mines.

Bristol also has the honour of being the home of the manufacture of lead shot. Lead was mined in the Mendip Hills and a small smelting industry was based in the city but lead shot was notoriously difficult to produce – it had to be cast in moulds, a laborious and difficult process. William Watts was said to have had the idea from a dream he had or, in some accounts, a dream his wife had. Either way, the upshot was that he perfected a remarkably simple process. Both dreams were supposed to be of a burning St Mary Redcliffe with molten lead pouring down from the roof onto the wet ground. Happily,

Watts' idea to actually manufacture the shot did not involve setting St Mary Redcliffe alight, rather he dropped molten lead through a sieve from a great height into cold water where the blobs of lead suddenly cooled to form perfect spheres. The size of the shot depended on the height of the drop so the process could be controlled relatively simply. Watts was so enthusiastic, he knocked out the floors and ceilings of his Redcliffe house then built a 60-foot tower above to make a high enough drop; he also dug down into the caves below. Watts had great ambitions to expand the process but unfortunately his business acumen was not as good as his invention and he made some disastrous investments in a building project in Clifton, which eventually led to his going bankrupt in 1794. The process continued, however, and his original shot tower was in use until 1967.

A rather strange mock gothic building is a reminder of Bristol's great metal-working industries. On the Bath Road, the A4 out of Bristol, is a bizarre castle, that looks like an overgrown children's fort. And it's black. As Bettey shows, Horace Walpole, writer and architect, visited in 1766 and recalled, 'Going into the town I was struck with a large Gothic building, coal

The Black Castle in Arnos Vale, built from blocks made from the waste slag from the local brass industry.

black and striped with white; I took it for the devil's cathedral. When I came nearer, I found it was a uniform castle, lately built, and serving for stables and offices to a smart false-Gothic house on the other side of the road.'

The Black Castle was built in the 1760s by Quaker copper merchant, William Reeves. He used blocks of black slag from his smelting works with lighter coloured stone dressing. This formed the stables and outbuildings of his grand house, Arnos Court, built at the same time, on the other side of the main road. The Black Castle, complete with turrets, crenellation and flag-poles, is now a pub and rather incongruously sits between the HTV televi-sion centre and a Sainsbury's store, surrounded by a car park. It does, how-ever, have a certain bizarre charm of its own.

All this industry needed finance and in the eighteenth century, Bristol's first banks came into being. They were originally goldsmith-bankers; these were goldsmiths who would accept money for safe keeping and give a receipt. The receipt could be used to withdraw the money or be passed on to some-one else – the forerunner of the banknote – or be assigned in the form of a written note to someone else – the forerunner of the cheque. A son of a gold-smith and bookseller called Wall ran a small bank in Bristol and a goldsmith called John Vaughan was, until 1750, banker to the Corporation. The Bank of England had imposed a restriction on the number of banks allowed in a provincial city – six – and in 1750 Bristol's banks formed a partnership, known as the Old Bank. By 1790, banking lay with businessmen and more banks had been established, so that by 1811, there were thirteen, all in the area between St Stephen's Church and the High Cross, which is still the banking quarter.

Of course, shipbuilding was also crucial to the city. Shipyards were sited near the open water and there were dry docks for repair work at Limekiln Lane, Canon's Marsh and Merchants' Dock. Support industries provided sailcloth and metal goods, with the shipyard workers living near the yards.

Bristol had various other industries, too many to mention in detail in this cursory survey of the more well-known industries associated with the city. But there was also the treatment and use of leather, with a thriving boot- and shoe-manufacturing tradition. There was a healthy brewing industry with over forty brewers and maltsters; breweries needed to be close to the river because they needed coal and in 1793 a group of merchants built a brewery near Bristol Bridge that became George's Brewery, later taken over by Courage. The woollen-cloth industry lingered in the Temple and St Thomas areas and the beginnings of cotton manufacture was gaining in importance. Yet, throughout the seventeenth and eighteenth centuries, the economic force behind the Bristol industries was trade with the

American colonies – trade that would depend on the export of Bristol-made goods, from clothes to building materials, from food and drink to sugar tongs, from tea urns to clocks, from boots to furniture. And it was this trade that led to the import of the raw materials – sugar, tobacco and chocolate – for Bristol's great processing industries, which in turn led to the huge growth in the city's wealth.

CHAPTER 14

VIRTUE AND VICE

One of the most prestigious hotels in Bristol, the Hotel du Vin, was opened in 1999; the building had been converted from a sugar refinery. The refinery was first built in 1728 and by the end of the century, the new steam technology was installed; what was the boiler room is now the hotel's reception and the engine house is now the wine cellar. The hotel stands on Lewins Mead, close to the shopping district of Broadmead and when the building was a functioning sugar refinery, the River Frome provided the waterfront needed for transporting coal and raw sugar to the refinery and the end product, white sugar, away.

For a city that was already prosperous, the eighteenth century made Bristol even more wealthy. And the goods that were to change the fortunes of the city were, essentially, goods that were bad for us. Along the lines of the

The Hotel du Vin, once a sugar refinery established in 1728, finally converted to a hotel in 1999.

saying 'All the good things in life are immoral, illegal or fattening', Bristol's prosperity flourished on the trade of tobacco, chocolate, rum and, of course, sugar. The luxuries of life, goods that appealed to the hedonists, were imported from the New World, processed and sold to an ever-increasing market in Europe. It seems fitting that the remains of a sugar refinery, having stood empty for over a decade is now one of the more luxurious hotels in the city.

The key to the increase in Bristol's import business lay with the new American colonies. By the mid-1600s, colonies had been founded at Virginia (1607), Plymouth (1620) and Maryland (1634). At the same time, islands in the West Indies including Antigua, St Kitts, Nevis and Barbados had been settled by the English and in 1655 Oliver Cromwell sent out an expedition which took Jamaica away from Spain.

It became obvious very quickly that the colonies were not going to survive by being self-sufficient. The colonists were a mixture of those seeking religious freedom, those seeking a quick way to get rich and those escaping from conditions in Europe, and none of these were obvious candidates to farm a strange land in an unfamiliar climate. Instead, their survival depended on a cash crop, something that suited the local conditions and would grow easily and, crucially, something that Europe wanted and was prepared to buy, or exchange for supplies. And the most profitable of those crops, for Bristol, was sugar.

Sugar had been considered a delicacy, even a medicine from 8000 BC. It is made from sugar cane, a tall grass that grew as a native crop in New Guinea in the East Indies. It was first seen by Europeans when Alexander the Great's army invaded India in 326 BC; before that, honey was the only available sweetener. The Moors spread cane sugar throughout Europe and it was growing in Spain by AD 714. Sugar cane needs a tropical or sub-tropical climate and lots of water; it can't be grown in the Mediterranean because it's too dry, and northern Europe is too cold but by the 1400s it was established in the Canary Islands, the Azores and Madeira. A consignment of sugar arrived in Bristol in 1456 but was prohibitively expensive and only available to the wealthy. By all accounts, a century or so later, Queen Elizabeth I was addicted to sugar – her teeth had turned black.

Sugar did not become available to the masses until it was grown on the plantation system of the New World. It is thought that Columbus took sugar-cane cuttings with him on his second voyage (1493) to the Caribbean and planted them on San Domingo; subsequent Spanish explorers took the cane to Jamaica as well as Cuba and Puerto Rico. The Portuguese were quick to follow, taking sugar cane to Brazil in the early 1500s, while the British planted sugar on Barbados and the French in Louisiana.

By the end of the sixteenth century, the primary sugarcane area was the Caribbean, which has the ideal climate. Sugar cane is not an easy crop to grow; it exhausts the soil so should be grown in rotation with other crops and from planting to harvesting is about fourteen months, which does not fit in easily with other rotation schemes. It also needs plenty of water and abundant fertiliser.

Generally, propagating sugar cane was done by taking cuttings and the new cuttings were planted by hand, in furrows a metre or so apart. They were continually tended, weeded and fertilised until ripe but once the cane is ripe and ready for harvesting, sugar cane is an unforgiving crop. As soon as the cane is cut and the juice exposed to the air, it can spoil in a matter of hours so the system of harvesting is very intensive.

To extract the juice, the cut cane was put through a press, a mill driven by oxen, wind or water close to the fields; the resulting liquid was boiled in a series of copper kettles, the scum from each kettle of boiling liquid ladled into the next kettle until it crystallised; this system was often known as the 'Jamaica Train'. The end result was a pale brown granular sugar, called muscovado, and a sticky, brown residual syrup, called molasses, out of which no more sugar can be crystallised.

This part of the refining process had to be done at the plantation because of the need to extract the juice and separate the crystals from the molasses immediately. But once the sugar is in crystal form, it can be shipped to its final destination for the next stage of purification and eventually, to the consumer.

Initially, from the mid-fifteenth century, Bristol imported refined sugar from the Portuguese Madeira and the Spanish Azores but after about 1612, raw sugar was imported from Spain and Portugal to be refined in Bristol. The first sugar house was St Peter's refinery, adjacent to St Peter's Church, built and operated by Robert Aldworth. But by the middle of the seventeenth century, Britain's representatives in the Caribbean had started settling and planting estates there, mostly with sugar. This gave Bristol the opportunity to import sugar from Barbados, Montserrat, Nevis and St Kitts and, later, Jamaica.

New sugar refineries sprang up everywhere in Bristol. The second sugar house was on the site of the Great House, where the current Colston Hall stands, and included thirteen cottages in the grounds as accommodation for the workers. A sugar house needed a constant supply of fresh, lime-carrying water so needed access to a well or to the streams that arose from springs on Brandon Hill and had been diverted to supply fresh water to Bristol's centre. The muscovado, or crystalline sugar imported from the plantations, was contaminated by caramel, lime and gluten and had to be further refined. The sugar was boiled and purified in a series of vessels similar to that used on the plantation but the eventual result was pure, white sugar. It was poured into cone-shaped moulds to crystallise and was sold to the retailer in this form, the 'sugar loaf'. This process is still commemorated in the pub at the bottom of Christmas Steps, the Three Sugar Loaves, built on the site of a sugar refinery. The retailer would then either sell the loaf whole or break off pieces to sell separately.

At the height of Bristol's sugar industry there were twenty refineries in the city and it was the city's lucrative import. The industry was not without its problems, however, not the least of which was fire. The risk was so severe, and the effects so devastating, that few insurance companies were prepared to offer cover to a sugar refinery and so the refineries formed their own insurance company in 1718. They also had to provide their own fire-fighting equipment and until the formation of the Police Fire Brigade in 1837, this was the city's only fire-fighting system. Fire was such a risk that in the most active period of Bristol's sugar imports, eleven refineries were burned to the ground.

But why was sugar so popular? Humans do seem to have a sweet tooth – even babies like the taste – and prior to the mass production of cane sugar, it was a luxury along with spices. It was even considered a medicine and a preservative. But the mass production of sugar coincided with the introduction of beverages that needed sugar to sweeten them.

Coffee, tea and chocolate all reached England at roughly the same time. Before that, across Europe, alcoholic drinks were the main alternative to water, which was not always clean, and certainly for social drinking, the pubs and bars were the common meeting places. Coffee became the popular alternative, not as a beverage for home consumption, rather, it was sold in coffee houses; the first coffee house opened in Oxford in 1650 and London followed in 1652 with the first of what would be thousands of coffee houses. Bristol's first coffee house opened in High Street in 1677.

Coffee houses were all-male domains, and quickly became popular meeting places for business as well as social gatherings. Incidentally, the custom of tipping originated in the coffee houses; a sign reading 'To Insure Prompt Service' was positioned over a tin on the way in and a customer was supposed to throw a coin in the 'TIPS' tin to guarantee being well served.

Not everyone was impressed by the coffee-house culture, however. Women were not best pleased about the amount of time their husbands were spending in them and, as quoted at www.realcoffee.co.uk, circulated a petition raging at coffee, protesting against 'the grand inconveniences accruing to their sex from the excessive use of the drying and enfeebling liquor'. Charles II even tried to ban them as a potential hotbed of revolutionary talk but to no avail. And it was the coffee-house culture that eventually introduced England's other favourite beverage – tea.

Tea had reached Europe in the early seventeenth century but at the time, Europeans preferred coffee. It wasn't until the middle of the century that the English began to trade in tea and it was first offered for sale in the coffee houses. When Charles II married a Portuguese princess, Catherine of Braganza, her affection for drinking tea out of delicate porcelain started a fashion and tea became popular. Thomas Twining entered the tea industry by selling the finest-quality tea at his coffee house but saw the potential for selling tea directly to disgruntled women who would not venture into bawdy, noisy coffee shops. And as people began drinking tea at home, they needed sugar to sweeten it, adding to the demand for the refined sugar.

The process of refining sugar generated molasses as a by-product – and molasses can be turned into rum. It was first discovered on the Caribbean plantations, where the molasses fermented naturally to provide a distinctive-tasting spirit and was a welcome distraction for the slaves. But the potential for profit was too tempting to ignore and the manufacture of rum was soon incorporated into the sugar-manufacturing process.

In the English colonies, the intoxicating and not very refined spirit went by the name of 'Kill Devil' for reasons that can be imagined, or 'numbullion', which was shortened and altered to today's word 'rum'. Sugar planters soon realised its market value, particularly to the British naval vessels in the Caribbean. By selling it at a discount to the navy, they were encouraging its warships to stay around and discourage pirates. Initially, the rum itself was part of the export from the West Indies into ports including Bristol, but the government tried to protect English distilleries and stop the import of cheap spirits so, later, the molasses were sold directly to distilleries in New England and the was rum made there for trade with Europe and the rest of the colonies.

Rum was not a major factor in Bristol's eighteenth-century economy but there was another import that became crucial to the port's development. For the chocoholics amongst us, Bristol holds an important honour. It was the site of the first ever edible solid chocolate bar – not particularly tasty and a bit gritty, but a milestone all the same.

This came about through the good offices of the Society of Friends, otherwise known as the Quakers. A Bristol apothecary, Walter Churchman, began to sell chocolate out of his shop in 1728; he was granted a patent by George II in 1729. At that time, chocolate was consumed as a drink; a piece of chocolate was put in the bottom of a cup and hot water or milk added – together with sugar to sweeten it. Walter Churchman's business was taken over by his son

Charles until his death in 1761 when it was taken over by a Dr Joseph Fry.

Joseph Fry was a young Quaker who had been apprenticed to an apothecary in Basingstoke and also qualified as a physician. He settled in Bristol in 1748, opened his own apothecary shop in Small Street and with its success, moved to bigger premises in Narrow Wine Street. Many of the successful businessmen of the time were Quakers, partly because as Nonconformists outside the state Church, they were excluded from attending universities, so the most intelligent turned their talents to commerce. Some became doctors, because in those days, physicians became qualified by following an apprenticeship rather than a university degree.

In the eighteenth century, chocolate was expensive, and considered to have medicinal properties – of course, there are those who maintain that is true today – but was only available to the wealthy elite. The Quakers approved of the drink as an alternative to alcohol.

Joseph Fry took over the design for Churchman's machine for making chocolate and, in 1793, moved to premises in Union Street. In 1795 his son, Joseph Storrs Fry, invented a new method of grinding cocoa beans using the Watts steam engine. The company became known as J.S. Fry and was the first company to bring modern industrial methods to chocolate manufacture. In 1847, the company found a way to mix sugar, cocoa butter and cocoa powder

The funeral procession of Joseph Storrs Fry in 1913; the barefoot boy on the left is fascinated by the cortege as it passes along Upper Maudlin Street.

to make a solid slab, the famous first chocolate bar.

A somewhat more palatable version was introduced in 1876, with the invention of milk chocolate by Henri Nestle and Daniel Peters. This was in production at Fry's in 1902.

Meanwhile, John Cadbury, another Quaker, had set up a chocolate factory in Birmingham, in 1824, that was a direct rival to Fry's. In 1905, Cadbury's company invented Cadbury's Dairy Milk which was an instant success.

The Fry's premises were in the centre of the city, at the Pithay, adjacent to Broadmead; by 1908 they employed over 4,000 people. After the First World War, in 1919, J.S. Fry and Cadbury's combined their financial interest and moved their factory to Keynsham, where the company still makes chocolate today.

Bristol's other major eighteenth-century import was tobacco. For Bristol's economy, tobacco shared a major advantage with its other import, sugar – both are addictive, creating an insatiable market.

The story is usually told that Walter Raleigh brought the tobacco plant to amuse the court of Elizabeth I but it is more likely that John Hawkins brought back the first samples, even if it was Raleigh who made it fashionable. Tobacco did not enjoy royal patronage, however, as women, including the Queen, simply did not smoke tobacco and her successor, James I, was rabidly anti-smoking. James wrote an anonymous 'Counterblast to Tobacco', which noted that smoking was 'a custom loathsome to the eye, hateful to the nose, harmful to the brain, dangerous to the lungs, and in the black stinking fumes thereof, nearest resembling the horrible stygian smoke of the pit that is bottomless.'

But in a breathtaking display of double standards, he realised that tobacco's growing popularity could bring him some much-needed cash by taxing the import of tobacco – rather like today's anti-smoking campaigns from the same government that rakes in the tax from the excise duty on tobacco products. Much of the imported tobacco came through Bristol.

For the English settlements in Virginia and Maryland, tobacco had become their very means of survival. They were on the brink of failure as self-sustaining farming communities; the get-rich-quick appeal of the colonies had drawn immigrants more interested in profit than a considered, long-term plan. Tobacco became more than just a cash crop, it became a form of currency within the colonies. And as tobacco became more and more popular in Western Europe, the colonies could turn to growing it for export. In hindsight, it would be interesting to speculate on what would have happened to the history of North America had Europeans not become addicted to tobacco and the English colonies had failed.

In the Virginia plantations, the tobacco leaves were hung to dry before being packed into barrels or hogsheads and sealed tightly before being exported. Large plantations used agents in England, usually in London or Bristol, to sell the tobacco and purchase household goods to be sent back to the plantations.

Initially, tobacco was smoked in a pipe, usually made of clay, but by the seventeenth century, snuff was becoming more popular, particularly among women and the upper classes. Several snuff mills sprang up in Bristol, including the building that is now the Clifton Observatory, a wind-powered snuff mill until it was gutted by fire in 1777. There were two snuff mills on the Frome, one at St James' Back and several others throughout the city.

The thriving trade with the American colonies was rudely interrupted towards the end of the eighteenth century; the American War of Independence – or American Revolution, depending on perspective – was one of several wars that affected global commerce. France was in uproar, with its own Revolution, and international tensions made shipping danger-ous for everyone. The loss of Bristol's trade with the American colonies hit tobacco imports more seriously than those of sugar from the West Indies. A note of sarcasm features in an advertisement that appeared in the *Bristol Gazette* in June 1777, as quoted in Peter Marshall's *Bristol and the American War of Independence*:

ADVERTISEMENT EXTRAORDINARY
To be lett
THE QUAY OF BRISTOL
For Particulars enquire of the Addressers for the
AMERICAN WAR
NB It will be cheap, there being little Prospect of any further
use for it, as plainly appears by the small number of vessels
now lying there.

Some merchants went bankrupt, others hung on by their fingernails. Some took advantage of the war, supplying rum and bread to the military but when the dust had settled, the tobacco industry had survived, to make its mark on Bristol.

By 1788, a small tobacco manufacturer had been set up by Henry Overton Wills producing smoking tobacco and snuff. It traded as Wills, Watkins & Co. but in 1789 Watkins retired and so the company became known as Wills & Co. Henry's sons, Henry Overton II and William Day Wills, took over the firm in

An early 19th century image of workers at the turn of the century in the Bedminster premises of W.D. & H.O. Wills.

1826 and the company was to emerge as the great empire of W.D. & H.O. Wills, one of the dominant tobacco manufacturers of the country. In the 1850s, cigarettes were supposedly brought to England by officers returning from the Crimean War who had been introduced to them by Turkish soldiers. The first manufactured cigarettes were of a strong Turkish type of tobacco but British smokers preferred the milder Virginian variety; by 1882, W.D. & H.O. Wills were manufacturing cigarettes and with the introduction of mechanised tobacco handling the firm was hugely successful. In 1883, the company had introduced a new cigarette-making machine, the Bonsack machine, which allowed them to undercut their competitors and they moved to bigger premises in East Street, Bedminster, in 1886.

The firm grew quickly and in 1906 moved into the Tobacco Factory on Raleigh Road in Bedminster. The Wills company was an enlightened employer, among the first to give its employees paid holidays, canteens, medical care and sports facilities. The company expanded and the factories extended with further sites at London, Swindon, Newcastle and Glasgow.

In the late-nineteenth century, however, a threat emerged from the American tobacco industry. The head of the American Tobacco Company, James Buchanan Duke, had created a massive company in America and had set his sights on British tobacco manufacturers. In 1901, he arrived in Liverpool and immediately bought Ogden's tobacco factory, with a view to doing the same to the other British companies. The answer was for thirteen

*The premises of W.D. & H.O. Wills in Bedminster; the company became an
part of the larger Imperial Tobacco in 1901 although it continued to trade
under its original name.*

family-run companies, led by Wills, Players and Lambert & Butler to form a
much larger company, Imperial Tobacco, to withstand the commercial
onslaught from America. The individual companies continued to trade under
their own names and brands, with William Henry Wills, later to become
Lord Winterstoke, as Imperial Tobacco's chairman.

The Wills company was under the leadership of the family until 1969,
when Christopher, the great-great-grandson of the first H.O. Wills retired. In
1974, the company moved to a new factory in Hartcliffe to the south of Bristol
where it remained until its closure in 1990.

The Wills family were hugely influential in the city and one of their main
contributions was the founding of the university. In 1908, Henry Overton
Wills offered to give £100,000 towards the founding of a Chartered
University, to be formed by amalgamating the University College on Park
Row with the Merchant Venturers' Technical College. By 1905, University
College had built more facilities on University Road; with the amalgamation

and the money from the Wills family, the University of Bristol received its charter in 1909 – with Henry Overton as its first chancellor.

The most striking legacy of the Wills family is the Wills Memorial Building that dominates the skyline at the top of Park Street. It was designed by Sir George Oatley and building started in 1911. The First World War interrupted progress so it was not finished until 1925. In the top of the sixty-five-metre-high tower is the huge bell, Great George, and today one of the most extravagant buildings in Bristol houses the Faculty of Law and the Department of Geology.

The old Tobacco Factory in Bedminster is now a thriving arts centre, with a theatre, café bar and creative work space, supporting local independent creative businesses.

Yet, the wealth of Bristol, based on the luxuries of the time, is also based on another legacy, a shadow that is cast over the profit made by sugar, chocolate and tobacco. The crops that were grown on New World plantations needed labour – intensive, demanding labour, often in atrocious conditions of heat and exhaustion and this labour had to come from somewhere. And that 'somewhere' took Bristol into the darkest chapter of its commercial history – the slave trade.

The Wills Memorial Building is a major landmark in Bristol; designed by George Oatley, it was completed in 1925

173

CHAPTER 15
THE TRADE

Among famous Bristolians, the name of Edward Colston is hard to miss. His statue stands in what is now 'the Centre', close to Bristol's war memorial and at the centre of the busy traffic roundabout.

Bristol's great philanthropist – and slave trader. Edward Colston's statue, by John Cassidy, was erected in 1895.

The nearby Colston Hall is one of his namesakes; first opened in 1867 it is Bristol's major concert hall and its exterior is much the same as when first built. It stands somewhat incongruously next to the Colston Tower, a glass and concrete building from the early 1970s. There are three schools in Bristol named after Colston as well as an almshouse on St Michael's Hill, legacies of a man who was one of Bristol's most generous philanthropists.

Edward Colston was born in the Temple parish of Bristol in 1636 into a merchant family and was baptised in the Temple Church. He grew up in the family home in Wine Street but his father, William, was a Royalist and his previous good standing in the city was diminished when the Royalists under Prince Rupert surrendered to Cromwell's forces in 1645. William was deprived of his office as alderman and sheriff and some time in the mid-1640s, the family moved to London, where Edward was educated.

After thirty years as a merchant in London, Edward returned to his native Bristol and lived in the city for a few years, importing goods in ships owned by his father and brother. However, this was only a brief interlude. From 1689 onwards he lived in his house in Surrey, staying there until he died, a lifelong bachelor living with his sister and growing more and more wealthy from his various dealings as a merchant.

If this was the total of his achievements, his would be just another name on the roll of seventeenth-century Bristol merchants yet, in the early 1700s, he began to make the donations that were to make him Bristol's most famous benefactor. He was concerned about the plight of the poor, paying for six sailors to be housed in the Merchant Venturers' almshouse, which is still a feature of King Street. He expanded Queen Elizabeth's Hospital school, sub-sidised some of its pupils and then set out to establish a school of his own. He took over the Great House that stood on the site of the current Colston Hall and turned it into a school, calling it Colston's Hospital. This school stayed on these premises until 1861 when it was moved to its current location in Stapleton. In 1891, the trustees of Colston's will established a school for girls, which still occupies its original position on Cheltenham Road, Colston's Girls' School.

He gave money for the repair of churches, the workhouses for the poor and founded another almshouse on St Michael's Hill. He established the Temple School for Boys in the parish where he was born; when he died in 1721 he left £171,000 to posterity, which, in today's currency, would be worth close to £15 million.

A benefactor indeed. In 1895, the statue by John Cassidy was raised in the Centre on Colston Avenue. Yet, in 1998, his statue was vandalised, one of many symptoms of the controversy that erupted in connection to Edward Colston's heritage. The graffiti wasn't obscene; it consisted of a single phrase that symbolised the moral ambiguity surrounding his gifts to the city: 'Slave trader'.

In the later decades of the twentieth century, a public awareness was growing of Bristol's role in the forcible capture, transport and sale of Africans to supply labour to the plantations of the Caribbean and the American colonies. The Trade. And Edward Colston's role in this?

He was an immensely wealthy man and although history does not give precise details of where all his money came from, he was known to be a shareholder in – and benefited from – the Royal African Company. There is no doubt that a significant amount of his income came from his shareholding in the company, set up in London to represent England's interest in the slave trade.

The slave trade in the seventeenth and eighteenth centuries was, at its simplest, a three-legged journey. Trade goods – cloth, metal objects and guns – were taken to West Africa and traded for slaves, which were then shipped across the Atlantic to the Caribbean. Here they were sold as labour for the plantations and the proceeds used to buy sugar, tobacco and other luxury goods which were then shipped back to England, usually at a substantial profit for the whole voyage. Hence the name 'Triangle Trade'.

Initially, the London-based Royal African Company held a monopoly on this trade but, seeing the potential for profit, other ports were soon clamouring for their slice of the action. In Bristol, the Merchant Venturers began to put pressure on the government to allow them to be part of the trade and in 1698, the Royal African Company monopoly was broken and Bristol entered its darkest period of commerce.

Local legend has conjured up vivid images from this era but many of them are complete nonsense. There were no slave markets on The Quay or on Blackboy Hill, no slaves manacled in Redcliffe caves. The complex system of underground cellars in the centre of Bristol was used for storage, and does not constitute a network of tunnels to take slaves under the harbour (it would be easier to cross by boat), or up to Blackboy Hill, which was some distance outside the city in the days of the trade. The street name of Whiteladies Road and its link to Blackboy Hill inspired legends of the 'white ladies' stepping out with their black page boys dancing attendance but this is just fantasy. Slaves were not bought and sold for the plantations in Bristol itself, this all happened on the second leg of the trade between Africa and the Americas. Blackboy Hill derives its name from the Blackboy Inn, which stands on the site of a former Blackboy Inn, demolished in 1874. The origin of the name has several possible sources; it could have been named after the swarthy Charles

II also known as the Black Boy, or it could have derived from the Blackamoor's Head (or Saracen's Head), named after the Crusaders' gruesome souvenirs of pickled Arab heads. No-one really knows. Likewise the origins of Whiteladies Road are obscure but at the height of the slave trade in the eighteenth century, Whiteladies Road was just a track. It might have been named after a convent standing in grounds adjacent to the road but is more likely named after a piece of land called White Lady's Field. A map of 1826 in the City Museum shows a narrow track with one building marked – 'White Ladies', possibly an inn, but this map is dated twenty years after the slave trade had stopped in this country.

However, there is no doubt that Bristol was involved in the biggest, wholesale, enforced migration of human beings that the world has ever known. Driven by the western greed for profit, it is estimated that between 9 and 11 million Africans were transported to a new continent in conditions of unimaginable cruelty, all to satisfy the European taste for luxuries such as sugar.

Yet the slave trade didn't appear out of nowhere, it didn't arise suddenly as a novel idea to sail to Africa and kidnap the natives. Bristol's dealings in slavery go much further back than the eighteenth century.

As early as the twelfth century, when Bristol was already a thriving port, one of its major trading outlets was Ireland. And Ireland was prepared to buy slaves, paying handsomely for fit young men and women. Unscrupulous Bristol traders were not above kidnapping likely victims, particularly young girls, pregnant women or strong-looking youths that would fetch a good price.

There are those that argue that trading in slaves was excusable by the morals of the time, that we in the twenty-first century are not justified in being judgemental from our position of morality. Yet, even in the twelfth century there were those who believed that trafficking in slaves was wrong, a violation of human rights.

At that time, Bristol was part of the diocese of Worcester, this trade in humans appalled its bishop, Wulfrun. He came to Bristol, living here for months on end, trying to preach against slavery to the good citizens. It was an uphill struggle; there was a tax on the sale of slaves and King William was quite happy for that to supplement the royal coffers. But a combination of the Archbishop of Canterbury persuading the King to manage without the slave tax and Bishop Wulfrun wearing down the people of Bristol brought this trade to an end – at least officially.

The shady world of slave trading was to apparently disappear until the expansion of the British Empire, which took place during the sixteenth century, created the vacuum that was to be filled with African slaves. The sugar plantations in the Caribbean and the tobacco plantations of North America were labour intensive and that labour was hard and demanding. When the plantations were first established, the local Native Americans were used as enforced labour but they were susceptible to European diseases and not used to the back-breaking work demanded on a plantation. The next stage was to create a labour force from white settlers.

Conditions in England were changing quickly. In just over a century, from 1520 to 1630, the population doubled and poor harvests led to rising prices, falling wages in real terms and a dramatic increase in poverty. In some cities and ports as many as half the population were living below the poverty line.

So, in what seemed like a golden opportunity, the chance to emigrate to the New World as an indentured servant presented itself as the answer to many prayers. The sea crossing, board and lodging were paid for, in exchange for a term of typically five years of labour, after which freedom was granted. In Virginia, over the seventeenth century, as many as three-quarters of English settlers were indentured servants arriving to work on the tobacco plantations.

Labour was also needed for the sugar plantations of the West Indies but planting and harvesting sugar was back-breaking, dangerous and disease-ridden in the tropical climate. Many Europeans simply could not survive these conditions and certainly did not want to take on this work if it could be avoided.

So, in the tradition of Bristol's early trade with Ireland, it was not unheard of for children and young people, particularly those on the streets, to be kidnapped and shipped to the colonies. However, this was not a particularly reliable means of supplying a labour force. Bristol became notorious for transporting criminals to the plantations; it was a well-organised racket that involved the justices and officials of the city, many of whom also owned plantations. The plight of the unfortunate felons, some of whom had only tried to steal food to survive, was to be offered transportation as an alternative to hanging.

But, ultimately, the horrific conditions on the plantations and the increasing demand for sugar led to a labour shortage. And there was a new way to make up such a shortfall.

The use of African slaves had begun in the 1440s when Portuguese men had bought African slaves from Africa to work on their plantations in Brazil. English (London based) and Dutch merchants had joined in by the 1600s. For a while, the African slaves worked alongside the white indentured servants in the fields but it soon became apparent that the Africans were able to withstand the tropical conditions and survive the back-breaking work better than the Europeans and the Triangle Trade was set to flourish.

Although the Royal African Company held the monopoly on slave trading until 1698, it is likely that Bristol merchants were trading illegally in slaves as early as the 1670s, taking the risk of being caught and fined because of the huge potential for profit. Once the monopoly had been broken, Bristol's first (legal) slave ship, the *Beginning*, owned by Stephen Baker, sailed for the coast of West Africa where the captain purchased enslaved Africans and took them to Jamaica to sell as plantation labourers.

Bristol didn't look back. By the mid-1700s, it had become the country's slave-trade hub and a city already prosperous from centuries of trade became even wealthier. In a sense, the whole city was involved in the trade, from the manufacturers of brass kettles in Warmley to the shipbuilders in the yards that were fitting out the ships, from the sailors chewing tobacco to the ladies putting sugar in their coffee or tea. But although the general principle of the slave trade was tacitly accepted, few who did not go to sea really understood the enormity of what they were condoning. Few knew the full extent of the horrors of the Middle Passage.

An unsettling aspect of the slave trade is that the system could not have survived without the existing slavery system in Africa and the collaboration of certain African chiefs. Slavery was a way of life among some African tribes; slaves were taken as prisoners of war in local disputes, in repayment of debts or as reparation for a wrong but it was not until European merchants sent ships to trade for slaves that the African slave industry became part of the Triangle Trade. The Europeans did not go searching the African bush for likely slaves – there were chieftains who were prepared to do that for them. Eager for the trade goods brought by the ships, a lucrative kidnapping system was established; not content with selling prisoners of war, the tribes sent scouting parties far inland, who grabbed anyone they could find who could not defend themselves and took them to the coast.

At the coast, a well-organised system of bartering was established. Forts were built, such as the Cape Coast Castle (built by Swedish traders in 1654 and captured by the British in 1664), along the coast from El Mina in Ghana. This fort, like many others, could hold hundreds of hapless slaves in underground dungeons, waiting purchase by the slave ships. Any slaves that looked underweight, and so were not as valuable, were force-fed to fatten them up. When a slaving ship appeared and the dealing was done, the slaves were shackled together by leg-irons, in pairs, and taken in longboats to the ships waiting off the coast. And once on board they were, simply, cargo.

There were two methods of transporting slaves: 'pack 'em loose' or 'pack 'em tight'. The object was to get as many slaves across the Atlantic alive as possible. So those who packed them loose took less slaves, gave them conditions that, although appalling, were not as bad as those who were 'packed tight' in the hope that fewer died on the voyage. Those who packed their slaves tight reasoned that although they would lose more from disease, infected wounds and the horrendous conditions, they would nevertheless transport enough across the Atlantic to make a profit.

The slaves were shut in the hold. The women and, occasionally the children, were able to move about but the men were held in leg-irons, attached to a chain running down the middle of the hold; this was to stop them attempting suicide by jumping overboard. They lay on boards with a vertical gap between each board of about half a metre. They lay side by side, unable to move to get to the buckets that served as a primitive hygiene system. Many of the slaves brought from the interior of the continent had never even seen the sea let alone been on a ship; seasickness was rife but there was no release. In the dark and heat of the hold, lying in their own piss, shit and puke, death would have been a welcome alternative.

Some captains brought the slaves up onto the deck when the weather permitted, to be hosed down and made to dance for exercise, while the crew cleaned the hold. But in rough weather, they were left alone in the heat, darkness and stench of the hold. The smell on a slaving ship could be so bad that passing ships would steer clear rather than get downwind of it. The ship's surgeon was responsible for checking the slaves for sickness – a vital job as an infectious disease could decimate the valuable cargo. Dead slaves were simply thrown overboard, to the circling sharks.

A slave ship would carry as many as 600 slaves and the voyage across the Atlantic usually took between 6 and 12 weeks depending on the weather conditions. When the slaves that survived reached their destination in the Caribbean or the North American plantations, life was no better.

Arrivals from Africa underwent a period known as 'seasoning', whereby slaves new to the Caribbean had between three and five years to adjust to the full workload expected of them on the plantation. Life was harsh for two reasons. The first was simply the exhausting and harsh working conditions, with twelve-hour days sometimes spent clearing the ground, or digging and cutting cane. The second is that because the white population was vastly outnumbered by the slaves, control became a crucial issue. Punishment, therefore, was extreme for anything that was considered a threat to the smooth running of the plantation and rebellion was punishable by death. It was common to be flogged. For some offences, including trying to run away, disfigurement, such as cutting off the ears, was used as a deterrent. The white plantation owners, managers and overseers, had to make it absolutely clear that they were in charge and did so by the use of force and cruelty.

There were many Bristolians involved in the trade, with such familiar names as the Smyth family of Ashton Court owning slaves on their Jamaica plantation. But probably the best known Bristolians involved in the slave trade are from the Pinney family. John Pinney owned sugar plantations on the small Caribbean island of Nevis that he had inherited from his cousin. Pinney visited Nevis in 1764 to take stock of his inheritance and the immediate impression was not encouraging. Many of the slaves on the plantations were too old or sick to work and were no use for harvesting sugar; Pinney freed them so he wouldn't have to pay taxes or doctors' fees for them, although he continued their food and clothing allowance.

He bought new slaves to replace them. In 1765 he bought four slaves from Joanna Jones: an African woman named Harriet, a twelve-year-old boy called Pero, and his two sisters, Nancy aged eight and Sheeba who was six.

Number 7, Great George Street – now known as the 'Georgian House', this was the townhouse built and owned by merchant John Pinney.

They had all taken the surname of Jones. Pero and his sisters were probably born on the island of black parents whereas Harriet had been brought from Africa and had gone through the seasoning period.

Pinney consolidated his plantations and concentrated most of his efforts on Mountravers, which consisted of about 270 acres with its own mills, boiling and distilling houses and workshops. By all accounts Pinney was not as harsh as some of the plantation owners. When he first arrived on Nevis he confessed to being uneasy about the idea of slavery but nobly convinced himself it was ordained by God. As Dresser and Giles explain in *Bristol and Transatlantic Slavery,* Pinney wrote a letter in 1765 stating:

> I have purchased 9 Negro slaves in St Kitts and I can assure you
> I was shocked at the first appearance of human flesh for sale. But
> surely God ordained 'em for use and benefit of us otherwise his
> Divine will would have been made manifest to us by some par-
> ticular sign or token.

Ordained indeed. This was typical of the logic of the time; any queasiness about the trade and forced enslaved labour of human beings was dispelled by the medicine of profit to be made from sugar.

Pinney turned his estates into profitable concerns and in 1783 he came back to Bristol. His legacy to the city and hence the familiarity of his name was the building of a fine new townhouse at number 7, Great George Street. Now known as the Georgian House, it is owned by the City Museum and is maintained as an example of the architecture and lifestyle of Pinney's time.

John Pinney had married and when the family returned to England he brought Pero, who had become Pinney's personal servant, as well as Fanny, Mrs Pinney's maid, to live with them at the townhouse. Pinney set himself up in business with a partner, James Tobin, who he had known in Nevis. They worked out of the Great George Street house, acting as agents for other plantation owners in the Caribbean, lending them money, handling sugar consignments and organising supplies to be sent to them from England.

Pero was a permanent member of the household and when the Pinneys went back to visit Nevis he went with them, once in 1790 and once more in 1794. It isn't clear why, but after this visit, Pinney implies in correspondence that Pero had started drinking to excess. By 1798 Pero was ill and was sent outside Bristol to Ashton to convalesce but Pinney knew he wouldn't recover. When Pero died, aged about 45 years, he had been a slave to Pinney for over 32 years.

Contrary to the lurid stories of slave markets on The Quay or on

Blackboy Hill, there were few black Africans in Bristol; as with Pero and Fanny, Mrs Pinney's maid, they came as servants, either with plantation owners or merchants, or with captains or officers of slaving ships who saw owning a black servant as a perk of the job.

The horror of the slave trade was not without its opponents, however. A growing realisation of the conditions and implications of this commercial venture drew its critics. Among the first to speak out against it were the Quakers, the Society of Friends, in 1760 and by the 1770s the founders of Methodism, John and Charles Wesley, were also preaching against the trade and were joined by the Anglican Dean of Bristol, Josiah Tucker, and the Evangelist Hannah More. Bristol was visited by the former slave Oloudah Equiano (1745–97) who, as a public speaker, shared his own graphic experiences of the trade.

Bristol's direct involvement in the slave trade was significantly reduced by the 1780s, partly because of the loss of trade to Liverpool with its superior port facilities. But the city still had a strong interest in trade with the West Indies and abolition of the slave trade would have a serious economic impact. A committee was formed, including John Pinney and James Tobin, to oppose abolition and this committee petitioned Parliament in favour of the slave trade.

A major figure in British politics, Edmund Burke argued against the slave trade and slavery. He was MP for Bristol from 1776 to 1780 and a friend of Hannah More, another anti-slave campaigner, but his relationship with the people of Bristol was not a comfortable one. He had taken the seat of Bristol as a way into Parliament and although he was in favour of peace and trade with the North American colonies, which was popular in Bristol, by 1778 he was speaking out against the slave trade, which made him less popular.

As the campaign gathered momentum, the public spokesman against the trade was politician William Wilberforce and he visited Bristol in 1791 to speak against slavery. Working with him was a young clergyman, Thomas Clarkson, who had written a prizewinning essay against slavery and visited Bristol in 1787 to gather evidence for Wilberforce and the campaign. Initially, no-one was keen to talk to him except for the Quakers but gradually, by hanging around bars and quays, he found sailors prepared to reveal the full horrors of the conditions on the ships. Through his investigations, Clarkson found that the crews were suffering almost as much as the slaves.

Reluctance to sail on a slaver meant that crews for these ships were obtained by dubious tactics, a practice known as 'crimping'. Often, with the connivance of local landlords, men with no money were given credit in a bar, plied with drink 'on the slate' and then, when the time came to pay up the only option was to be arrested or to be handed over to those recruiting for the ships. Other recruiting tactics involved the simple expedient of kidnapping someone who was too drunk to resist and bundling them on board, where they were forced to sign a document that they were not allowed to read – even if they could read. Clarkson befriended the landlord of the Seven Stars, a dockside pub still serving customers today, close to the church of St Thomas. The landlord did not join in with the enforced recruitment techniques and introduced Clarkson to those who could give the evidence he needed against the cruelty to slaves and the nightmarish conditions endured by the crew.

Wilberforce brought a proposal to Parliament to abolish the slave trade in 1791 but it was rejected – and Bristol celebrated. Legend has it that the church bells were rung when the news reached the city. The campaign against slavery suffered a hiatus with the economic crash that was started in 1793 by war with France but eventually, on 25 March 1807, the Act of Abolition became law. It was now illegal to trade in African slaves.

Stopping the slave trade, however, did not yet mean the end of slavery itself. It took until 1834 before slaves working on the plantations of the Caribbean were actually freed and it took another two decades of vitriolic campaigning on both sides before the Emancipation Act was passed. In America, it took a Civil War to bring an end to the conditions on the plantations of the South and the hard-earned freedom of former slaves brought further problems of poverty and social prejudice that took decades, if not a century to overcome.

Nothing can make amends to the countless millions that lost their lives, their souls and their dignity in the name of profit. Nothing can give back what was taken away; the only thing left is the memory. In Bristol, in 1999, a new bridge over the Frome was named after John Pinney's servant Pero Jones. Pero's Bridge stands as a reminder, not just of one slave who lived and died in Bristol, but also of all the slaves that died in bringing prosperity to a city they would never know.

The Seven Stars, the inn whose landlord met Thomas Clarkson in 1787 and helped him gather evidence of cruelty on board the slave ships; evidence that eventually contributed to the abolition of the slave trade in 1807.

CHAPTER 16

FLOATING HARBOUR

Nowhere in the centre of Bristol is very far from the tranquil surface of the water that forms a complex system of waterways. Ferries carry tourists around the docks, and commuters across the water, while narrow boats come and go, local rowing teams practice and visiting boats make their leisurely way around the quays. Yet before 1809, the whole of the central waterway was drained twice a day by the tides, exposing the muddy river bed and dumping ships and boats berthed at the quays onto their keels.

A vivid reminder of the problems of the tidal approach to Bristol; even after the Floating Harbour was completed, a steamer in the river is still grounded by the tide.

The end of the eighteenth century was a difficult time for Bristol. Although the campaign against the slave trade was gathering momentum, it was not to have the effect on Bristol that had been feared. Other factors were having a much more disastrous effect on Bristol's trade – and hence wealth.

The problem was the river. The Avon had been the reason for Bristol's existence in the very beginning and had kept the city safe from raids from the sea when other ports were suffering pirate attacks. Yet the river created two problems that became more and more pronounced as merchant ships got bigger. The first was that the six miles of river between the port and the Bristol Channel is narrow and winding and, in part, follows a route through the course of the gorge. It was near impossible to sail along the river, and bigger ships had to be towed up and down the Avon. The community of pilots, based at Pill (meaning 'creek' or 'inlet') a small town further downstream of the Avon, grew up to service this need. Pilots were skilled navigators, brought on board a ship returning up the Severn to bring her into port, a necessary service that cost the shipowners dear but was crucial to the safety of the ship and cargo. Each pilot worked for himself, with an apprentice, so when a returning ship was seen approaching the mouth of the Avon, they would race out to meet it, the first one there getting the job – and the fee. Because of this rush to the west, the pilots were also known as 'Westernmen' and their boats were built for speed. The pilot would be taken on board the returning ship and the apprentice would take their boat back to Pill. When the pilot brought the ship towards the Avon's notorious Horseshoe Bend near Pill, it had to be navigated with precision or things could go horribly wrong.

The second problem for Bristol was, of course, the tide. It wasn't just that twice a day, all the water disappeared from the port, it was more complicated; there was a 'window' either side of high tide when the water was

The harbour at the village of Pill on the river Avon, home to the pilots that brought the ships safely into Bristol.

deep enough for a ship to be brought in. It took some organisation to bring the ships in systematically when they had been waiting, sometimes for weeks, either at Kingroad in the Bristol Channel, just outside the mouth of the Avon, or at Hungroad, a stretch of the river near Pill, downstream of the Horseshoe Bend.

The tides don't just vary on a daily cycle; there is also the monthly cycle of spring and neap tides. Twice a month, the spring tide is more 'extreme' – when high tide is higher and low tide is lower, and between them, twice a month, is the neap tide, when the tide is less extreme than normal. The complex shape of the Avon and Bristol Channel also affects the tides, as does the direction of the wind, so shipowners and crews were totally dependent on the local knowledge of the pilots.

The development of shipping was bringing in larger ships so it became more likely that a ship would have to wait until a spring tide before the water was deep enough for her to enter Bristol. When she did come into port, the low tide caused her to settle, often at an angle, with the potential for damage to her timbers, as well as the added risk of everything not actually fixed down sliding around.

To make matters worse, Bristol had a rival. The port of Liverpool, with its deep natural harbour, provided a less hazardous and stressful berth for the new grade of merchant ships. The Industrial Revolution had seen the building of a canal network throughout the centre and north of England, which meant large consignments of cargo could go by water to ports such as Liverpool, rather than use the river system that connected central and South West England, and which brought trade via the Severn and Avon to Bristol.

With an increase in Bristol's prosperity, mostly due to trade with Africa and America, the volume of shipping increased – so congestion in the port became a third problem. During the eighteenth century, the Merchant Venturers, who were responsible for the upkeep of the port, made a half-hearted effort to improve the situation. They had installed cranes for unloading ships, extended the quay wall along the Frome and built a wharf on Welsh Back. They attempted to relieve the congestion by building a wet dock at Sea Mills, with the idea that ships could unload cargo there, but it was not popular with shipowners who still had to transport their goods into the city. The Merchant Venturers' lease on the harbour was renewed in 1764 on condition they made more improvements, which resulted in quays along the Grove and St Augustine's Reach. All this, however, made very little difference.

All through the eighteenth century, schemes were discussed and dis-

A view of Bristol's working harbour, looking along St Augustine's Reach with the tower of St Stephen's visible in the background.

cussed some more and proposals were made to improve the harbour, but nothing further happened. In 1765, the engineer John Smeaton, who had rebuilt the Eddystone Lighthouse off Plymouth Sound and whose tower, Smeaton's Tower, stands as a memorial on Plymouth Hoe, submitted a proposal. He suggested damming the river across the mouth of the Frome with a channel across Canon's Marsh also providing berthing for further ships. Then, in 1767, William Champion extended this idea, proposing a dam across the river at Rownham and a lock system on what would become the Cumberland Basin. Yet the Merchant Venturers and Common Council were loath to commit themselves. They were to turn dithering into an art form.

By the end of the eighteenth century, it was obvious to everyone that something had to be done but the worry was still what – and by whom – and where the money would come from...

The problem of damming the Avon made the scheme something of an engineering challenge but in 1802, engineer William Jessop proposed a way of creating a floating harbour by digging a second channel to carry the tidal Avon – the 'New Cut' – and a lock system to maintain the old river bed at a constant water-level. In 1803, an Act of Parliament was passed that allowed

As the harbour was developed to take larger ships, Welsh Back remained the berth for local trade.

the formation of a new company, the Bristol Dock Company, and a slightly revised plan from Jessop was given the go-ahead, with him as chief engineer.

It took five years to build the new harbour. There was no shortage of labour; the Napoleonic Wars had created a convenient surplus of prisoners, of which at least 5,000 were languishing in Stapleton prison, but it was exhausting work. The New Cut was two miles long and the digging was through the wet mud into the bedrock.

Jessop's design called for a huge earth dam to stop the flow of the Avon itself; this was at the site of the present Underfall Yard, where the harbour-master's office is today. At the time, it was designed with a weir to take the overflow from the river, so was known as the 'Overfall' yard (the name change will be explained shortly). A set of locks created what is now the Cumberland Basin and a system was built to stop the spring tides overflowing into the harbour. At the other end of the new Floating Harbour, the New Cut rejoined the river to the east of Temple Meads, at Totterdown Lock, and a canal was built to maintain the water-level in the harbour and – hopefully – alleviate the problem of the water becoming stagnant. This was the Feeder Canal, just over a mile long, which, at its far end linked to the Avon at Netham Lock.

All this construction had not gone at all smoothly and the costs had soared. The original estimate had been for £212,000 and a succession of problems, including a bridge collapsing, killing two workers in February 1809, drove the final figure to nearly £600,000. Much of the money had been raised by the Dock Company taking investments and promising high dividends on the return but by the time 'the Float' was finished, they were unable to pay this back. In the meantime, the Merchant Venturers and the Corporation were still charging their own fees to shipping and the only way the Bristol Dock Company could even begin to recoup their layout was to charge their own – additional – fees. It doesn't take an economist to work out that, for a commercial operation such as the port of Bristol, this was not a good policy. Rather like trying to get commuters to use public transport today, increase the prices too much and clients will decline the invitation. Bristol was not the only port on the west coast of England and if other port fees proved much cheaper there was no need for ships to put up with the inconvenience of the river as well as the exorbitant costs.

The Chamber of Commerce was well aware of the disastrous effect of these charges and tried to present the Corporation with some hard evidence to prove this. They showed that on a typical selection of imports, the equivalent fees at Hull would be £147,587; at London they would be £210,098; Liverpool would cost £231,300 and Bristol would be nearly double at £515,608. The Corporation still refused to admit there was a problem and by 1835, a report noted that the fees due on expensive items such as sugar, brandy, rum, tobacco and wine were still more than twice that of Liverpool.

It all became very acrimonious, with the Corporation refusing to admit that their stubborn grip on their right to collect dues was counter-productive; they would not publish their accounts or co-operate to solve the problem. Eventually, a Royal Commission became involved and its report was damning. The Merchant Venturers and the Dock Company had refused to co-operate and the Corporation was busy spending money on pomp and ceremony when the docks and city were crying out for investment. The end result was a reformed Corporation, elected in 1836. Even after all this the Merchant Venturers and Dock Company still refused to address the problem of the port pricing itself out of business.

It wasn't long before another problem that had been niggling away since the Float was created became too obvious to be ignored – the small matter of the water flow and sewage. Now the story gets gruesome. Whereas once the Avon's tide had flushed the city's waterways clean twice a day, the Floating Harbour was rapidly becoming a stagnant pool fed by the Frome, to all intents and purposes, an open sewer.

The summer of 1825 was unseasonably hot. Sweltering, in fact. The smell – and sight – of the water in the Float and the mud of the New Cut at low tide cannot be fully described in case, gentle reader, you are eating while reading this. Suffice it to say that even the good Bishop of Bristol was forced to retire from his palace at times. The attempts by the Commissioners for Paving, Cleansing and Lighting to force the Dock Company to do something about it met with turgid resistance; the Dock Company even claimed they had affidavits from physicians claiming that the water produced 'no unhealth-iness'. The whole situation ended up in court, with a ruling that the Dock Company was to sort out the mess.

The Company brought in engineer William Shadwell Mylne to propose a plan, which resulted in a culvert – an underground pipe – to take the water from the Frome under Broad Quay, Narrow Quay and the harbour before emptying into the New Cut; there was also a facility to flush the Frome when things got really grim. This now moved the sewage problem to another part of the city – those south of the New Cut suffered the worst, particularly along Coronation Road – and the sewage outlets flowed into the channel above the low-water mark. With the wind in the wrong direction, the experience of low tide at Bedminster or Southville needed a strong stomach. But, at least, the tide regularly washed the New Cut clean.

In fact, the water-management policy was a complete shambles. As well as the sewage problems, industry around the harbour and along the Feeder Canal emptied all sorts of effluent and toxic waste into the water; for other industries such as the tannery that needed a clean water-supply, complaints about water quality led nowhere.

The new Floating Harbour meant that Bristol was just about holding its own in terms of shipping figures but it was a precarious stability. And, in addition to the high fees and the sewage problem, yet another difficulty was causing headaches for everyone using the Float.

The harbour was fed by not one river, but two, and both the Frome and the Avon carry silt – a lot of silt – which, once caught up in the static water of the Float, just sank to the bottom. It didn't take long for the harbour to start to gum up with mud, so that ships could not approach the quays in safety.

Yet again, the Dock Company had to be prodded into action. This time it requested proposals for ways of clearing the mud and stopping it silting up again; various ideas surfaced, including one by an engineer by the name of Edward Casey. He proposed a deviously cunning scheme whereby new gates would allow the Frome to be flushed out at high tide but in the process the whole Float would come to a standstill to shipping, which rather defeated the object of its design.

Enter the hero of Bristol's engineering challenges – Isambard Kingdom Brunel. The impact that Brunel had on Bristol deserves a whole chapter (which it has), but as far as the problems of silting up the Float were concerned, Brunel was the answer to the Dock Company's prayers. In 1832, he was asked to report on the situation and recommend a solution. He agreed with Casey in principle but his idea reflects a simplicity that seems, in hindsight, to be a blinding flash of the obvious; the water would be stagnant if it wasn't kept moving. His solution was less disruptive than Casey's yet would still move the silt.

He realised he needed to create some way for the water to flow out of the Floating Harbour so that it could carry at least some of the silt and stop the water stagnating. To do this, he recommended raising the boards at the dam at the east end of the Floating Harbour, at Netham Dam, to give a higher head of water. He also proposed a series of sluices – large pipes that could be opened or closed either manually or automatically to carry water from the Float to the New Cut. It would then be possible to use dredgers (boats) on a regular basis to move the mud into the centre of the harbour where it would be sucked away by the sluices.

Of course, there was yet more dithering on the part of the Dock Company but by 1834, even though the height of Netham Dam was never altered, the sluices had been cut and were working. A sluice was installed at Prince Street Bridge, which had been built in 1809, and four were cut through the dam that Jessop had built, known as the Overfall Dam because of the weir that took the Float's overflow. These sluices ran from the Float to the New Cut; there were three sluices that were used to control the Float's water-level depending on weather conditions and one deep sluice that was opened at low tide. The undertow of the river then created a powerful sucking effect that forced water – and silt – through the sluice and into the New Cut, to be carried away by the next high tide.

And, in an inspired leap of logic, what used to be known as the Overfall Dam became known as the Underfall Yard – and still is today. In 1842, Brunel added further improvements to stop silt building up near Redcliffe Back, which included another, larger dredger. In principle, Brunel's method is still in use. The harbour is dredged regularly and some of the silt is now pumped to the sluices through a more sophisticated pipe system while the rest is carried away in barges.

Brunel also contributed to the harbour facilities by the redesign of the original South Lock. The lock still exists but it is no longer in use and has been sealed with a concrete wall. As far back as 1835, Brunel had warned that the South Lock was too small and needed rebuilding. Both the Chamber of Commerce and the Great Western Steamship Company supported him in this view but the Dock Company refused to acknowledge the problem. Again. It wasn't until 1844 when the lock was in a terrible state of disrepair that Brunel was brought in to build the new lock. The building started well but by then Brunel was preoccupied with other, larger, projects and the work dragged on, beset by technical problems. It was finally opened in 1849.

The hazard of the river Avon as the approach to Bristol – the ss Gypsy, on 12 May 1878; she became stranded on a falling tide and broke her back. It took explosives to clear the river of the obstruction to traffic.

In 1848, the Dock Company was taken over by Bristol City Council, after a period of yet more acrimony between the Dock Company and those fearing that the exorbitant charges were driving shipping away.

In the end, though, the improvements to the harbour could not stop the decline of the port as no amount of improvement to the harbour could solve the problem of the river. The limitations of waiting for the few hours around high tide, and the problems of bringing large ships around the Horseshoe Bend were not to going to go away and as the new generation of ships was getting bigger, the end of the port's glory days was inevitable.

Those enlightened souls who had seen this coming had already been discussing plans for a completely new approach. The plan was to build a new dock at the mouth of the Avon, able to take large ships and thus avoid the problem of navigating the river. Plans included sealing off the Avon at its mouth to create a giant Floating Harbour, building a large dock at Pill and a dock at Portishead, on the Bristol Channel. Nothing happened until two private companies took on the task of building a new dock at Avonmouth (which opened in 1877) and at Portishead (which opened in 1879). Initially,

A paddle steamer in the Cumberland Basin, with the district of Hotwells to the left of the photograph.

they were in competition with each other until, finally, a wave of common sense washed over Bristol and the Corporation bought them both out. Further investment led to expansion at Avonmouth, with the building of the new Royal Albert Dock which opened in 1908. With the ever-increasing size of ocean-going vessels, the Royal Portbury Dock was built in the deeper water on the west of the river mouth. Today, it is a successful cargo port, and the dock system can be seen in all its activity from the M5 motorway that passes overhead on the Avonmouth Bridge.

As Portbury went from strength to strength, Portishead could not be sustained as a viable dock; it lost most of its trade in the 1980s due to the closure of the power stations and the resultant end of the need to transport coal. It is now a marina. And the life of the Floating Harbour as a commercial port was also at an end. There was a brief flurry of activity during the Second World War when all available space was needed to bring supplies into the country but by 1974 it was no longer a commercial port. Yet it still has the draw of a harbour in the centre of the city, and today's regeneration projects have given it back a new, if very different, life of its own.

CHAPTER 17

BRUNEL'S BRISTOL

The ss *Great Britain* is, put simply, magnificent. She sits in her original dry dock, surrounded by glass at the water-level that supports a shallow layer of water, which gives the impression she is afloat. But the glass isn't just there to enhance the look of the ship, it also provides an airtight seal so that the ship's hull, below the glass, can be maintained in a special atmosphere; mas-

The ss Great Britain, *in her original dock in Bristol, restored and open to visitors.*

sive de-humidifiers keep the air as dry as the Arizona desert. This is crucial to stop the further deterioration of the iron hull from rust. The ship is in her very own purpose-built glass case – the ultimate ship in a bottle – with the difference that visitors can descend to the dry dock and see the massive hull and propeller up close and personal.

The SS *Great Britain* was the first iron-hulled, steam-powered ocean liner, a great achievement of her day, and the brainchild of Isambard Kingdom Brunel. The ship will never sail again but the restoration project has brought her home and shows her off to a perpetual stream of visitors. The interiors have been recreated with loving detail and give an atmosphere of the ship as she was when she first sailed.

The ship is important to Bristol for many reasons. She is a celebration of Brunel and his legacy but she is also a symbol of Bristol's decline as a commercial port. In July 1843, when she was ready to be launched, she was the biggest ship in the world. For the facts and figures enthusiasts, she was just over 98 metres long – a full 30 metres longer than any other ship of her time – and displaced 3,066 tonnes.

At the launch, as the docks were thronged with spectators, the 'fit' was so tight, the ship was in danger of scraping her sides on the quay; it needed crews of men to push against the hull to guide her into the Floating Harbour. This was in the presence of the Prince Consort, Prince Albert, who had come to Bristol for the occasion; the whole city had come to a halt to watch the event in an atmosphere of jubilation and triumph.

Yet, eighteen months later, when the time came to move the ship out of the Floating Harbour, into the Avon and out to sea, there was a near disaster. It was crucial that they wait for the high spring tide, giving a slightly higher water-level than a normal high tide. The ship was to be taken out of the northern lock into the Cumberland Basin and then onto the Avon itself. But the locks weren't big enough.

Now the logically minded would ask, why didn't Brunel simply design the ship so that it could get out of the locks? Not an unreasonable question, but to be fair to Brunel, the question had been addressed as the building began and, in yet another superb display of incompetence, the Dock Company assured Brunel that by the time she was ready to launch, the locks would have been widened. But this did not happen. Over two years of procrastination and committee meetings had achieved absolutely nothing and the only solution was for Brunel and his team to dismantle the stonework of the lock. With the permission of the Dock Company, Brunel had removed some stonework from the north junction lock allowing the ship to squeeze

'The Launch of the ss Great Britain' *by Joseph Walter. It seems to have been
the occasion for quite a party.*

out of the Float and into the Cumberland Basin, so that she could move into
the tidal Avon on the spring tide of the morning of 10 December 1844. A tug
started to pull *Great Britain* out through the north Cumberland Lock and on
board the tug was Christopher Claxton, one of Brunel's partners in the enterprise. Looking back, he suddenly realised *Great Britain* was not going to get
through the lock – and was stuck. This would have been a disaster. With the
lock gates open and the ship wedged, they would not have been able to close
the gates, the water would have drained out as the tide went out and left the
ship stranded. The ship would have been left supported only by her contact
with the sides of the lock; she probably would have sagged and possibly fallen
and broken. Claxton was quick enough to get the tugs to haul her back into
the basin and the lock gates closed before the water-level fell. But this left
Brunel and Claxton with the problem that if they didn't get her out on the
next high tide, the water-level would not be high enough and they would
have to wait another month for the next spring tide.

Brunel and Claxton worked frantically to remove more stonework and by
the next high tide she was pulled through – but night had fallen and, as the
tide ebbed, the *Great Britain* was grounded in the river bed. In his publication

Isambard Kingdom Brunel, Rolt reveals that Brunel missed an appointment the following day, with good reason, as he explained:

> We have had unexpected difficulty with the *Great Britain* this morning. She stuck in the lock; we did get her back. I have been hard at work all day altering the masonry of the lock. Tonight, our last tide, we have succeeded in getting her through; but, being dark, we have been obliged to ground her outside and I confess I cannot leave her until I see her afloat again and all clear of her difficulties.

If it was going to be so difficult to build and launch the *Great Britain* in Bristol, why was Brunel here at all? His decision was the end result of a long relationship with the city that had started decades earlier. Born in 1806, the only son of French engineer Marc Brunel, he had been educated in France and joined his father in 1822 to work on the ambitious Thames Tunnel. An accident during the building of the tunnel left Isambard badly injured and in need of recuperation. At first he went to Brighton but then came to Clifton to convalesce. While here, he first heard about a competition to design a bridge over the Avon Gorge at Clifton. In 1753, William Vick, alderman of the city, had died leaving the sum of £1,000 in trust; his intention was that it should accumulate interest until there was enough money to fund a stone bridge over the gorge. He was nothing if not optimistic. By 1829, the sum had reached £8,000 and the Merchant Venturers, realising there would never be enough to build a stone bridge, set up a committee to organise a design competition for a suspension bridge. They thought it would be cheaper. In November 1829, Isambard entered four possible designs to the competition, illustrated by sketches.

But the judge – the only judge – was the engineer Thomas Telford, and when he rejected all the submitted entries and proposed his own, the good men of Bristol were justifiably suspicious. Telford insisted that there was a theoretical maximum span for a suspension bridge and that happened to be the span of the Menai Straits Bridge in North Wales that he had designed, a span of 600 feet. Brunel's designs included spans across the gorge of at least 760 feet. When Telford submitted his own design it relied on two huge towers rising straight out of the bedrock on the river bed to a height of 200 feet.

Telford's design was eventually rejected and a new competition announced. This time Brunel won, but his new design was still influenced by Telford's reservations. Rather than designing a span crossing the gorge in its entirety, which still made everyone nervous, he reduced the span by designing the abutment on the Leigh Woods side of the gorge.

Incidentally, it was always assumed that this abutment was made of solid sandstone. A test bore was taken in 1969 and it went through solid stone but in 2002, a discovery was made that was something of a surprise as there were no complete plans of the abutment. It was discovered to have twelve chambers in two tiers; they are linked by tunnels and narrow shafts and the biggest chambers are 57 by 18 feet, and 35 feet high. The lower of the two tiers is built directly onto the rock of the gorge. The sudden realisation that the abutment was riddled with 'holes' sounds slightly alarming but engineers have checked it; if it has stood this long, it implies that Brunel, of course, knew exactly what he was doing. The chambers were sealed so there was nothing living in there but the air was clean.

Work began on Brunel's bridge with a 'ground-breaking' ceremony in June 1831 but didn't get very far. There wasn't enough money. Brunel was in Bristol during the fateful October 1831, and was caught up in the riots; he was drafted in as a special constable in an attempt to restore order and also gave evidence at the subsequent trial of the mayor, Charles Pinney. But an effect of the riots was economic chaos in the city and building work was not started again on the bridge until 1836.

By 1840 the piers had been finished yet only three years later the money had run out again and the work stopped once more, leaving the two piers dominating the landscape. They remained so for twenty years; Brunel never saw his bridge completed.

In the meantime, Brunel had been taking on other work. In 1833, a company was formed to take on the rivalry with Liverpool, already developing direct rail links with London. The Great Western Railway set out to build a direct link from London to Bristol. The company was incorporated after the Act of Parliament in 1835 and the twenty-seven-year-old Brunel was appointed as engineer. Brunel surveyed the route he planned for the railway himself, on the punishing personal schedule that drove him most of his life. His decision to take the line north of the Marlborough Downs, which at the time was not particularly heavily populated, was controversial, but not as controversial as his decision to use 'broad gauge', a distance between rails of 7 feet $\frac{1}{4}$ inch rather than the standard gauge of 4 feet $8\frac{1}{2}$ inches already in use by George Stephenson. Brunel's autocratic approach to his engineering work led him to resist others' attempts to contribute ideas or opinions. He even tried to design his own locomotives which weren't altogether successful until he accepted the young engineer Daniel Gooch as Superintendent of Locomotives. Between them, Brunel and Gooch chose the small village of

The unfinished tower of the Clifton Suspension Bridge on the Leigh Woods side of the river. The abutment supporting the tower was recently found to be partially hollow.

Swindon for their engineering works. This was the highest point the route would take between London and Bristol.

The progress of the GWR was by no means a smooth ride. The route involved new bridges, embankments, the laying of 118 miles of track, plus new stations. Landowners had to be appeased – and paid – where the line ran over their land and, not surprisingly, the costs spiralled. Brunel's insistence on the broad gauge over the narrow gauge of other rail networks developing in parallel with the GWR was a cause of tension; an interest from some who wanted the GWR to be linked to these networks added further to the pressure.

But, despite the opposition, Brunel was determined to stay with broad gauge. He was convinced that greater speeds could be reached in safety and comfort and that the broad gauge was also more efficient and economical. He might well have been right but the problem was that George Stephenson was already building railways and Stephenson had based his gauge on the width of the coal wagons on Tyneside. He then used this gauge for the Stockton and Darlington railway and as 'railway mania' hit the country, new rails were built on his existing system. Brunel fought long and hard to keep the GWR on broad gauge, arguing that the system was self-contained and did not need to link physically to the other new rail systems. Eventually, in what became known as the 'gauge war', a Royal Commission was set up in July 1845 to sort it out once and for all and, since there was more narrow gauge track than broad gauge in the country by then, they came down on the side of

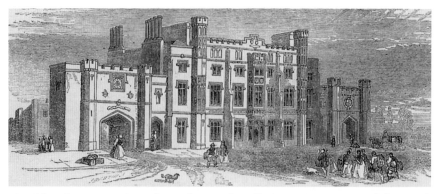

A mid-19th century view of Temple Meads railway station as Brunel designed it; the station was enlarged at the end of the 19th century and this part of the building complex now houses the Empire and Commonwealth Museum.

Stephenson's system, which became the national standard.

The first trains ran on the GWR in June 1838, between Paddington and Maidenhead and, by 1841, with the opening of the Box Tunnel between Bath and Bristol, the line was complete.

Although the line was crucial to Bristol, Brunel spent little time in the city, usually only staying a day or two for a meeting. Yet he left his legacy throughout the city, not the least of which is his terminus, Bristol Temple Meads. It was built on the land owned, long ago, by the Knights Templar (hence 'Temple Meadows') and which, in 1830, was designated as the site of the city's cattle market, hence Cattle Market Road that runs alongside the station complex.

Bristol Temple Meads is the oldest railway terminus in the world. Brunel was able to indulge his design for a sweeping roof that was seventy-two feet wide to create a train shed with no columns. He included a Tudor Gothic-style building for administration offices. Bringing the railway to Bristol also meant bringing new and accurate timetables. And therein lay a problem that hadn't been important before. Until then, time was measured locally; noon was determined by the sun's highest point in the sky and the clocks calibrated to this, but because of the distance from London to Bristol, 120 miles or 2° 35′ of longitude west of Greenwich, the rotation of the Earth means noon occurs 10 minutes later in Bristol than it does in London. This had the potential to create mayhem with train timetables. The problem was solved by the introduction of a new clock, which can still be seen on the front of the Exchange building in Corn Street – it has three hands, an hour hand and two minute hands, one showing the exact time in Bristol and the other showing the time in London.

*GMT comes to Bristol; the clock on the Exchange has three hands, to show the
10 minute difference between Bristol and London*

The railway was a tremendous success and by the mid-1840s, GWR was
one of the leading rail systems in the country, still running on broad gauge
and extending as far as Cornwall, and into Wales and Gloucester. But with
the Royal Commission deciding against broad gauge in 1846, any new track
the GWR laid was of mixed gauge whereby both types of trains could run on
it. The last broad gauge train left Paddington for Cornwall on 20 May 1892;
that night, work started to convert all the broad-gauge rails to standard gauge
and within twenty-four hours, the whole of the GWR had been changed and
broad gauge no longer existed.

It was almost a chance remark that introduced the idea of the first of
Brunel's great ships. In October 1835, Brunel was at a dinner for the directors of the GWR and became exasperated when the discussion raised mis-
givings about the length of the line from London to Bristol; his retort was
meant to be sarcastic – why not make the line even longer, with a steamboat
from Bristol to New York? It could be called the *Great Western*. Apart from
being something of a conversation stopper, the remark was then politely
ignored until after dinner when Brunel was accosted by Thomas Guppy, a
member of one of Bristol's richest merchant families. Guppy was convinced
the idea was brilliant and the two talked about how to turn this crazy plan
into reality. They approached the Bristol shipbuilder William Patterson and
the Quay Master, Christopher Claxton, an ex-Naval officer. It didn't take long
for them to raise the money from other Bristolians who saw the potential of
the direct link to New York. By the following June, much of the capital had
been raised and the keel was being laid at Patterson's shipyard at Prince's
Wharf on the Floating Harbour.

The *Great Western*, as she was officially named, was to be big – much bigger than any existing ship. That such an ambitious project could even be considered was due to Brunel's challenge to existing engineering wisdom that said the bigger the ship, the more coal would be needed to fuel her and there was a point at which the amount of coal needed to take a ship across the Atlantic would make the ship too heavy. The consensus was that it couldn't be done. Yet Brunel, in a typical flash of insight and mathematics, realised the fallacy of this argument and, going against all the perceived engineering wisdom of the day, insisted a bigger hull would actually be more efficient than a smaller one.

The *Great Western* was a paddle-steamer with a hull of copper-sheathed oak. Built over two years, in July 1837, she was launched into the Floating Harbour, followed by a celebration dinner on board, and a month later set sail for London where she was to receive her engines.

The *Great Western* was built to replace sailing ships that had made

A hansom cab waits outside Temple Meads railway station; today, passengers are picked up by taxi from the same place.

transatlantic crossings since 1818 and this did not go down well with rival companies in Liverpool, who intended to monopolise the route. The British and American Steam Navigation Company was already building ships for this purpose but hearing of the progress of the *Great Western*, adapted an Irish steamer, the 700-ton *Sirius*. In a bid to be first to cross the Atlantic by steam, the *Sirius* left London on 28 March 1838 and after taking on coal at Cork, set off across the Atlantic on the 2nd of April. Meanwhile, the *Great Western*, en route from London to Bristol, suffered a fire on board and Brunel, trying to find out what had happened in the engine room, stepped onto a charred ladder that gave way and he fell; happily, Claxton was at the bottom of the ladder and broke his fall, saving Brunel's life, although he sustained serious injury and had to be confined to bed for weeks.

The *Great Western* was not seriously damaged, however, and was able to continue her maiden voyage, setting out on the 8th of April, four days after the rival *Sirius*. It was undignified but the maiden voyage had turned into a race. Yet, although *Sirius* did arrive in New York first, on the 23rd of April, *Great Western* was only hours behind her, having made the journey in 15 days. Legend has it that the crew of *Sirius* had burned cabin furniture and children's toys to eke out the fuel to complete the journey, but in reality, when she arrived, she had about 15 tons of coal left. The *Great Western* still had nearly 200 tons of coal in her hold.

The *Great Western* went on to establish a regular steamship crossing to America, just as Brunel had envisaged. But what he hadn't envisaged was the mismanagement of the Bristol Dock Company; while the *Great Western* was moored at Pill, unable to come back into the Floating Harbour because of her size, the Dock Company was still charging full dues, and extortionate ones at that. Negotiation broke down completely so the *Great Western* upped anchor, as it were, and headed for Liverpool. Another own goal for the Dock Company.

However, things had gone so well for the *Great Western* that Brunel and his colleagues were immediately thinking about their next project, a sister ship. He had proved his point about the efficiency of large hulls and set out to make the next ship even bigger. Yet SS *Great Britain* was originally intended to be another wooden-hulled paddle-steamer.

Much of Brunel's genius lay in recognising an existing idea and adapting it for his own ends. In 1838 a paddle-steamer, the *Rainbow*, visited Bristol's Floating Harbour; and, although iron-hulled ships had been in service since 1821, this was the first time Brunel thought about the possibility of an iron hull. Claxton and Patterson joined the *Rainbow* on a voyage to Antwerp to monitor her performance and the results were promising. It was a way of solving the problem they faced in designing the *Great Britain* to be bigger than the *Great Western* – such a large hull was proving difficult to design with timber to give it the necessary strength. So Brunel, Guppy and their team set about redesigning the *Great Britain* in iron and to accommodate her size, the shipyard itself had to be modified and expanded, and new machinery designed and built.

Orders were placed for the massive engines that would drive the paddles but, as building progressed on the hull, in May 1840, another visitor to the Floating Harbour caught Brunel's attention. She was the ss *Archimedes*, and instead of paddles, was driven by a screw propeller. Again, although the technology had been around for nearly two years, this was the first time Brunel had seen the technique in action and, again, seized on the idea with enthusiasm. Brunel chartered the *Archimedes* for six months to carry out tests and persuaded the Company directors of the Great Western Steamship Company to allow the suspension of the work on the *Great Britain* while the design was reconsidered once more.

Brunel and Francis Pettit Smith, the designer of the screw propeller system, with interest from a few enlightened individuals in the Royal Navy, carried out further tests and were commissioned to design and build a ship specifically to test propeller designs. The result was the *Rattler*, and during its tests became famous in 1845 for being set in a tug of war against a conventional paddle-steamer of the same size, the *Alecto*; the *Rattler* towed the *Alecto* backwards. No contest.

It took four years to build the ss *Great Britain* and, as already seen, the launch in July 1843 and her departure from the harbour in December 1844 had sounded warning bells for Bristol's viability as a commercial port. She journeyed to London to be fitted out and was never to return to Bristol as a working ship, instead working out of Bristol's arch-rival, Liverpool.

The *Great Britain's* working life nearly came to a premature end only two years after her launch. Leaving Liverpool for New York, she went aground on a reef at Dundrum, in Ulster; it seems there had been an error in the captain's charts. The passengers and crew were rescued but the ship was stuck fast and the Company seemed to have no idea as to what to do. Brunel was tied up with work on the railway and his many other commitments so William Patterson visited the scene to report on the situation. Brunel wrote to him and suggested at least protecting the stranded hull from the pounding surf with wooden breakwaters. But it took a visit from Brunel and his determination in forcing the Company not to abandon her to finally get the ship afloat. They would have to wait out the winter until the weather improved before making the necessary repairs and it was the salvage engineer James Bremner and his son Alexander who eventually helped with the operation, so that in August 1847, the *Great Britain* was once more afloat.

The finances involved had crippled the Great Western Steamship Company. They had sold the *Great Western* to finance the salvage and repair of the *Great Britain* and in 1850 they sold the *Great Britain* to the Liverpool firm of Gibbs, Bright & Company. She became an emigrant ship, taking hopefuls to Australia and, apart from a two-year stint carrying troops to the Crimea in the mid-1850s, made thirty-two round trips to Australia, carrying the ancestors of a quarter of a million of today's Australians.

By 1876, she was no longer viable as a passenger ship and was sold again, this time for use as a cargo ship. The engines were removed to make space and, under sail, she carried coal from South Wales to San Francisco, around Cape Horn. In early 1886, struggling round Cape Horn against the prevailing winds, in mountainous seas and laden low in the water with cargo, it became obvious she was in trouble and had to seek refuge in the Falklands.

It was too expensive to repair the damaged ship and so, at the end of her days, she was used as a store ship, for wool and, later, coal. But by 1933, even this was no longer viable and the decision was eventually made to scuttle her; she was beached on Sparrow Cove in the Falklands and left to rust.

The story of her recovery and restoration is one of determination worthy of Brunel himself. Funds were raised and studies made of the best way to get her home and eventually, with the financial help of philanthropist Jack Hayward, and a massive effort by salvage experts, the ss *Great Britain* was secured onto a massive pontoon. In May 1970 she was towed the 7,000 miles home. She was initially taken into Avonmouth Docks for her hull to be made seaworthy and then, on the 5th of July, was towed up the Avon to the Floating Harbour, watched by a crowd of 100,000. On the 19th of July, the spring tide was high enough for her to be eased back into the Great Western Dock, where she had been built 130 years earlier.

Undaunted by the financial difficulties of the *Great Western* and *Great Britain*, Brunel went on to design the *Great Eastern*, a bigger ship yet again and this time there was no question: she could not be built in Bristol. The task went to a purpose-built dockyard in London and the great shipbuilding engineer John Scott Russell. This was Brunel's last project. The building of the *Great Eastern* was a long, protracted saga of financial and technical difficulties and, by 1859, it was apparent that Brunel's health was deteriorating. Even when he was very ill, he insisted on hearing news of *Great Eastern*'s progress. On her maiden voyage from her Isle of Dogs mooring to New York in 1859, an explosion in the English Channel destroyed one of her funnels and killed five of the crew. Brunel was told about the accident and, ten days later, he died, never seeing the *Great Eastern* at sea.

The question quickly arose of a fitting memorial to the great engineer. Various plans were submitted but it was Brunel's colleagues, members of the Institute of Civil Engineers, who proposed completing the Clifton Suspension Bridge. Another suspension bridge Brunel had designed and built at Hungerford had to be demolished to make way for railway improvements to the South Eastern Railway so the chains were bought for use in Clifton. Engineers William Henry Barlow and Sir John Hawksaw revisited Brunel's design and adapted it, using a triple-chain system, instead of Brunel's double chains, and a stronger deck. The towers had already been built in Brunel's day but had not been completed with his planned ornamentation; the engineers decided to leave them as they were. Five years after Brunel's death, the bridge was opened with great ceremony on 8 December 1864 and has been open for traffic ever since.

As well as the Clifton Suspension Bridge and the ss *Great Britain*, there are other glimpses of Brunel all over Bristol, features that almost go unnoticed as integral parts of the city. On St George's Road, at the bottom of Park Street, Brunel House was conceived as a hotel especially for rail passengers on their route to New York on the *Great Western*. The building closed as a hotel in 1855 and is now home to Bristol City Council's planning department.

The Floating Harbour now operates its dredging system much as Brunel designed it. His redesigned lock is still there, and the swing-bridge he designed over the lock is no longer used but is nevertheless intact, lying beside the north lock under the roadway carried above by the Cumberland Basin bridge. And Brunel's original Temple Meads railway station, superseded in 1878 by the adjacent terminus, is now the site for Bristol's Empire and Commonwealth Museum.

One of Brunel's original buildings for the GWR made international headline news in 2005. Used as a warehouse, a fire started during the night of Sunday 9 October and by the Monday morning the whole building was ablaze. The fire made news because the warehouse was in use as storage space for the animation company Aardman Animations, makers of *Wallace and Grommit*, *Chicken Run* and *Creature Comforts*. Although the main base of operations is on Gas Ferry Road, near the ss *Great Britain*, the props and models used for previous films were archived in the warehouse and, as a result of what is thought to have been an electrical fault, all were lost in the fire.

For Bristol, the Clifton Suspension Bridge has become the symbol of the city; as a logo, on postcards, badges, mugs, tea towels. It can be seen from the approach to the city from the south-west, and when lit up at night, the iconic shape that makes it so recognisable is displayed at its finest. The city was founded on a bridge, Bristol Bridge, and 1,000 years later, a masterpiece of engineering crosses the Avon some 200 feet above what was once a ford, the only other crossing available when Bristol Bridge was built.

Originally the Great Western Hotel, designed by Brunel to accommodate passengers en route to New York via rail and steamship; the hotel closed in 1855 and the building now houses Bristol City Council offices.

A NOTE ON SOURCES

The sources for this book have been many and varied; the list below gives the published works that have been the most relevant. In particular, the collection of booklets published by the Bristol Branch of the Historical Association, some of which are included below, are a superb source of historical detail.

Aughton, Peter, *Bristol A People's History*, Carnegie, repr. 2003

Awtrey, Hugh R., *Blackbeard the Pirate Breaks into Print*,
    www.cr.nps.gov/history/online__books/regional__review/vol2-6e.htm, 07-Sep-05

Ballard, Martin, *Bristol – Seaport City*, Constable Young, 1966

Belsey, James, *A Small Light in the Far West*, Cartwrights Solicitors, 1996

Benbrook, Ivan, *Bristol City Docks: A Guide to the Historic Harbour*, Redcliffe Press, 1989

Bettey, Joseph, *Bristol Observed*, Redcliffe Press, 1989

Bettey, Joseph, *St Augustine's Abbey*, Bristol Branch of the Historical Association 88, 1987

Bettey, Joseph, *Royal Fort and Tyndall's Park*, Bristol Branch of the Historical Association 92, 1997

Branigan, K., *The Romans in the Bristol Area*, Bristol Branch of the Historical Association 22, 1967

Brindle, Stephen, *Brunel, The Man who Built the World*, Weidenfeld & Nicolson, 2005

Brown, H.G. & Harris, P.J., *Bristol England*, Burleigh Press, fifth impr. 1967

Buchanan & Williams, *Brunel's Bristol*, Redcliffe Press, 1982

Carus-Wilson, E.M., *Medieval Merchant Venturers*, Methuen & Co., second edn 1967

Clinch, Rosemary, *Unknown Bristol*, Bossiney Books, 1987

Crawford, Anne, *Bristol & the Wine Trade*, Bristol Branch of the Historical Association 57, 1984

Crossley, Evans M.J., *Hannah More*, Bristol Branch of the Historical Association 99, 1999

Cunliffe, Barry, *Facing the Ocean*, OUP, 2001

Dresser & Ollerenshaw, *The Making of Modern Bristol*, Redcliffe Press, 1996

Dresser, M. & Giles, Sue (ed.), *Bristol and Transatlantic Slavery*, City of Bristol Museum & Art Gallery, 2000

Eickelman & Small, *Pero*, Redcliffe Press with City of Bristol Museum & Art Gallery, 2004

Farr, Grahame, *Bristol Shipbuilding in the Nineteenth Century*, Bristol Branch of the Historical Association, 1971

Firstbrook, Peter, *The Voyage of the 'Matthew'*, BBC Books, 1997

Fleming, Peter, *Bristol Castle a Political History*, Bristol Branch of the Historical Association 110, 2004

Fleming, Peter, *Bristol and the Wars of the Roses*, Bristol Branch of the Historical Association 113, 2005

Fleming, Peter & Costello, Kieran, *Discovering Cabot's Bristol*, Redcliffe Press, 1998

Foyle, Andrew, *Bristol*, Pevsner Architectural Guides, Yale, 2004

Grant, Neil, *Kings and Queens*, Collins (Keys), repr. 2003

Green, G.W., *Bristol and Gloucestershire Region* (British Regional Geology), BGS (Stationery Office), 1992

Grinsell, L.V., *The History and Coinage of the Bristol Mint*, City of Bristol Museum and Art

Gallery, 1986

Harris-Sacks, *The Widening Gate*, University of California Press, 1991

Hill, John C.G., *Shipshape and Bristol Fashion*, Redcliffe Press, 1983

Horrox, Rosemary (ed.), *The Black Death*, Manchester, repr. 1995

Hunt, W., *Bristol (Historic Towns)*, Longmans Green & Co, 1902

Ison, Walter, *The Georgian Buildings of Bristol*, Kingsmead, 1978

Jenks, Stuart, *Robert Sturmy's Commercial Expedition to the Mediterranean (1457/58)*, Bristol Record Society, 2006

Jones, F.C. & Chown, W.G. *History of Bristol's Suburbs*, Winstone, 1977

Jones, Donald, *Bristol: A Pictorial History*, Phillimore, 1991

Jones, Donald, *Bristol Past*, Phillimore, 2000

Jones, Donald, *Bristol's Sugar Trade*, Bristol Branch of the Historical Association 89, 2003

Jones, Donald, *A History of Clifton*, Phillimore, 1992

Jones, Donald, *Captain Woodes Rogers' Voyage Round The World*, Bristol Branch of the Historical Association, 1992

Jones, Evan T., *Illicit business: Accounting for Smuggling in Mid-Sixteenth Century Bristol*, Economic History Review LIV 1 (2001) p.17–38, 2001

Jones, P. & Youseph, R., *The Black Population of Bristol in the 18th Century*, Bristol Branch of the Historical Association 84, 1994

Kelly, Andrew, *Queen Square Bristol*, Redcliffe Press, 2003

King, Andy, *The Port of Bristol*, Tempus, 2003

Klein, Herbert S., *The Atlantic Slave Trade*, CUP, 1999

Kurlansky, Mark, *Cod*, Vintage, 1999

Little, Bryan, *The City and County of Bristol*, Werner Laurie, 1954

Little, Bryan, *The Story of Bristol*, Redcliffe Press, 1991

Lord, Evelyn, *The Knights Templar in Britain*, Pearson Longman, repr. 2004

Lynch, John, *For King & Parliament*, Sutton, 1999

Macdonald, Peter, *Cabot and the Naming of America*, Petmac Publications, 1997

MacInnes, C.M., *Bristol: A Gateway to Empire*, David & Charles, 1968

MacInnes, C.M. & Whittard, W.F. (ed.), *Bristol and its Adjoining Counties*, British Association for the Advancement of Science, 1972

Manson, Michael, *Bristol Beyond the Bridge*, Past & Present Press, 2000

Manson, Michael, *Riot! The Bristol Bridge Massacre*, Past & Present Press, 1997

Marshall, Peter, *The Anti-Slave Movement in Bristol*, Bristol Branch of the Historical Association 20, 1998

McGrath, Patrick, *Bristol & America 1480–1631*, Bristol Branch of the Historical Association, 1997

McGrath, Patrick, *Bristol and the Civil War*, Bristol Branch of the Historical Association, 1992

McGrath, Patrick & Cannon, John (ed.), *Essays in Bristol and Gloucestershire History*, Bristol & Gloucestershire Archaeological Society, 1976

Moorcroft & Campbell-Sharp, *Bristol from the Fred Little Collection*, Budding, 1988

Moorcroft, D. & Campbell-Sharp, N., *Bristol in Old Photographs*, Sutton Publishing, 1998

Morgan, Kenneth, *John Wesley and Bristol*, Bristol Branch of the Historical Association, 1990

Morison, S.E., *The European Discovery of America, The Northern Voyages*, AD 500–1600, OUP, 1971

Nicholson, Helen, *The Knights Hospitaller*, Boydell Press, 2001

Powell, K.G., *The Marian Martyrs*, Bristol Branch of the Historical Association, 1972

Press, Jonathan, *Merchant Seamen of Bristol 1747–1789*, Bristol Branch of the Historical Association 38, 1995

Price, Denis, Normans in Gloucestershire & Bristol, Brewin, 1983

Quinn, David, *Sebastian Cabot, Bristol Exploration*, Bristol Branch of the Historical Association 21, 1997

Quinn, Phil, *Holy Wells of Bath and Bristol Region*, Logaston Monuments in Landscape Volume VI, 1999

Ralph, Elizabeth, *The Streets of Bristol*, Bristol Branch of the Historical Association 49, 2001

Ramsey, Keith, *The Bristol Coal Industry*, Bristol Branch of the Historical Association 106, 2003

Reid, Helen, *Chronicle of Clifton & Hotwells*, Redcliffe Press, 1992

Reid, Helen & Stops, Sue, *On The Waterfront*, Redcliffe Press, 2002

Richardson, David, *The Bristol Slave Traders: A Collective Portrait*, Bristol Branch of the Historical Association 43, repr. 1996

Robinson, Derek, *Shocking History of Bristol*, Abson Books, third impr. 1987

Rolt, L.T.C., *Isambard Kingdom Brunel*, Longman, 1964

Sherbourne J.W, *William Canynges*, Bristol Branch of the Historical Association, 1985

Sherbourne, J.W., *Port of Bristol in the Middle Ages*, Bristol Branch of the Historical Association 13, 1999

Shipsides, Frank & Wall, Robert, *Bristol: Maritime City*, Redcliffe Press, 1981

Sivier, David, *Anglo Saxon & Norman Bristol*, Tempus, 2002

Smith, Brian & Ralph, Elizabeth, *A History of Bristol & Gloucestershire*, Phillimore, 1996

Smith, Graham, *Smuggling in the Bristol Channel 1700–1850*, Countryside, repr. 1994

Stoddard, Sheena, *Bristol Before the Camera: The City in 1820–1830*, Redcliffe Press, 2001

Swanton, Michael (tr. ed.), *The Anglo-Saxon Chronicle*, Dent, 1997

Thomas, Susan, *The Bristol Riots*, Bristol Branch of the Historical Association, 1995

Thomson, E.V., *People and Places in Bristol*, Bossiney, 1986

Vanes, Jean, *Port of Bristol in the Sixteenth Century*, Bristol Branch of the Historical Association 39, 1986

Vanes, Jean, *Bristol at the time of the Spanish Armada*, Bristol Branch of the Historical Association 69, 1988

Vanes, Jean, *Education and Apprenticeship in Tudor Bristol*, Bristol Branch of the Historical Association HA, 1982

Vaughan, Adrian, *Isambard Kingdom Brunel: Engineering Knight Errant*, Murray, pb 2003

Waite, Vincent, *The Bristol Hotwell*, Bristol Branch of the Historical Association 1, 2002

Walker, David, *Bristol in the Early Middle Ages*, Bristol Branch of the Historical Association, 1971

Watson, Sally, *Secret Underground Bristol*, Broadcast Books, second edn 2002

West, Jean M, *Sugar and Slavery: Molasses to Rum to Slaves*, www.slaveryinamerica.org, 06-Sep-05

Wilson, Ian, *The Columbus Myth*, Simon & Schuster, 1991

Winstone, Reece, *Bristol's Earliest Photographs*, Winstone, 1974

Blackbeard the pirate and the Presumed Wreck of the QAR, www.ah.dcr.state.nc.us/qar/default.htm, 27-Jul-05

INDEX